RED CARD ROY

RED CARD ROY

BY
ROY McDONOUGH
WITH BERNIE FRIEND

VSP

Published by Vision Sports Publishing in 2012

Vision Sports Publishing
19-23 High Street
Kingston upon Thames
Surrey
KT1 1LL

www.visionsp.co.uk

ISBN: 978-1-907637-56-8

Editor: Jim Drewett
Copy editor: Alex Morton
Cover design by Doug Cheeseman

Typeset by Palimpsest Book Production Limited, Falkirk, Stirlingshire

Printed in the UK by TJ International Ltd, Padstow, Cornwall

A CIP Catalogue record for this book is available from the British Library

CONTENTS

In loving memory of Iris and Jim,
the best parents anyone could wish for.

And John Lyons, a class act who
still makes me laugh in my thoughts today.

Dedicated to my guardian angel, Lizzie.
I may not be here today if
I had not found the love of my life.

ACKNOWLEDGEMENTS

It has long been my ambition to have my football career recorded in a book, as I always believed I had a good story to tell. But I didn't have a clue about just how much work it would take, and how much help would be needed to start the pages turning on my tale.

The biggest thank you goes to my ghostwriter, Bernie Friend, for remembering me fondly from his teenage years standing on the Roots Hall terraces, then flying out to Portugal and Spain some 25 years later to listen to my stories. This book would never have been brought to life without his dedication and hard work, and there were plenty of laughs and tears shared along the way. Bernie certainly lived up to his surname, as my wife and I thoroughly enjoyed the time we spent in his company. Thanks, Friend.

I would also like to express my gratitude to Jim Drewett, Toby Trotman, Alex Morton, Henry Firth and everyone else at Vision Sports Publishing for their devotion to real football stories, and believing in the potential of an old footballer whose career was played out a million miles away from the Premier League. Special thanks also to Jeff Whitehead for help with additional research, and Ian Tuckey for lending another set of eyes to read over the pages. Another big thank you goes to the *Southend Echo, Colchester Evening Gazette, Essex Chronicle* and *East Anglian Daily Times* for the kind use of their pictures to illustrate my career, and Dave Shields for getting the photos into a publishing-friendly format. The *Daily Mirror* and *People* have also been a huge help, allowing access to their football libraries to piece together the timeline of my story. For additional guidance, advice and inspiration, thanks also to Will Price, David Wilson, Mick Walsh and Chris Holmes.

I would also like to thank the following people, who have all helped to get this book on the shelf in one way or another: Dick Godwin, Francis Ponder, Mark Wallis, Jon Waldron, Matt Plummer, David Selby, David Simpson, Trevor Beal, Jon Weaver, Dave Ward, Glen Eckett, Peter Miles, Dave Goody, Matt Hudson, Andrew Poole, Gary Sutton, Kevin Drury, Andrew Bennett, Mike Blackstone, Chris Daines, David Crown, Steve McGavin, Paul Brand, James Brown, Dave Kidd, Julie Porter, Gareth Cox, Dean Morse, Paul Carter, Paul Abdale, Martin McNeill, Rob Sambrook, Paul Douglas and Carl Marston.

PROLOGUE

Blotchy, red pressure marks appeared on my terrified opponent's sweaty skin as I tightened my grip around his throat. His muddy football boots scythed through thin air as I lifted him off the grass with one hand. It was an incredible display of strength for a 16-year-old schoolboy. Especially when you consider my ghoulishly white-faced victim was a fully-grown man. He was vastly superior to me in height and build, and had been on my case right from the first whistle. This bloke just would not get off my back, questioning every move I made on the pitch and stifling my attempts to play football and win the game. But he'd pushed it too far this time, and I couldn't stomach that. Something inside me snapped, the red mist descended and it was time to take the law into my own hands, to snuff out this irritating presence once and for all. The trouble was, this wasn't a troll-like centre-half who had punched me in the ribs from behind, or a bone-crunching midfield enforcer who had been handed a pre-match dossier to take me out. The man I was throttling one-handed – his horror-filled eyes popping out on stalks – was the referee of my local secondary school cup final, and a teacher too. But in these flashpoints of rage which would later plague my career as a professional footballer, respecting status and obeying authority didn't matter to me. I couldn't care less about the punishments that followed my acts of aggression; the suspensions, club fines and trips to Lancaster Gate for a dressing down from the FA's big beaks.

My wife will tell you that I am one of the softest, most easy-going people in the world when I'm not in a football kit. I've only ever been involved in one nightclub dust-up in my life. But when I crossed that white line I was at work. The football pitch was my office, and I was willing to go that extra mile to win the game for my club, team-mates and fans. It didn't matter if it was a flat-nosed centre-half kicking me up in the air, or an incompetent referee failing to do his job properly – I couldn't let them take liberties. The violence was rarely premeditated. It was all about self-preservation. I pride myself on the fact that my nose still has its natural shape. All of my teeth are my own and I've only ever had a dozen stitches in my head. That's because I looked after myself. I was more than happy to crack skulls with an opponent and if we legally contested the ball for 90 minutes there wouldn't be any trouble. If I got clattered by a defender who was trying to win the ball honestly, then I didn't have a problem with that. But I have been spat at, nutted, elbowed and punched in the face on far too many occasions. In those instances – when a player was not trying to win the ball fairly, in an attempt to cause deliberate damage to my body – I had to start taking liberties with them. If the referee wasn't offering me the correct protection as I scrapped for my team, I dished out my own brand of justice. A warning was usually issued first. 'Behave yourself fella and we'll get along fine'. Most defenders knew my reputation and would instantly cut out the cheating. Some of the thicker ones held back for 10 or 15 minutes, thinking they had got away with it. But the next time the centre-back tried to land a sly one on me, or left a foot dragging late against the back of my leg, that was it. Bang! I would go straight through him like a dose of salts, without uttering a single word. The offender would end up in a claret-stained heap on the floor nursing the blow from a swift hook to the jaw, a razor-sharp elbow driven hard into his hooter or the studs of my boot raked down the front of his face. Then I'd deal with the shell-shocked official, who was just as much to blame for this brutal reprisal. Before the referee had time to reach for his top pocket, I would inflict a four-lettered blast of GBH on his ear holes, turn away and start making the all-too-familiar slow trudge back to the players' tunnel – the angry jeers of the crowd ringing around the ground.

Avenging this strong sense of injustice on the football pitch earned me a longer crime sheet than the Great Train Robbers. During a turbulent 20-year career as a professional footballer, before winding down anything but gently on the non-league circuit, I clocked up an English record 22 red cards. This pinnacle of untamed indiscipline is a record that still stands today, leaving the snarling and spitting efforts of other so-called 'football hardmen' way below the summit of my many misdemeanours.

But my career could easily have followed a more stellar path, as I was a promising striker at big clubs like Aston Villa, Birmingham City and Chelsea, before falling from grace and beginning a violent trawl through the rough seas of the lower divisions. My bitter disappointment of failing to crack the top level degenerated into a bread and butter voyage through a journeyman world of birds, booze and bungs. In a career that surpassed 650 games, 150 goals, 400 women and thousands of beers, I played for three England World Cup winners, tried to clog Dutch master Johan Cruyff and pulled a Miss UK finalist with half a pint of lager and £1 petrol money. There were promotions, relegations and a cup final appearance at Wembley as a player-manager. I also managed two marriages; one to a club chairman's daughter, before running off with the groundsman's wife. But these highs and lows were littered and lost amongst a bad-tempered volley of painful elbows, punches and kicks, resulting in a catalogue of early baths and the infamous nickname, 'Red Card Roy'.

1. VILLAN OF THE PEACE

etting sent off for grabbing the referee by the throat in the schools' cup final wasn't my first dismissal. But, looking back, it defined my long journey along a controversial career path which spanned four decades of football.

It was a March afternoon in 1975 and 300 teachers, parents and pupils had congregated at the Henry Road playing fields to watch the fifth-year Birmingham Schools' Cup Final. My school, Lyndon High, from Solihull, were up against one of our main foes, the Sir Wilfrid Martineau School, who fired themselves into a 2–0 lead. I was captain, playing centre-half, and hadn't got off to the best of starts. They had this chirpy little Pakistani kid up front, who was giving it all the mouth, so I started kicking him from pillar to post. I might have been playing at the back, but I was streets ahead of the rest at school level, so I would run around all over the pitch. But, playing like that, there is always the chance of getting caught out, and while I was still in their half, the gobby striker broke from the centre circle and shouted, 'Catch me, if you can!'

'Cheeky fucker', I thought, 'you're not getting away with that.' So I pushed down hard on the accelerator, caught up and volleyed him right in the side of the body, giving a penalty away. The referee booked me, but luckily they fluffed the spot-kick.

Feeling calmer, I managed to pull a goal back for us. But I

knew that, with the booking hanging around my neck, I was a dead man walking. That was because the man in the middle was also the headteacher of our other arch rivals. He knew I was one of the best players in the area, as he'd witnessed me take his boys apart enough times. This was his chance to level the scores. I was spitting feathers and spelt out just how unhappy I was with his performance. But he just told me to get on with it. Halfway through the second period, he penalised me in favour of the motormouth forward, who laughed in my face, so I took a swing at him and missed.

The referee blew his whistle furiously, before frantically ushering me over to him. But I was completely gone by this stage. For the first time in my life, at the age of 16, I had lost control. I don't know what happened, as everything blanked out for 20 seconds. But when I came round and the red fog started to clear, I had the referee by the neck and was lifting him off the floor with one hand as if I was the Incredible Hulk. This bloke was 6ft 3in tall and must have weighed 15st, boots dangling above the floor. What was I doing? How had this even happened? Fully conscious and back in a sobering reality, I released the grip on my stunned victim, who pointed to the showers and sent me off as soon as his studs had sunk safely back into terra firma.

We lost the match 2–1 and, despite being the disgraced captain, I still had to lead all the players through an appalled crowd up some steps to collect their runners'-up medals. One of the teachers handed me a medal, but I wasn't interested in taking home something which would remind me of second place. I looked down at the watching parents below, some of them shaking their heads in disgust, and chucked the medal across the park, before heading off alone.

I wasn't proud of my aggressive reaction, especially the manner in which I had lost the plot without warning. It left me in total shock. And it wasn't long before I came to realise that I had screwed up big time. I was on schoolboy forms with Aston Villa and was considered one of the brightest prospects in the area, playing alongside little Gordon Cowans in the Villa youth team. I had been top scorer for both the Birmingham Schools and Warwickshire county teams for three years on the trot, and had a plethora of scouts scrambling for my signature on a schoolboy contract. All the local professional teams had sent spies down to games to monitor my progress. Coventry, Derby and Wolves had all invited me to visit them, but Aston Villa had pushed the boat out by sending a scout round to our shack of a house and getting me to sign. I'd pretty much given up school – indeed the headmaster had rung me up telling me not to bother coming in any more – and becoming a footballer was my main focus.

The dreaded phone call from my headmaster came a few days after my cup final dismissal. He was forming a disciplinary panel with the referee and two other independent teachers to decide how they were going to punish me. I sat there listening to this bloke bleating down the receiver, but it was just noise to me. I was finished with authority – school, referees, everything – and I would do things my way from now on. Inside my head, I wrote it off as John McEnroe syndrome. If the world's greatest tennis player could haul the officials over the coals, screaming and shouting like a madman when he felt so passionately that he was being cheated, then so could Roy McDonough.

The headmaster called back with a hearing date for my case and asked me to confirm I would be attending. 'Oh yeah, of course,' I told him. But I didn't bother showing up. I wasn't going to stand there in front of a kangaroo court of teachers, who had already made their tiny little minds up. Those smug, clueless bastards were all happy enough to lick my backside when I was breaking numerous sporting records for them, raising the profile of their school in the Solihull area. Every year hundreds of kids would compete at the schools' area sports finals at the Tudor Grange athletics track. I had broken the 100m hurdles record for Solihull and won the race three years in succession. Lyndon High didn't have a pot to piss in and couldn't even afford to buy hurdles for us to practise jumping over. I just ran it and won it on the day. I was their Sport Billy, the ace in the pack, and they loved the kudos they got from my achievements, the one-upmanship they got over rival schools. Now they wanted to hang me out to dry. I wasn't going to give them the satisfaction.

An envelope dropped through the letterbox a few days later. An Education Authority Discipline Board recommended I should receive special behavioural lessons after school. Well, that was hilarious, as I hadn't shown my face around Lyndon High for months. As far as I was concerned, my future was mapped out. I was going to be a footballer and would be starting life as an apprentice at Villa Park in a few months' time. They could all stick it where the sun doesn't shine. But then I got the really crushing news. The Birmingham Schools' FA had also held a summit to discuss my cup final conduct, and it hit me with the one punishment which really hurt – a six-month suspension from playing any competitive football.

So that was my first proper ban in football, but my first sending off had come a year earlier. I had signed schoolboy forms for Aston Villa which made my Dad proud as punch, and he was especially proud when I cracked a grown man square on the chin to earn my first-ever red card.

Villa had entered an under-15 nursery team as their youth side in the Premier Division of the men's Sunday League. We were called Stanley Star XI and played our home matches during the afternoon at a small ground close to Villa Park. Gordon Cowans, who would lift the European Cup for Villa and pull on an England shirt in the future, and Mick Rathbone, who went on to play for Birmingham City and ended up physio at Everton years later, were in the same side. And we all thought we looked the bee's knees wearing Villa's famous claret-and-blue kit.

It would be fair to say our adult opposition didn't quite share our enthusiasm. Having a bunch of flash kids prancing around with Villa's strip on was like waving a red rag at a herd of bulls. These were big, bruising men with points to prove, who had often necked three or four pints in the pub before

VILLAN OF THE PEACE

the game to top up the tank. Fuelled by alcohol, they wanted to kick seven bells out of us and show they were better players who also had what it took to be on the books of a pro club. We were fitter and more skilful, cockily running rings around most of these teams. But they were much stronger and took great delight in letting us know we had been in a game, no matter how many goals they had shipped.

But Villa's ploy was clever. By watching how the young boys reacted they could see which boys were tough enough for the job on these mean pitches, marshalled by blokes in their twenties and thirties, who wanted to return to the pub with a souvenir – a boast for their drinking buddies about chopping one of Villa's future stars in half. It was give as good as you got, or get hurt, during a 90-minute scrap. A prime example of the value of this exercise was Gordon Cowans. He was just three-stone wringing wet and had the biggest target on the front of his face – a huge conk weighing just as much as his body – which any one of these angry buggers could have hit smack on the bullseye from any part of the pitch. But he was as brave as a lion and reaped the benefits of weekly combat on these muddy battlefields. Gordon could tackle like a monster and, as his legs got stronger, could use both feet to score goals from anywhere. It was crystal clear to anybody standing on the side of the pitch that this boy had a great future ahead of him.

Playing for Stanley Star XI helped transform most of us into men, as we grew more determined to defeat the armies of ogres with beer-breath put in front of us. It's a real shame football clubs don't employ the same tactics now. It would straighten out the pampered little pussies who get spoilt rotten at all levels these days, showing off a glittering Rolex and driving round in a BMW before they have achieved anything at all in the game.

Anyway, Villa's 'sink or swim' team was also the birthplace of the disciplinary problems which would pollute my career. I was 15 and we were playing a rough old mob called the Sparr XI. All they wanted to do was kick and fight us, and it was like World War Three all the way to the last minute. We were 8–0 up and I'd helped myself to four goals, which hadn't gone down too well. I loved a bit of banter and made a sarcastic passing comment to their centre-half every time I beat their goalie, 'Come on mate, keep up. I bet you can't even tackle your missus.' I was laughing right in his face, which was boiling red with increased rage, as I knocked the ball past his lumbering legs and gave him a wave. Then I spotted a big enough gap open up between his boots for a nutmeg – the ultimate humiliation for a defender – and he totally lost it after I played the ball through his legs and shouted 'nuts', grabbing my shirt and spinning me round, before punching me on the chin. This guy was much bigger than me – he was 6ft plus, 10 years my senior and must have weighed around 14st – but I didn't go down. I took everything he had on the jaw and hurled one straight back at his face.

It all happened so quickly and the referee swiftly nipped any further trouble in the bud by sending us both off. I was distraught, with tears rolling down both cheeks, as I sat on the touchline among the water bottles and balls with a coat draped over my shoulders. Dad stomped across from the other side of the pitch where he had been watching, and I was bracing myself for a loud bollocking. But it never materialised. He was dead chuffed with me for not being intimidated. In his eyes, I had proved I was a chip off the old block, and he said, 'Well done, son. You took a punch from a fully-grown man, stayed on your feet and got one back in. Don't worry about the red card. I'm proud of you.'

Dad didn't ever do praise, so his response left me feeling happy and relieved, but mostly confused. He had never once patted me on the back for anything I had achieved within the laws of the game. But, driving back home, he was like a broken record, drumming into me how proud he was that I had stood up for myself. I couldn't believe what I was hearing.

When I was a third-year at Lyndon High I had played against the fifth-years of Alston, which was one of the biggest secondary schools in the area. We'd thrashed them 6–1, and I'd blasted all six goals. But Dad had the right hump after the game and slaughtered me because of the one chance I had missed, which I had smacked against the crossbar.

From a very young age, I didn't just participate in sports, I had to win at them, because I was so driven to please Dad. Raised in a dog-eat-dog environment, I was competing against three other brothers and two sisters for a meagre scrap of Dad's affection. I was Mum's blue-eyed boy, but Dad was rarely at home as he was always working away or playing cricket. So, spending any quality time with him meant excelling at sport. Then he couldn't do enough for me. He would always drive me to games, no matter how far away, which can make or break a young footballer's career. Dad watched all four of his sons play football – my older brothers James and Keith, and my twin Gaz, who was also on Villa's schoolboy books. All of them were good players, but Dad saw something different in me. He knew I had that extra fire in my belly, and he would do whatever it took to fan the flames and help me succeed.

Dad could be embarrassing on the sidelines at games, working himself up into a right old frenzy, screaming abuse at the opposition coaching staff and players. There was no special treatment reserved for his sons, however, and we copped plenty of flak, too, as he ran down the touchline ranting and raving at us. In his mind, he was doing us a favour, giving us a gee up. It didn't make Gaz try any harder, though. It just destroyed him. He would tell Dad to 'fuck off', sulk and give up. But it had the opposite effect on me. I was even more determined to stick two fingers up at the old man by pushing on a gear and scoring another goal. If I was up against Gaz in a five-a-side match now, I would break his leg to score the winning goal, brother or not. Gaz would fight anyone off the pitch, but he would just step aside during a game and let me score. He had enough raw talent to join me in the pro ranks, but didn't have that darker edge which can be the difference between success and failure.

Looking back now, Dad could have reacted differently to my first dismissal and should have given me a fierce dressing down that I wouldn't forget in a hurry. But I don't honestly think it would have steered me away from trouble. I was desperate to earn his all-too-rare words of praise, which, ultimately, gave me added licence to go out and win at all costs. I craved that extra attention. And if it meant getting nasty on the pitch to make Dad notice me above the other brothers, then the opposition team was in big trouble.

After they were informed of my suspension following the schools' cup final sending off, Villa weren't impressed, but the suspension would expire before the new season started and I could still train with the rest of the boys. They knew I was a promising talent – I was scoring 20–30 goals for the Warwickshire team in seasons of only 16 games – so they weren't going to let me go. How could they?

I missed a large chunk of the pre-season fitness sessions at Villa, making a brief return to the school hall to sit my exams. My revision schedule was non-existent, but I managed three O-Levels, in Art, English Language and Literature. I only really bothered to take the exams to evade the merciless Villa coaches. They would carry out military-style 'beasting' drills in a bid to build up fitness for the season ahead, running the boys into the ground until they were puking up on the floor. However, I hadn't entirely dodged the bullet and would feel sick to the pit of my stomach soon enough when I returned to the Villa regime.

Vic Crowe had failed to guide Aston Villa back into the First Division, so the Manchester City manager, Ron Saunders, was brought in during the summer of 1974. He was an instant success, winning the League Cup Final at Wembley, as well as taking the club up in his first season, finishing runners-up to Manchester United, who had taken a mighty fall from grace. I don't think Saunders had seen many of the younger lads play. But one summer morning he trotted over to watch us taking part in an eight-a-side practice match at the club's Bodymoor Heath training ground. After we had finished, all the boys who had signed apprentice forms under Vic Crowe were called into the canteen, where the first-team players were sitting down scoffing their lunches off plates on wooden trays. There were seven of us expecting to make the move up from schoolboy forms to challenging for a professional contract the following season, as the club had promised in writing. But it turned out that the forms we had signed were invalid under the new regime.

We were each told to take a seat, and one by one the lads were called into a room for a showdown with the gaffer to learn our fate. The first four came out blubbing like newborn babies, and I was thinking: 'This ain't looking good.' The next one also came out crying, his dreams shattered too, which left just me and Gordon Cowans. Now there was no doubt about Gordon, as he was a different class and everybody knew it. Gordon was a Geordie, but his future at Villa was set in stone the day his folks moved lock, stock and barrel to the Midlands. To get the boy firmly under their wing, Villa had given the Cowans family the security of a house and jobs in Sutton Coldfield, where they looked after the apprentices who had upped sticks from Ireland and Scotland. There was no way Gordon was going to slip through the net, they made sure of that. Sitting there awaiting my audience with Saunders, I was convinced they had left the best two players – the ones Villa were going to keep – until last. My name was called out and I walked confidently into the room to face Saunders, who was sitting there with his big, bald head and long sideburns. This is it, I thought. Everything I have worked so hard for. Playing football eight times a week, catching all those late-night buses back alone from training, ignoring the temptation of a sneaky drink with my brothers, and even sacking off school for the solitude of kicking a ball against a wall for hours on end to improve my touch and power. Here it comes. The confirmation. Everything was going according to plan.

'Sorry, Roy, you're not quite up to the right standard and we won't be taking you,' said Saunders, without the slightest hint of emotion. This was a new era, Saunders was in charge, and he was making his mark by clearing the decks.

I didn't say a word to him, or shed a tear. I just turned around and steamed out, thinking, 'I'll show you Saunders, you slaphead.' Seeing my dry-eyed face, one of the earlier rejects was quick to congratulate me, 'I knew they'd take you, Roy.' I just shook my head and carried on walking, while Gordon went in and took hold of Saunders's pen, the only one to sign on a far from magnificent day for the rest of the seven lads, all nursing broken futures. But Villa meant nothing to me now.

A volcano of rage was building up inside as I caught the bus home. Houses and shops flashed past the window and I kept repeating in my head: 'How dare that bald fucker tell me I'm not good enough.' When I got home, I ran straight to the bedroom I shared with Gaz, ripped the claret-and-blue scarf off the wall and chucked it in the bin. I was more determined than ever to make the grade now. This wasn't the end – it was just the beginning.

2. BLUE-EYED ROY

Football is in my blood. My uncle, Fred Harris, played for Birmingham City before and after the Second World War, still turning out for the first team at 38. He was captain at St Andrew's and had a reputation for being a strong tackler, clocking up more than 300 games for Blues as an inside-forward and wing-half. Dad had also been on the books at Birmingham, before turning out for Bath City when they were top dogs on the non-league scene.

Dad's name was James, but everyone called him 'Macca'. He had dark hair and a hard face, but he was a good-looking bloke and a bit of a 'Jack the Lad' around Solihull. Never a big drinker, he was always striving to win at something on the sporting field, be it tennis, cricket or football. But his biggest conquest was a blonde stunner called Iris, my mum, who looked like Marilyn Monroe through my young eyes. Dad had survived the Second World War as a tank driver in Italy, and Mum would often tell us stories of hiding underground in poorly lit shelters as the German bombers cast an evil shadow over the Midlands during the Blitz. Mum and Dad met at a dance in Solihull during the Fifties, and it was their first waltz down a lifelong married path, which was always feisty and full of arguments. But like all decent fighters, they went the distance, and still loved each other right until the final bell sounded. And that love produced six children. Four years my senior, Jim is No.1 brother, with Keith second in command, and I have two beautiful younger sisters, Lindsay and Lisa.

Then there's my twin brother, Gaz. Connie Francis was No.1 in the UK charts with *Stupid Cupid* when we scrapped our way into the world at Solihull Hospital, on 16 October, 1958. But Gaz won the baby bout on points as he popped out 10 minutes ahead of me – a delayed delivery weighing in at 7lb 2oz. We're not identical, far from it in fact. I'm 6ft 1in tall with square shoulders, while Gaz is a good few inches shorter. He has almost olive skin and dark hair, while I'm pale around the cheeks and as grey as a badger on top. I always claimed to be the better-looking one. But that wasn't hard, as Gaz had a droopy eye as a kid, which needed quite a few operations to fix, and horrible Bugs Bunny teeth. I must have landed the first blow inside Mum's belly.

People often ask if we ever feel any of that supernatural twin telepathy stuff; sharing the same thoughts, or Gaz getting a sharp pain in his shin when I was clobbered by a defender's boot playing football hundreds of miles away from him. The only thing I ever felt was his right hand or foot in my face. Gaz loved nothing more than a ruck, and we were always having tear ups as kids. The golden rule was never to play on opposite teams during break-time football at school because our ultra-competitive natures meant it always ended up in tears. Neither of us could handle losing and I had a right tasty school punch-up with Gaz – which he started – on the one occasion we ignored the rule. The cheering circle of children gathered around us was quickly broken up, but I still had enough time to blacken both his eyes and make his nose swell up. I knew Gaz wasn't going to let that go and would want to start round two as soon as the school bell rang at home time. He would be waiting for me, so I sprinted all the way back to our house, shoved the bolt tight across the door and locked myself in the toilet. Not because I was scared of Gaz, but because he was my brother, who meant the world to me, and I didn't want to fight him.

Life at school was tough for the McDonough clan – even in the junior ranks. Solihull was home to the Land Rover manufacturing plant and the Triumph motorbike factory, as well as Birmingham Airport. Our four-bed semi was in Richmond Road, Olton, in one of the working-class streets. We attended St Margaret's, which was a Church of England primary school. I hated being forced down the church pews twice a week to appease the school's hierarchy, especially as the bible-clutching parents hadn't taught their little devils God's Great Commandment, 'Love thy Neighbour'. Most of the other pupils were snobby rich kids, and they would rip the backsides off us as they walked past our ramshackle house with its overgrown garden, broken wall and unpainted window frames. We were all shoehorned into shared bedrooms and hand-me-down clothes. Being technically the youngest brother, I got to wear all of Jim and Keith's patched-up old cast-offs. The other children dismissed us as the poor family, the 'smelly kids'. But that couldn't have been further from the truth. Mum and Dad were grafters and didn't have time to cut the grass or mend the wall, because they were always working their socks off to feed six hungry mouths. Mum ran a lady's boutique, while Dad flogged dresses out of a van, before opening his own shop in Wednesbury, near Walsall's football ground. We weren't the sort of family who kept telling each other, 'I love you'. In fact, nobody ever said that. Nor were we hugging and kissing each other every five minutes. But we always had fresh food on our plates and Dad silently crept into our rooms every Christmas and left pillow cases next to the beds, stuffed with top-quality chocolate selection boxes and new footballs. He also bought us a three-quarter-length snooker table, which took pride of place in the back room and that faded green baize got a right battering from four highly competitive brothers.

Sport was always going to be critical in breaking down social barriers in my life. Being laughed at in the St Margaret's playground wasn't the nicest thing to go through on a daily basis. But one school football match, playing as a 10-year-old rookie striker against rivals Chapel Fields, finally made me the biggest talking point across the classrooms for positive reasons. We trounced them 4–0 and I got all the goals. Suddenly, all the other kids wanted to be best mates with their favourite figure of fun. And I loved every minute of it.

Those goals were my most valuable school lesson – better than anything I ever gleaned from an English, maths or science book. They showed me I could earn the respect of my young peers through success on the sporting field. So I tripled my efforts, generating a burning desire to be the best I could at sport and win my biggest battle – acceptance from other children. I smashed all the school records for the long and high jumps, 100m sprint and hurdles, as well as for throwing a cricket ball. My first piece of silverware was the Victor Ludorum Trophy – awarded to the school's best all-round sportsman of the year – which I know other great competitors like Ian Botham, Jamie Carragher and Steven Gerrard all won at their schools and cherished.

Learning to bounce back from the spiteful 'poor kid' ridicule at such a formative age developed my drive to show my tormentors just how rich in sporting talent I was. As I approached the end of senior school at Lyndon High, Gaz and my older brothers had started boozing and hitting the clubs. But I never let a drop of alcohol touch my lips. The most excitement I had outside of my complete dedication to football was a fumble in the cinema with my childhood sweetheart Jane. Late nights and beers were completely alien to me. Football was all that mattered in my life. There really was nothing else.

Good old Dad may have had his faults, but he came up trumps for me when I was down in the dumps after being rejected by Villa. He still had connections at Birmingham City from his playing days and got on famously with the chairman, Clifford Coombs. He also knew the chief scout, Don Dorman, who had been desperate to tie me down on a schoolboy form, before I opted for Villa. Dad rang him on the Friday afternoon that Ron Saunders delivered his bombshell, and by Monday morning I was on trial with Blues, who at that time were an established First Division club.

I trained all week with the apprentices, who were all complete strangers to me, and was told to report at the ground on Saturday morning because I had booked a seat on the club minibus to play for the youth team at Mansfield. I couldn't have got off to a better start, exorcising some of those Villa demons straight away by claiming both goals in a 2–0 win over the Stags' youngsters on a training pitch in the car park next to Field Mill's main stand. The door was pushed halfway open now, with the light starting to stream through on a second crack at an apprenticeship. Three days later, at City's Damson Lane training ground, I belted another brace in a 5–2 victory over Stoke, who included another young striker making his way in the game, Garth Crooks. That was four goals in two games, and I believed I had ripped that St Andrew's door off its hinges and was just waiting for one of the coaches to throw me a pen. But nothing happened.

By the Friday, I still hadn't been offered a deal, so Dad got back on the blower to Don to find out what was going on. 'The kid's done great,' said Don. 'He's scored goals and everyone likes him. We're just a bit concerned about whether he's going to mix or not.' They were worried that I was a loner because I wasn't socialising with the other lads back at the ground after the matches. There was a simple reason for that. When the club bus left Damson Lane, I would ask the driver to stop at the traffic lights by the Wheatsheaf pub, in Coventry Road, as it was only a two-mile walk home from that point. If I'd gone back to the stadium with the rest of the apprentices, it would have been double the distance, and I had no money for public transport. But after scoring again on the Saturday, I stayed on the bus, travelled back to St Andrew's and tucked into beans on toast with the other boys, before playing a few games of pool. And hey presto . . . I signed an 18-month apprenticeship as a 16-year-old with Birmingham on the Monday morning for a princely sum of £10 a week, just 17 days after being kicked out of big city rivals Villa.

My reputation as a half-decent targetman was growing – somebody who relished winning his headers, could protect the ball with his back to goal and link the play, as well as get on the end of crosses to finish himself. Even England were sitting up and taking notice, after I hit both goals in a 2–0 friendly win for Birmingham's youth team against the Three Lions' Under-18s at St Andrew's. I'd terrorised their defence and the international scouts came to watch my next few games, with an FA Youth Cup replay at Wolves expected to be my gateway into the England set-up. But I smashed my knee up in training before the match, sliding across a wet pitch to meet a cross and colliding painfully with the goalkeeper. I was lowered into a bath filled with boiling hot water that I could only just about stand in to try and reduce the swelling, before being patched up and sent into battle at Molineux. The knee was strapped so tightly I could barely move the joint as I tried to take on Bob Hazell and George Berry. But I was struggling and was put out of my misery after an hour – signalling the end of my England ambitions.

Equally important in the development department was sharpening up my image. All footballers need one. It helps catch the eye, especially with the birds. But I failed miserably, as my far from carefully crafted look remained the same for the next 20 years. Even at that age, I had shoulder-length hair, which was rapidly turning a white shade of grey, and a matching moustache. Both would become my trademark, so I'm told. A lot of people thought it was cleverly planned – part and parcel of the tough-guy persona. Especially the fur on my top lip, which I've seen quoted in football hardmen polls as being 'immaculately well trimmed, sending out the hard as nails warning that Roy would take on anyone outside in the car park after the game'. I thought I looked about as scary as Dick Dastardly from the *Wacky Races* cartoons. The honest truth is that I've got a round blemish just below my nose. Mum used to call it a 'beauty spot' to make me feel better, but I had a complex about it as a child. As soon as I could muster the power to sprout facial hair, I slapped a moustache over the top to hide it.

People linked the colour rapidly draining out of my hair

with the pressure of trying to make it as a footballer, which was a joke as I couldn't even spell 'stress' at the time, let alone know the meaning of the word. None of my brothers went grey until they hit their forties, so I'm sure I got their share as well, too bloody early. As for the long hair, music was my biggest love after football, and I wanted to look like my favourite guitar heroes, whose faces filled a poster shrine on my bedroom wall. I was a rocker at heart and bang into all the noisy ear-splitting Birmingham bands like Led Zeppelin, Thin Lizzy and Black Sabbath.

There was only ever one slight variation to the hairstyle during those early days at Blues – and that was to prove my sisters wrong. They said that I didn't have the bottle to go the whole hog and have a rock star perm. So I cockily toddled along to a salon all full of myself and asked this bent-as-a-nine-bob-note hairdresser to make me look like Robert Plant or Roger Daltrey. He sat me under the dryer with all my hair pulled through this plastic cap. But when he whipped it off, I had a microphone head – like the Golliwog off the jam jars. I just sat there horrified, staring at the mirror in utter disbelief. But the hairdresser was chuffed with his handiwork, and smiled, 'Oh, it's taken just lovely, Roy.' I had started to attract a few female admirers on the touchline, but the next time I trotted out for the reserves there wasn't any swooning, just incessant giggling. There would be months of laughter at my expense before that curly abomination grew out and disappeared.

Life as a Birmingham apprentice was mundane. All we wanted to do was play football, but we were handed the most boring jobs to knock us into shape – scrubbing the toilets, sweeping the stands and mopping the changing room floors. I got to clean Trevor Francis's boots and prided myself on making them look perfect for him on a Saturday afternoon. He wore Adidas World Cup boots, with Stylo stripes stitched on the side, as they were his personal sponsors. Trevor was Mr Birmingham City and everything at the club revolved around him. As a young forward trying to make the grade, I couldn't have asked for a better pair of boots to clean. They would be worn by the first £1 million player when he joined Nottingham Forest a couple of years later. Trevor was 21 when I started buffing up his footwear, but was Birmingham's highest-paid player and had a top-of-the-range club-sponsored Triumph TR6 in the car park, which was the best motor there by a country mile. He looked after me at Christmas, giving me a £10 bonus, which matched one week of my apprentice wages, and he was always happy to chat about football.

There was one occasion when Trevor didn't have it all his own way at Birmingham, however, which was the worst training-ground bust-up I have ever seen. Trevor was a big moaner and would let everyone know he wasn't happy if the ball didn't go straight to his feet. We had a feisty Scouser, Archie Styles, and the two of them had already been involved in a couple of minor altercations. Archie caught him late again, and Trevor, who was never a fighter, threw back his shoulders and started shouting the odds. But Archie never said a word, he just punched Trevor straight in the nose and as he went down rubbed six studs across his pretty-boy face. Both of his eyes were blackened and he was left with tramlines down his nose. Archie had put him in his place and that was the end of it.

I was making good progress now and had found a second – and much calmer – father figure in one of the coaches, Ken Oliver. He was a Geordie who took an instant shine to me, with a keen interest in teaching a devoted pupil the striker's trade. He could see one of my biggest strengths was holding up the ball, so he taught me to 'guard it with my life'. This was also a time when the boozing culture at clubs was legendary, and there were no hi-tech diets to keep players in shape, so he also passed on plenty of advice about looking after my body. He could see how dedicated I was to football, and it was a massive plus to have an ally on the coaching staff. But Ken didn't need to worry about the temptations of drink affecting me. I was still leading a monk-like existence, taking Jane out when I wasn't playing football and steering well clear of joining my brothers on the beer trail. I didn't even know what a pint of lager tasted like, and I wasn't interested in finding out.

I had never realised the true meaning of the word pain until I reported back to St Andrew's for my first proper serving of torturous pre-season training at the start of the 1976/77 season. After a gruelling summer work-out, which left my calf, thigh and stomach muscles sore to the touch, I was well prepared for the new campaign. The manager, Willie Bell, obviously thought so too, as he began picking me for the weekly reserves-against-first-team match on a Friday. These games were supposed to be a gentle workout for the senior lads ahead of Saturday's First Division match, and we were expected to hold back. But I wasn't going to give any of them an easy ride, as this was my golden opportunity to stake a claim for a first-team place. Knowing full well the manager was watching every kick, I would try and run the bollocks off the two centre-halves, Joe Gallagher and John Roberts. They were both powerful lads who were silent as statues but would quite happily clump you without warning.

One player who didn't welcome my youthful exuberance was Kenny Burns. He was in his mid-twenties, six-months short of joining Brian Clough at Nottingham Forest, where he reverted from striker to centre-half as the lynchpin of back-to-back European Cup triumphs. Burnsy was one of the big cheeses at Birmingham, a law unto himself and a typical fiery Scot. A senior member of the club's drinking squad, I'd heard stories about him going ballistic and smashing all his clubs up against a defenceless tree after hitting one bad shot on the golf course.

But he was calmer on a Friday. That was the problem. He just wanted a nice, easy knockabout and shower, before playing Leeds or Liverpool the next day. He hated me for making him sweat more than he deemed necessary and made my life hell. Every time I saw him – on the training pitch, during games, or around the ground – he would shout derogatory remarks, or stand there pointing and laughing at me. It was just like being back at school. But this wasn't a spiteful child I had to deal with – it was the biggest loose cannon at the club. It was daunting enough going into the changing room to pick up the first-team players' dirty kits, because they could destroy you with their rapier-like banter. But on one occasion Burns decided to turn up the intimidation meter a few hundred notches by throwing a football boot straight at my head, which whizzed just past my ear and smacked against the wall. He did his best to make my life extremely uncomfortable, and I did my very best to avoid that wavy hair, squashed nose and mean handlebar moustache at all costs. But there was no escaping my chief tormentor when we were paired up front together for a reserve outing at Hereford.

Burns had been injured and suspended, so was pencilled in for a rust-shaking run-out for the stiffs at Edgar Street. I can't say I was looking forward to partnering him in attack, but inside me there was also a big chunk of, 'Right Burnsy, I'm going to show you'. The pitch was a mudbath, and Hereford had a giant 6ft 4in centre-half who couldn't play, but could kick, bollock and bite. He was giving me – the young spunk – a hard enough time, but regarded Burnsy, a Scottish international, as a scalp worth collecting and was booting lumps out of him. Burnsy didn't want to be there and was going through the motions, but I sparked him into life after overpowering the defender at the far post and winning my header so he could tuck the ball past the goalkeeper.

The celebrations were muted, but I was in my element now, having it off verbally and physically with this towering centre-half. I just wanted to fight him. This was my chance to show bully-boy Burns what I was made of, so I kept putting my head in with the defender to try and batter him all around his half of the pitch. I was buzzing and the adrenaline nearly burst out of my veins when I climbed above their colossus once again to head in the winner. Tramping off the gluepot pitch after the final whistle, the defender came looking for me, not to give me a thump, but to shake my hand, and say, 'Well done'.

This game defined my style of play. It hit home to me just how much satisfaction I got out of dominating defenders. It didn't matter how much bigger than me they were, because whatever they chucked my way they were going to get back bucket loads more. From that moment on, I wanted every centre-half I played against to come off the pitch physically and mentally defeated, despite giving it everything he had during a bruising 90-minute duel. I wanted to leave that pitch owning his respect, otherwise I hadn't done my job properly.

Before I got back to the changing room, a beefy arm swung itself around my shoulders, 'Fair play to you, son. I owe you an apology'. My all-action display had won Burnsy's respect, too. That filled me with immense pride, as it meant I had won two huge battles – on and off the pitch. From that day on, he was good as gold with me. There was no more abuse or intimidation tactics. In fact, he started to make a big fuss of me, and we went out for a round of golf. He didn't feel the need to give the poor old clubs a bashing this time, either.

With Burns off my back, everything started to click into place. Birmingham were treading water mid-table in the First Division. I'd already been offered a one-year professional contract, quadrupling my apprentice wage to a bumper £40 a week, and I suddenly found myself being gently introduced into the senior set-up. Teams only had one substitute in those days, but two or three extra bodies would be part of the squad. They were usually youngsters, and it would give them a taste of the big-match atmosphere; travelling on the coach, sitting in the dressing room and, of course, picking up the dirty kits at the end of the game. I'd been conscripted for a couple of overnight stays on away trips, along with my pal Mick Rathbone. But there was never much threat of gate-crashing the first-team party as a shock starter, or stealing onto the bench. At 18 years of age, I had to be better than Kenny Burns or Trevor Francis to force my way into the team. Talk about mission impossible.

When my chance did come, it was a complete surprise. We were playing Sunderland and I'd travelled up on the coach to the team hotel in Durham, gawping at the blatant flaunting of wealth taking place. The executive members of the drinking squad were Howard Kendall, Joe Gallagher and Kenny Burns. Trevor Francis also had his feet firmly under the top table, but wasn't much of a drinker. Kendall, an energetic box-to-box player and probably England's best uncapped midfielder, loved a good booze-up and was the team's social secretary. Gallagher was the bookie and if anyone wanted a bet, whether it be on football, the horses or little green men landing a flying saucer in the centre circle at St Andrew's, he would give you the odds and cover it. On this coach trip, the four of them were grouped round a table playing three-card brag as we chugged up the motorway. Trevor had emptied a stash of cash from his trouser pockets and was sitting there with a lap full of notes; tens, twenties and fifties. I watched him lose £200 in four hands, money I could only dream of stuffing in my wallet.

At the team hotel there were whispers that I might have a more important role than laundry boy for the match at Sunderland. Joe Gallagher was struggling with an injury, and if he failed a fitness test Burns was expected to slot in at the back as cover. Three hours before kick-off on the Saturday, we had a team meeting at the hotel and Willie Bell broke the news that Gallagher hadn't made it, so I would be starting up front with Trevor Francis. It didn't sink in at first and it just seemed surreal. I was actually going to get a crack at the First Division, lining up alongside Blues' megastars – who were still so far detached from my life – as a complete equal.

My initial feeling was one of disappointment, as I was gutted none of my family would be there to see me play. Solihull was 200 miles away and they would never make it up north in time. There was no internet or mobile phones, so a stunned Dad heard about my inclusion on the kitchen radio. It must have killed him not being there after all the dedication he had put into my career. My silent reaction was soon punctured by Kendall, 'Well done, mate. You'll do well out there', and Francis, who shook the hand of his former boot boy and said, 'Good luck, Roy. We'll look after you.' But I didn't need taking care of, I was raring to go. I wasn't nervous at all, just massively excited, ready to run out at

Roker Park for a real game and show the football world just what I was all about.

After the brief meeting finished, we headed straight to the dining room for a pre-match meal. There was no healthy pasta dish, or high-energy liquid potions. Not even beans on toast. The choice was chicken or a fat sirloin steak, with an omelette or toast. Barely able to believe that the best day of my life could get even better, I demolished a steak treat, which rarely materialised on a plate at home.

The team coach was given a police escort by cops on motorbikes as it slowly pierced a sea of red and white flowing all the way down to Roker Park. There were Sunderland fans swarming all around the ground, edging their way through the turnstiles to build a 34,193 crowd. Some of their supporters waited for us to leave the coach. First off was our goalkeeper Jimmy Montgomery, who was a legend on Wearside, playing over 600 games and winning the FA Cup, and he got a great ovation from Sunderland's fans. The rest of us hurriedly sought refuge in the changing rooms, as we were showered with apples, drink cans, spit and general dog's abuse. It didn't bother me. Nothing was going to ruin this milestone day – Saturday, 7 May, 1977.

As I walked out of the tunnel for a peep at the ground, it dawned on me how normal it all felt. Here I was, on the verge of my First Division debut, and there were thousands of people standing on concrete terrace steps smoking fags, and others with backsides going numb on wooden seats flicking through programmes. But in the centre of it all, it was still just a grass pitch, with white lines painted across it, a goal at each end and flags in all four corners. It was just a game of football. I returned to the changing room and there was my kit, the blue shirt of Birmingham City, hanging up waiting for me. I was going to pull that over my body – this really was happening.

Ten minutes before kick-off, Willie Bell came in for his pre-match talk, but I didn't hear a word of it. I was already fully focused on getting on that pitch and rattling the cages of a few First Division reputations. As I stood in the tunnel, waiting to jog out with the rest of the lads and start the game, the famous Roker Roar reverberated around the stand above my head. It was the loudest thing I had ever heard in my life and it made the hairs on the back of my neck stick up. It wasn't anxiety, it was the buzz of hearing that crowd and knowing this was what I was in the game for. All the hard graft I had put in since primary school was about to pay-off – all the sacrifices had been worth it.

And it was so nearly a dream start. In the eighth minute, I cut inside a defender from the wing and hit a shot from 16 yards across goalkeeper Barry Siddall. Howard Kendall was square and going berserk, screaming at me to pass: 'Give it here, you little shit!' But this was my chance to make a lightning-quick mark on the big time. Dad always told me I was too generous, that I created too much for others by passing the ball when I should have been selfish, had another touch and fired at goal myself. The shot was creeping all the way inside the far post, but Siddall hadn't read the script and got half a hand to the ball, which agonisingly rolled inches wide of the upright.

We got beaten 1–0, with Mel Holden grabbing the winner. I had missed my one and only chance, but felt I had played well, winning plenty of headers and making a nuisance of myself against wily old defenders. There were plenty of encouraging back slaps from the lads in the changing room after the game – including Kendall, who had calmed down by then. I believed I had done enough to merit keeping my place for the next game on Tuesday night – the grudge match against city rivals Aston Villa at St Andrew's – which I was desperate to be involved in for obvious reasons. I wanted to stick it right up Ron Saunders in the best way, by doing over his team in front of 43,000 fanatical punters. But I never got the chance. Gallagher had an injection to take the sting out of his injury, releasing Kenny Burns to go back up front with Trevor Francis, who got the winner from the spot. I was completely bombed, not even making the bench.

Willie Bell pulled me to one side after training on the Monday morning and told me I was out: 'If you'd have scored, son, I would have played you.' It was the ultimate anti-climax, after having a nibble at the First Division banquet just a few days earlier. The only positive thing about it all was my reaction. When I was younger, I would have withdrawn deep inside myself and sulked, not talking to anybody for days. But this rejection had the complete opposite effect. I knuckled down even harder in training and was rewarded with a second bite of the cherry before the season finished. And, best of all, everybody would be there to see it this time.

Birmingham and QPR were both sandwiched snugly in the middle of the First Division pack. Pre-match, the most important thing about the final game of the season at Loftus Road for the QPR fans was bidding a fond farewell to former Arsenal legend Frank McLintock, who was hanging up his boots. But I was ready to gatecrash the party. Burns was being rested for international duty, so after getting the official nod from Bell I made sure my family had plenty of notice to travel to west London. They did this in style, of course, all jumping in Dad's brightly-painted camper van, which suffered a flat tyre on the way down. But the whole clan still made it in time.

Partnering McLintock in the QPR defence was the ex-Chelsea hero, David Webb, who was a hefty old unit and had always been able to handle himself. McLintock was a good few years Webby's senior, but both of them were on the wrong side of 30 and I was rubbing my hands with glee, thinking, 'I'll have these old fuckers.' We got off to a great start, with Howard Kendall giving us a half-time lead, but Rangers hit back, with Don Masson and Webb getting on the scoresheet. The clock was ticking down and their boys were already counting a win bonus to top up the summer holiday fund. But I stole the cash out of their pockets. With three minutes to go, I laid the ball back to John Connolly wide on the left, who skinned their full-back Dave Clement and curled a peach of a cross to the back post. I was always taught to move into space after releasing the ball, so I carried on running to the box and launched myself above Webb and Ron Abbott to bury a header in the top corner of Phil Parkes's goal.

The Birmingham fans went crazy, but I didn't know what to do. I had nothing special planned and my goal celebration was naff. In a complete daze, I just carried on running back to the halfway line, as my bemused team-mates tried to catch up with me. The final whistle soon blew and I'd earned us a point with my first league goal. After the game, all I could think was, 'That one's for you Saunders, you bald bastard'. I wanted him to choke on his Cornflakes reading the morning papers, which had my name plastered all across them in bold black headlines: 'Roy Robs Point for Blues' and 'Young Mac is Blues' Saviour'.

On the coach home, the end-of-season piss-up got into full swing. The beer cans were passed around and, despite not being a drinker, I was the new goalscoring hero and had to go with the flow. So I sunk a few tins as we headed back to a notorious nightclub in the Small Heath area of Birmingham called the Garry Owen. The place had a poor reputation. A bouncer had recently been shot outside and on another occasion a headcase had attempted to drive his car straight through the club's front doors. But it was a regular haunt of the first team and all the lads were out on the razz.

I sat at a big table with all the senior players, some of whom would disappear every now and then to visit the massage parlour next door. I honestly believed they were going there for a relaxing post-match rub down. I really was out of my depth and my head was spinning all over the shop from my first adventure with alcohol. I still polished off one of the venue's trademark T-bone steaks and drowned the meaty monster with pint after pint, still worrying about who was going to pay for what was an extravagant outing for me. The club had the bar bill covered, of course, and paid for my taxi home as well, which some of the players bundled me into at 5am. It was the first time I had been completely pissed out of my head.

And as the day's glorious events whirled around my stewed teenage brain in the back of the cab, all the way home to the bedroom I shared with Gaz, I had a little smile to myself. I was on my way. I'd got my goal – the first of many in Blues' colours – and all the other lads loved me now. I'd proved I was good enough to be a First Division striker. Next season, I would keep my place in that team and become a top-flight star. I'd almost cracked it.

3. BARREN KNIGHTS

The club doctor had me down as a medical marvel just a few days after opening my goalscoring account at QPR. Everyone had to report back to St Andrew's for a summer weigh in, with the threat of a club fine for anybody piling on too many extra pounds during their holidays. I was only 12st and expected to be in and out as quick as a flash. But the doctor starting buzzing around me, running all sorts of tests, before plonking a bottle of pills in my hand to, 'Clear it up'. That wouldn't be the last time I would hear those words, but it turned out that on this occasion I was one step away from pneumonia. I had a congested lung and the doctor was at a complete loss to understand how I had managed to last 90 minutes at Loftus Road. I didn't really give it a second thought. I felt fit as a fiddle and was more interested in the improved contract I had just signed. A two-year deal, which more than trebled my wages to £150 a week, plus a £50 appearance bonus – a great wage for a young lad just shy of his 19th birthday.

The summer flew by as I kept myself ticking over, playing cricket with Dad. The *Birmingham Sports Argus* published a few complimentary articles with pictures, earmarking me as one of Blues' hot properties for the future. People were even starting to recognise me in the street. So, with the season over, I started to socialise a bit more, but still only having a couple of pints at a time when I went out. I was in the Faces nightclub with Gaz one night when the DJ announced over the loud speakers that they were honoured to have Birmingham's brightest new star in the house. Gaz shook my shoulder and said, 'They're talking about you, Roy. You're a big face around town now.' The DJ repeated the message over and over again for an hour. I just leant against the bar lapping it up, waiting for the inevitable horde of beautiful women to throw themselves at me, like helpless moths attracted to a flame. I had a stupid Cheshire Cat grin right across my face. But it soon fell off sideways, as a large crowd of screaming girls tried to get their paws on a young bloke with long, dark hair at the other end of the bar. It was John Taylor, the Duran Duran guitarist – he was the big attraction, not me – and fair play to him, he was prettier than most of the birds.

Pre-season training before the 1977/78 campaign was still painful, but definitely felt easier second time round. There was one notable absentee, Kenny Burns, who had been flogged to Forest for £150,000. His departure was great news for me and I believed that it surely made me a shoo-in for first-team action, a view strengthened by the usual round of warm-up fixtures. We played seven games that summer, including matches against Sheffield United and the Saudi Arabian national team. With Burns defecting to the City Ground, I was thrust straight back into the limelight, partnering Trevor Francis for the friendly programme. It couldn't have gone any better, as apprentice and master hit it off straight away. I held the ball up and linked the play, ploughing through the donkey work, while Trevor worked tirelessly up and down the channels. The pairing reaped instant rewards, with Trevor netting eight goals, while I chipped in with six more. I was already scanning the First Division fixture list to see which teams Trevor and I would shoot down in tandem. We had Manchester United, Chelsea, Leeds and Liverpool in our first four games. Massive matches, and I was going to be starting them all. There wasn't a shred of doubt in my adolescent mind. But that was before one of the directors – who also just happened to be the greatest England manager of all time – absolutely killed my chances. Sir Alf Ramsey, who had led us to World Cup victory against West Germany on that famous day at Wembley in 1966, was now on the board at St Andrew's. I don't think he ever put tuppence into the club, but just having his name associated with Blues was a big deal, as he was one of the most iconic figures in football. He still lived in Ipswich, where he had won the First Division title before taking over as England manager, and attended games at Portman Road. It was during these regular sojourns to his old stomping ground that somebody caught his eye, somebody who could fill Burns's boots, but somebody who wasn't me. So, on Sir Alf's glowing recommendation, Blues splashed out £135,000 on another forward, Keith Bertschin, and I was a crushed squad player again. I suppose it had been naive to think a First Division club was going to start the season with an untried teenager as their main second striker. But it didn't mean I had to like it, especially after such a great pre-season. An overwhelming cloud of bitterness set in.

Without me, Blues made a terrible start to the season, getting stuffed 4–1 at home by Manchester United, before losing the next couple of games to Chelsea and Leeds. I can't say I was that bothered, though. I'd had the guts ripped out of me and my mentality had completely changed. I wasn't even making the bench, and sat in the stand listening to the fans slagging off the team, with Keith Bertschin already coming in for a lot of stick. He still hadn't scored a goal and I sat there seething, hoping he'd have a stinker and miss sitter after sitter. He was only a couple of years older than me and had hardly been pulling up trees at Ipswich. Keith was a nice lad, but too soft in my opinion, and watching him skip around the pitch with his demi-wave hair blowing about in the wind made me so angry. I was much more aggressive than him, which was what a team under the cosh needed, not some prancing pony. It was the same in training, I couldn't stand seeing the geezer and just wanted to break his legs. I really had to hold back. But it wasn't because I hated him, I just wanted his shirt. I had the same attitude to Birmingham's results; I wanted them to get hammered 6–0 every week, because then the manager would have to change things. It's the football mentality – the whole point of your existence is to chase the next ball, score the next goal and play in the next game. I wasn't doing any of those things, sitting on my backside among the restless natives on a Saturday afternoon. To make matters worse, I was scoring regularly in the reserves, netting a hat-trick in the Football Combination against Reading, as well as getting on the scoresheet at such prominent venues as Highbury and White Hart Lane. At the start of September, Willie Bell told the *Birmingham Mail* that four of the club's youngsters would be in the squad to face league and European champions Liverpool at St Andrew's, and their story had my picture printed alongside it on the back page, which temporarily lifted my spirits. Kevan Broadhurst, Steve Fox and Mick Rathbone, who were all a similar age to me, started the game, which we lost 1–0. I didn't even make the bench and was exiled to the stand again. The fans sitting around me were laying it on thick, saying, 'You should be out there, Roy', which just gave me the hump even more.

The frustration continued to simmer until I exploded in a second-string match at Luton. The centre-half was a real handful, mobile on the ball and had me in his pocket. I was getting crap service and putting in an even worse performance. The hot steam was bubbling away at 2–0 down, but I finally erupted when the referee awarded a free kick against us that I didn't agree with. 'You fucking cheat,' I shouted. Top pocket, red card, straight off. It was the start of a career-long campaign against what I judged to be incompetent officials. But it's not easy staying calm in the heat of battle, and they didn't have a clue about all the other stuff going on around me during the match. Some Herbert was permanently camped in my ear, telling me he was shagging my missus and that she takes it up the arse, and that he's going to do this and that to her – anything to try and get me going. I used to hear loads of that, as people knew I had a short fuse. But I could handle the verbal assaults, as I classed myself as being pretty sharp, able to quickly come back with an even better line to shut them up. But the arrogance of a referee who can't accept his brainless ruling is wrong, maybe costing my team the game after I'd sweated my nuts off, well, that was a different matter all together. There was no amount of relaxation therapy that could teach me to switch off from that.

Back at St Andrew's, I wasn't the only one in hot water. Willie Bell got the bullet after the disastrous start to the season – five successive defeats and no goals for Keith Bertschin. I felt sorry for Bell, despite his reluctance to pick me, as he was a straight guy and a decent coach, but he was never a good man-manager. I was surprised to learn that he had turned to religion after leaving Blues, following a short stint bossing Lincoln City. Bell got ordained as a minister in the US and started delivering sermons at prisons, which must have been like visiting holiday camps compared to the goldfish bowl of St Andrew's. But there was precious little time for any crocodile tears, as the mental merry-go-round was spinning in my head again.

Bell's demise was my opportunity to impress a new manager and get back in the picture. His successor had already been lined up – one of the biggest football gods on the planet, in fact – and we really should have seen it coming. Sir Alf Ramsey had gone from floating around the periphery to becoming an increasingly visible presence at the club. He had sporadically watched our home games in the past, but was now attending all of them, as well as appearing at the training ground as an interested spectator. His arrival was both unorthodox and amusing. We were training in the pissing rain at Damson Lane – which had a slight slope, making the pitch a sloppy old mess – when this figure slowly tip-toed through the sludge. He was kitted out in a shocking combination of dark blue pinstriped suit and trousers – which he pinched above the knees to keep them out of the mire – and a mud-splattered pair of brown Brogues. Sir Alf was from east London originally, but there wasn't a hint of the Cockney barrow boy in his posher than posh voice. He was like a living, breathing exhibit plucked from another time zone. Ken Oliver stopped the game, allowing the legendary manager to make his address. 'Good morning gentlemen,' he said. 'I take it that you know things have been happening. Well, I wanted to let you know that I will be taking charge of the first team, and Ken will be assisting me with the coaching. I'm sure we'll do well and enjoy ourselves together. So, enjoy your training, and I'll see you all on Saturday.' He then made an immediate about turn and slid back across the pitch to find shelter.

I was a bit star struck. It was Sir Alf Ramsey after all, the manager who had won us the World Cup. I had watched every kick of those finals as a seven-year-old boy, huddled around the TV at home with my family. To have the architect of that famous victory taking over the managerial reins was a massive boost to everybody at the club. Sir Alf was very humble, but commanded instant respect, and he definitely got another 20 per cent out of everyone just by being at the club a few times a week. We never saw him between Monday and Wednesday, as he stayed in Ipswich and let Ken run the show, which I was more than happy with. But on the Thursday before his first game in charge at Middlesbrough, he approached me. 'Roy, do you have a minute please? Just to let you know, you're in my squad at Middlesbrough tomorrow because I think you're a jolly good footballer.' And then he was gone again, as I stood there with my mouth wide open. Sir Alf Ramsey knew my name, he had called me 'Roy'. I boasted about it to everyone I knew – Mum, Dad, my brothers and sisters, the bus driver, milkman and postman. Anyone whose ears I could burn.

Being involved at Ayresome Park held another fascination for me – the chance to mix it with a player I regarded as the hardest ever to walk the earth, Graeme Souness. The tough-tackling Scot was the complete package. He was a scrapper who wanted to win at all costs, whether that meant going over the top of a player, or punching or elbowing his opponent to force the upper hand. I had so much respect for Souness, as I shared his win-at-all-costs attitude, which must come from the genes of my battle-hungry ancestors. McDonough is an anglicised form of the Gaelic name Mac Donnchadha, which means 'son of a strong warrior'. Dad told me our name was inherited from rough Irish travellers, who hit the road seeking out bare-fisted bouts to earn a living. But Souness was more than a street-fighting thug, he was an exceptional footballer too, and if you let him play he would murder you.

Souness was five years my senior and I was desperate to get in a scrap with him on the pitch, even though I'd probably end up second best. I fantasised about our clash on the team coach, him giving me 10 stitches in my leg, then I would try and give him 12 back. The reality was very different, though. Sir Alf breezed into the changing room at 2.50pm, bouncing a ball on the floor before throwing it to the captain Howard Kendall. There was no blackboard with magnetic pieces arranged in puzzling formations, or translations of complicated diagrams explaining how to breach Boro's backline – the closely guarded tactical secrets of a World Cup-winning master coach. It was all very 'Mr Cholmondley Warner' again as Sir Alf spoke softly in his plummy tones: 'Howard, take the boys out now. Do what you do best as professional footballers. And, most of all, enjoy yourselves.' That was it, over in a few seconds, and then he did his usual disappearing trick.

I'd made the bench at last, but the nearest I got to pounding the turf was running up and down the touchline to warm-up. I got the usual welcoming hospitality from the northern monkeys – an apple core against the back of the head, half a brick flying past my ankle as I stretched by the corner flag and the highly original call of, 'Go back home and do your paper round you Brummie bastard.' It was slightly amusing the first 50 times.

Trevor Francis got a double and we won 2–1 – our first success of the season – but Keith Bertschin drew another blank. He broke his duck in the next game, a 3–0 home success against Newcastle, and it seemed that Sir Alf's sprinkling of stardust was working its magic. Birmingham won three of his first four games in charge and started climbing the table. I was still involved in the squads as I passed my 19th birthday, but wasn't getting anywhere near a substitute spot again, which was being hogged by John Connolly.

My highlight of the season came at Old Trafford in January, when Francis poached another goal to beat Manchester United in their own backyard. I'd had a soft spot for the Red Devils after crowding round the goggle box with my family again for their maiden European Cup win at Wembley in 1968 against Benfica and the mighty Eusebio. Connolly had failed his audition for the Theatre of Dreams, with Ricky Sbragia deputising on the bench, so the closest I got to following in my childhood idols' footsteps was being 14th man in Blues' squad, with a seat in the main stand alongside the 15th man, Steve Fox. Surrounded by Mancs, it nearly turned ugly when Francis nicked the winning goal, as we both jumped out of our seats cheering like a couple of away fans. It was like a scene from a Clint Eastwood cowboy movie when he swaggers into a hostile saloon and everything goes deathly silent, as hundreds of United supporters shot us angry daggers. What they didn't know was that it wasn't the goal which had had us jumping about screaming like school kids. It was because Francis's strike had pocketed us half a win bonus each just for sitting on our arses – £100 for being part of the squad, £200 if you actually played. So, I'll always have fond memories of my only trip to Old Trafford, and not many opposition players can say that.

At the final whistle we hurried down to the changing room before we got lynched. Sir Alf popped his head around the door and said, 'Jolly good show chaps. Enjoy your trip home and I'll see you all on Thursday.' Then he turned on his heels, not to get cosy on the team bus, but back into his own car to head straight home to Ipswich for a few days. A sweet little number, indeed.

Travelling with the team every other week without getting near the bench, and finding myself dumped back in the reserves on a Tuesday, was starting to take its toll. I began questioning whether all the effort and dedication was worth it. I was feeling depressed, a black state heightened by not having anybody to turn to for advice. We didn't have agents in those days to give us career guidance and I certainly couldn't call on Dad, who would have dismissed my cry for help as an embarrassing weakness. That ruled out Mum too, just in case it got back to Dad, and my brothers were out of the equation as well. How could I tell them I was feeling sorry for myself, when they were getting up at 7am to do nine-hour shifts in dirty old factories for less money? They would have given anything to roll out of bed at 9am, go and kick a football around for a few hours and be back home by early afternoon. If I had tried to confide in them, they would have bashed my brains in. I was so alone in this football world and nobody could ever understand how hard the rejection was.

On a Thursday, the weekend squads – firsts, stiffs and youths – were pinned on a notice board outside the dressing rooms. But when the starting line-up was announced on a matchday it was always the same, that heavy rock of despair crashing into the pit of my stomach. I'd warm my usual seat next to the fans at St Andrew's, or travel to another alien football ground, cast adrift in a cold, blowy old stand, going through all the rituals of being a first-team player, but not getting a kit on or kicking a ball. Just parking my bum on a creaky wooden seat, watching the lads out there playing, which is just about as cruel as it gets. So I decided to take solace in the arms of something that wouldn't let me down – alcohol, which started to anaesthetise the pain.

As my drinking steadily increased, football began to take a back seat without me even realising it. I started tagging along with my brothers to the pub, which just turned into a competition, as I had to match them drink for drink, sloshing away eight or nine pints on a week night, before shovelling down a plate of hot lava in a curry house at 2am. Things got out of hand very quickly, and we were a nightmare combination. We would race each other home pissed in our cars, hammering it up the middle of the A34, two or three of us side-by-side, playing chicken with the headlights of other motors zooming towards us. Gaz had a Ford Anglia 1600 with a Cortina engine, which he believed was the fastest thing on four wheels in Birmingham, but I'd still give him a run for his money in my Austin 1100. That car didn't last long, though, because of an incident involving another sport that beer had opened my eyes to – the fairer sex. By now I'd split up with Jane, who I'd been seeing since secondary school, and was knocking about with three girls from the Crown pub in Stratford Road, Solihull, which had crumpet hanging from the rafters. Playing the field off the pitch was another welcome distraction from football, and I was soon dubbed the 'German Porn Star' because of my long hair and moustache. It was a nickname I did my very best to live up to, as I was sleeping with two of these girls, who were best mates, which led to all sorts of ructions when they found out I was two-timing them. I was also teaching one of the younger lads at the club, Kevin Oakley, to drive. So one night, after a few too many lagers in the Crown, I told him to get behind the wheel, while I sat in the back entertaining the three girls. We had a blowout in one of the back tyres as we headed down a country lane towards one of their houses and Kevin ploughed into three garden walls, writing my car off.

I rattled into training the next day with the side hanging off my motor and bloodshot eyes betraying the shenanigans of the night before. Ken Oliver didn't need a radar to read the danger signs. I might have been going off the rails, but he still cared about my career. He knew I was still a rookie drinker and wanted to get me straight back on track. 'Go out last night, Roy?' he asked.

'Yeah, Ken, just out with my brothers,' I replied.

'Have a drink, did you?' he prodded. 'Yeah, lager, Ken.' The interrogation continued: 'How many, Roy? And be honest.' I lied. 'Four or five.' He pointed straight at a groundsman's rusty fire bucket on the floor, which had all sorts of filthy old crap swilling about in it. 'So, if I poured five pints in that shitty bucket, would you drink it?' he asked. 'Never in a million years,' I said. 'Well, that's what you did last night Roy,' he replied.

Ken was just trying to mark my card, and he was about the only person I did actually care about letting down. The problem was that I had a taste for it now and was living for the thrill of the feeling that drinking gave me, plus the attentions of female admirers. I had convinced myself I was only young and could still turn up for training the next day and run the legs off all the old gits. I didn't even know what a hangover was, then. I really couldn't see what harm I was doing. But Mum could. She knew I was letting my career slide down the pan.

Mum had sussed I was out all night drinking and shagging birds and tried to lay down the law by imposing a midnight curfew. It didn't make any difference, though, as Dad was always up late and I would throw stones at the window to get him to unlock the door. Football and fighting were in my genes – and so was fucking. Dad was the porn king of Solihull, with a shop full of grubby videos shelved under the bed and a black bag full of dirty mags hidden in the wardrobe. There wasn't much I didn't know about the birds and the bees as a kid with that explicit library to browse through. I lost my virginity far too early, as I put my periodical knowledge to use. The failure to keep my trousers zipped up was a curse I inherited from Dad, as he was a terrible womaniser. As a child he would tell me to wait in the car, while he popped inside a strange house 'on a job'. He would be greeted at the door by an attractive blonde in her silk nightie, before disappearing for 30 minutes, which I thought was odd at the time. But I realised just what a handyman he was as I grew older.

Dad's general disregard for authority, especially when it involved cars, also rubbed off on all the McDonough brothers. He wouldn't drive around in a death trap, but rarely bothered paying out for tax discs or car insurance, as he didn't want to 'waste the money'. Following his lead, topped up by a string of speeding fines, throughout my life I've accumulated a list of motoring offences as long as the M6, plus a criminal record to go with it after a handful of court appearances. And what was Dad's take on it all? He just laughed at me and said, 'What are you worrying about son? It's not like you've murdered anyone.' I really did need a strong guiding hand back then, but unfortunately it was never going to come from my old man.

The downfall of a living legend briefly reignited my footballing desire as I approached the end of my teens. After making a solid start, Birmingham had begun to stutter under the part-time tutelage of the Ipswich-based Sir Alf Ramsey. The fans had turned on him, and he stood down after a 4–0 defeat at Coventry on 4 March, 1978. Health concerns was the excuse offered for this most noble football king's abdication. But the truth was that Sir Alf was never in it for the long term, he just wanted to help out. Blues had already got their next man lined up, Jim Smith, whose Blackburn Rovers side were going great guns in the Second Division. He steadied the ship at Blues instantly, losing just one game out of 12, including a draw at league champions Nottingham Forest on the final day of the season. Keith Bertschin stumbled to 11 goals as Birmingham finished in a comfortable 11th position, and 12 months had evaporated since I had scored at QPR. I hadn't been given a single second to build on the highs of my first-team break-through the previous season. But I was now taking great comfort in the medication of alcohol and sex, which was nursing me through the lows. I was a young buck who thought I should be out there enjoying myself and that I could still burn the candle at both ends and be a First Division footballer. Smith had done a great job since coming in, so I couldn't question his team selection, but pre-season would be another clean slate and a chance to prove my worth. And I learnt soon enough that there was never a dull moment being under the wing of this 'Bald Eagle'.

4. FLYING ON EAGLE'S WINGS

Jim Smith worked hard and played hard. He was approaching his forties, a short arse with a big bald head and giant bulbous hooter spread across his battle-worn face. I always smile to myself when I hear people refer to him as the Bald Eagle, like it is some affectionate term for a popular, kindly uncle. That's because Smith could be a vicious bastard, who would rip you apart with his sharp vocal talons like a bird of prey if you did something wrong on his watch.

If you were in his team on the five-a-side pitch and gave the ball away he would hammer you to within an inch of your life. Almost bursting a blood vessel, with a red face like a bulldog chewing a nest of wasps, he would scream, 'What the fuck are you doing McDonough, you useless cunt? Don't ever fucking do that. Don't ever fucking give the ball away if you want to be in my team, you fucking stupid wanker.' So, at the age of 19, I never wanted to give the ball away again. It was a harsh lesson, but Smithy was only doing his job. He knew you needed a thick skin to survive in football, and he was trying to get inside our heads. But I didn't mind that, as he was my sort of bloke – down to earth and straight talking. There was never any bullshit, and if you made a mistake he would destroy you verbally. But he never held a grudge. Once he had ferociously made his point, it would be all forgotten.

During the first summer after Smith's arrival, I excitedly joined the rest of the Birmingham first team in jetting out to a five-star hotel in Albufeira, Portugal, for a week-long booze and cards marathon. I'd only previously got one stamp in my passport, and that was with Blues as well, when I travelled to France by ferry to play in a youth tournament in Dunkirk. I was only 17 and all my previous holidays had revolved around following Dad's summer cricket tours to the West Country in his camper van. It would be fair to say that my second experience of leaving English soil was much better – heading to Portugal with Smith & Co. was like running away with the circus.

I shared a room with our goalkeeper, Dave Latchford, who had played over 200 games for Blues and was a sound guy. He was happy to hit the tennis courts every day and kept an eye on me during the trip, which was a direct order from Smithy regarding all the younger lads. It was a week-long party, with Keith Bertschin, Malcolm Page, Garry Pendrey and Tony Towers all on the piss most of the day, playing three-card brag at £40 a hand. But it was easy to drink yourself silly in the sunshine when the club was picking up the tab. As the lads sat in the bar, necking lagers and dealing cards, the club secretary was at a nearby table, guarding a black briefcase. When any of the players needed another round of beers, they would simply walk up to him and he would hand over a wad of money from the case. Before he closed it shut again, you could see a thick bed of crisp notes lying on the bottom. There must have been at least £10,000 sleeping in there. It was the sort of case and contents you imagined being pushed slowly across a table at an edgy drugs deal, not the club expenses for an end-of-season jolly-up in Portugal.

With everybody well stewed from a day on the juice in the sun, it was no surprise that we got banned from the hotel restaurant on the first night. Smith had sunk a few drinks with his No.2, Norman Bodell. They were sitting there like Beauty and the Beast – Smith, the brutally hard-nosed baldy, and Bodell, a handsome specimen, who always looked immaculate, like something from a Kay's catalogue. They also had a good cop, bad cop routine going on, with Bodell acting as the calmer go-between, smoothing things over when Smithy upset someone. Everyone was sitting at the same long table when these two diamond blondes walked in. They were both English and looked like a couple of models. Neither of them had bras on and their tits were pointing through their tops in all directions. Bodell was a right ladies' man and got talking to the girls, buttering them up by explaining that we were First Division footballers, before inviting them to come and join us for a free drink. It was a recipe for disaster, as all the boys were well tanked up, and it wasn't long before one of them got bored making small talk and wanted to get a good feel of the merchandise. A hand came out of nowhere and copped a handful of breast. Its owner went bananas, clouting the groper around the head, who fell straight off his chair. It nearly caused a riot, as Bodell rapidly took on peace-keeping duties, wedging himself between the two girls and the floored boob grabber, before we got turfed out by the waiters, never to return for an evening meal all week.

The plan for the morning was to keep a lower profile, to make sure we didn't get sent packing on day two of the holiday. It was the end of May and the temperature was rising, so most of the players sat outside, camped around the hotel swimming pool, still drinking and playing cards. Above the pool area was a flat open-roof terrace, where a Portuguese couple were getting married, and a flight of wooden stairs ran down a cliff to the hotel's private beach below. Floating around in the pool sunning themselves were a couple of American beauties, who were in their late thirties and definitely worth a few bob. Both of them were in good nick and must have been a plastic surgeon's dream, as they had matching pairs of perfectly sculpted knockers, which were browning off just nicely. Relaxing on a lounger was the au pair, who was looking after the ladies' kids, and she was an attractive little thing too. The wedding was underway now, with the priest directing the elevated bride and groom through the proceedings in front of their seated guests. All the boys were behaving themselves and the American glamour-pusses carried on cooking their buns. What could possibly go wrong? Well, some of Birmingham's main cast members were missing from the tranquil pool scene, namely the manager and his drinking-squad entourage.

Smithy, Bodell, Towers and Bertschin had all gone to stretch their legs, walking along the sun-scorched beach into Albufeira. They'd been gone a few hours and had obviously stopped off somewhere to quench their thirst. On the way back, Towers had dropped his watch as they wobbled along a narrow cliffside path. Spotting it over the side of their steep climb, he'd got on his hands and knees to reach down for it at full stretch. Smithy was holding on to him as he extended further over the edge, but both of them lost their balance and tumbled down the cliff, luckily only falling a few feet on to a rocky ledge below. When Bertschin and Bodell had stopped laughing, they fished them back up again, before making their way back to the hotel. As we all sat peacefully by the pool, a topless Smithy came steaming up the private stairs cut to pieces. His knees, elbows and shoulders were all bleeding, and his hairless, red bonce was criss-crossed with scratches. Smith stood there for a few seconds, with just a pair of torn white shorts on. He looked up at the wedding party, before turning his attention back to the pool, complete with its surgically enhanced buoyant American goddesses. Then, he ripped off his shorts and dived into the pool stark-bollock naked, before breaking into an aggressive breast stroke. All the card-playing boys dropped their hands as they doubled over in laughter, and the roof-top marriage ceremony came to a complete halt. The wedding couple, priest and guests all pushed to the front of the balcony to look down at this bald head and white backside lapping backwards and forwards in the pool. All of a sudden, Smith stopped swimming and climbed out. His body was scuffed all over, but the traces of blood had washed away. He then started walking towards his abandoned shorts. At that exact moment, three new women reached the top of the beach stairs and saw him standing there in all his glory trying to pull his shorts up, before running off screaming around the pool. It was like being in an episode of *Benny Hill*.

The day's events left me with a glow-in-the-dark smile when

I got into bed. You just couldn't make up what had gone on, and I felt like I was living in a cartoon. 'This is definitely much better than Dad's cricket tours,' I thought to myself.

We had another expedition abroad that summer to polish off the pre-season preparations. Smith took us to the island of Gibraltar for a tournament, where we were most certainly caught between its famous rock and a very hard place. The continental competition was top drawer, featuring Slovan Bratislava from Czechoslovakia, plus Spain's Sporting Gijon and Real Zaragoza. Their inclusion meant the whole thing would be televised live by the neighbouring Spanish stations, and viewers were treated to an explosive semi-final between us and Gijon, with fireworks galore. The match was played at a huge sports arena, with a pitch circled by a large red running track. There were loads of Spanish fans in the crowd, desperate to see their side repel another English occupation of Gibraltar. I was sitting on the bench between Mick Rathbone and one of the younger apprentices, Pat Van Den Hauwe, a half-Welsh, half-Belgian defender who had come up from London and was earning a growing reputation as a scrapper.

A nasty niggle was creeping into the game, with a few naughty challenges from the Spanish players adding to the anti-English vibe filling the place. There was a horrible undercurrent running right through the stadium, with every late opposition tackle raising a cheer from the spectators, who were baying for our blood to be spilt. They got their wish soon enough, as a vicious attack on Don Givens – another forward, who had joined us from QPR – lit the touch paper for a mass brawl. As Givens backed into one of their defenders, the dirty Spaniard smacked him in the gob, splitting his mouth open. As he went down clutching his bleeding face, another Gijon player ran over and booted him in the head. Our players went mad, led by Tony Towers, who volleyed the defender straight in the chest, sparking an all-out punch-up.

We all ran off the bench, following a screaming Smithy into battle, with Van Den Hauwe throwing fists at anybody who got in his way. I was doing my best to avoid the flying punches and kicks, as nearly 30 men, including the coaching staff, started smacking the crap out of each other. Two of the officials had taken sensible evasive action, but the remaining linesman was sitting at the side of the pitch, watching the action unfold. That was before two fans climbed out of the stand and knocked him spark out with a chair, which ignited even more ugly scenes. The police didn't bat an eyelid as the linesman was hurriedly stretchered off through the mayhem with a busted head.

As we tried to retreat to the safety of the changing room, the punters started chucking red wine bottles at us from the seats. Van Den Hauwe chinned another couple of people as we punched a hole through the ruck to reach the other side of the ground, while glass rained above our heads. He ran up the stairs to the changing room, but stubbed his toe on the top step, fell back down and cracked his head. A few of the lads dragged him safely behind closed doors before a growing stream of angry fans could join the Gijon players in trying to tear us apart. A queue of hooligans tried to kick their way through the locked, but shaking, changing room door, while another irate mob had got on to the roof and were stamping on the ceiling. We were backed into a corner with no way out, waiting for them to breach the doors, or fall through the ceiling. With all the racket going on, it sounded like there were hundreds of them. I can't say it wasn't scary – all the shouting, screaming and banging – but we'd have fought our corner if necessary. Then it all stopped. The police had finally decided to lift their batons and break up the skirmish, before escorting us out of the stadium, as the last few stragglers hurled abuse but held back on the vino throwing. We got awarded a place in the final, which was a much quieter affair, beating Zaragoza and winning a trophy as big as a dustbin. The 'Brummie Battle of Gibraltar' had helped the lads forge a shackle-like bond, but it was the beginning of the end for me at Blues.

When we got back home, Jim Smith summoned me to his office. He said other clubs were interested in signing me, but

I was still under contract and could stay if I didn't get fixed up. But he told me to go and have a chat with them to see if any of the moves were appealing. Now I was really confused. I'd had a great summer with the lads and, despite the past disappointments, had never felt so much a part of the first-team set-up. And the manager wasn't making a concrete commitment as to whether he wanted me or not. I really didn't want to leave Birmingham, as it was where I was born and raised. It was my security bubble, a city I had rarely floated away from in nearly 20 years, and I didn't want to be anywhere else, in strange and far-away places.

I begrudgingly took Smith's advice, though, and visited a few of the clubs who wanted me. I was particularly keen to meet former Leeds cruncher Billy Bremner, who wanted me at Doncaster Rovers. But as we walked out of the tunnel together at Belle Vue, the gigantic size of the pitch put me right off. I didn't fancy running horseshoes on it, which Bremner warned me was a favourite exercise of his training regime. This gut-slogging fitness exercise sends you galloping down a length of the pitch, from one corner flag to the other, before sprinting behind the goal to the next flag, then breathing out of your arse back up the other side. Repeatedly doing that drill on that pitch was a one-way ticket to the knacker's yard, so I politely said no to his offer. I didn't want to nosedive all the way down to the Fourth Division doldrums either, and I had another invitation to remain in the top flight from Bristol City. But Dad's road atlas showed me that Ashton Gate was 100 miles away, which was too far from home. However, within the first month of the new season unshakeable disillusionment had set in again, and I took my boots 13 miles up the M6 to Walsall.

5. GOING TO THE WAL

My head was in a right mess after Jim Smith had allowed me to speak with other clubs, despite insisting he wasn't in any rush to kick me out of St Andrew's. I was totally confused. Smith was struggling too, as three games into the 1978/79 season Blues hadn't won a game – which would eventually stretch to a disastrous run of 14 matches. I was back in the Football Combination, playing reserve-team football against the stiffs of professional clubs anywhere south of Birmingham. I was drained of all enthusiasm and desperate to lash out and release my frustration.

Fortunately, I didn't have to wait long, as the second-string Chelsea centre-half volunteered himself as a human punch bag, repeatedly leaving his foot in later than it should have been. I didn't even want to be there, and this bloke was winding me right up. After feeling the pointed toe of his boot stab the back of my calf muscle once again, I span round and cracked my knee into his bollocks with all the force I could muster. It was walkies time again, and a nice hot bath, although without any bubbles, to relax and calm down in.

Smithy ordered me into his office for a red card debriefing on the Monday morning. I wasn't worried about facing him, despite knowing what a monster he could be, because I didn't give a fuck anymore. I'd worked hard for success at this club and believed in my juvenile mind that I warranted it tomorrow, if not yesterday. Smith told me he wasn't happy with my behaviour, but I also sensed a shred of sympathy in his tone, because he liked the fact I had a bit of spunk about me. But my time with Blues was coming to an end, advanced by the magnetic calling of my old mentor, Ken Oliver, who had become No.2 at Third Division Walsall. Ken had sounded me out at the start of the season, but knew I wasn't in the right frame of mind to make such a big decision, so he advised me to bide my time. But now Blues were at the bottom of the table – struggling hopelessly – and I still wasn't involved. Rotting in the reserves, I was further away from the first team than ever. And if I couldn't get a game playing in such a shit team, then there was no point in sticking around. So, the short drive up the M6 to Fellows Park became increasingly attractive. Dad had a shop close to the ground, but I only knew two things about the Saddlers – they had been in the Third Division forever and stole a few headlines in 1975 after giant-killing Manchester United in the FA Cup. But Walsall ticked all the boxes.

I could commute from home, Ken promised me regular first-team football and, most importantly, I could piss it at that level, which wouldn't interfere with my extra-curricular activities.

I was living a second life by then – on the beers and on the birds – making up for all those lost teenage years of being sober, faithful and completely dedicated to football. That didn't mean I had lost my ambition – in my mind I was dropping down to fight my way back up again. Walsall would give me the platform to relaunch myself back into the limelight. I'd go there for a season, knock in a few goals, and one of the First Division clubs would soon come and rescue me. In that era of football, the top flight wasn't flooded with foreign Carlos Kickabouts, mercenaries washing up on our shores on rafts stitched from £50 notes. There was a wealth of untapped talent in the lower divisions – players like Kevin Keegan and Ray Clemence at Scunthorpe, or Ian Rush at Chester, who were all snapped up by Liverpool. The major clubs would regularly mine these raw diamonds and polish them up into First Division gems. Geographically, Walsall was another plus, as it meant staying in the Midlands, the centre of the football universe, with a plethora of top clubs just a few miles up the motorway in neighbouring counties. So, my mind was made up, I was signing for Walsall, who paid Blues £15,000 for my services, which was a decent fee back then. The Saddlers had made a poor start, but were ambitious and already had a proven goal-scorer at the club in Alan Buckley. They also splashed out £15,000 on my Blues team-mate Ricky Sbragia, a solid defender who I drove to training every day, before spending another £35,000 on Stoke midfielder Steve Waddington, which was a lot of dosh at that level. The club even had a pedigree gaffer in place, Alan Ashman, who had guided West Brom to an FA Cup Final victory over Everton in 1968. When he got the push at the Hawthorns, the news was broken to him by a waiter while he was on holiday in Greece, but he must have liked it out there as he went back to manage Olympiakos. And with Walsall pushing that many boats out, I was certain we would be sailing to the Second Division by the end of the season. The wages and signing-on fee weren't too bad either, £450 a week, which was treble my salary at Blues, and a £5,000 lump sum, which I lavished on a racing green Dolomite Sprint, the fastest saloon car on the road back in the late Seventies. But quitting Birmingham would turn out to be the biggest mistake of my life and my old man should have grabbed me by the scruff of the neck and ordered me to stay at St Andrew's.

Compared to Birmingham City, Walsall was run like a holiday camp. Alan Ashman was a nice bloke and very softly spoken, like a big Honey Monster. But he was far too laid back, and after serving under somebody as driven as Jim Smith it was a massive culture shock. Training was all off the cuff. There was no tactical preparation, we just did a bit of running, crossing and shooting practice and played endless five-a-side matches. Fellows Park was a decent ground, just a corner kick from the M6, with three covered stands, towering floodlight pylons and a bank of open terracing behind one of the goals. I'd convinced myself I wasn't going to be playing there long, though, a cock-sure attitude backed up by a triumphant home debut against Swindon Town on Saturday, 9 September, 1978. I ruffled the Robins' feathers by laying on two goals in a 4–1 hammering, picking up the Man of the Match award in the process. Fifteen months had passed since my last taste of first-team action at QPR. It felt so good to be playing proper football again in front of a real crowd – 5,000 plus – not clowning around in the one man and his dog world of the Combination. I'd taken the game in my stride, just like I had known I would, and it wouldn't be long before a higher football power elevated me to a loftier status. But the buzz soon went flat when I picked up the morning newspapers to gauge the printed superlatives about my debut. The main headlines were hogged by the striker crisis at Birmingham. Keith Bertschin had broken his leg and would be out for the best part of six months, closely followed by Trevor Francis, who had ruptured knee tendons. I nearly spat out a mouthful of sausage. What had I done? If I'd just remained patient, I could have been back in the first-team picture at St Andrew's, answering their striker SOS. After all those months of frustration and kicking my heels in the reserves, desperate for a chance to shine, I couldn't believe they had lost their two main forwards within seven days of my exit. I was hovering above the Third Division trapdoor when I should have been filling the First Division boots of Bertschin or Francis.

Getting my first goal in the next game at Hull didn't improve my sullen mood, although getting thumped 4–1 might also have had something to do with it. But there was no point in sulking about what might have been, and I still had the consolation prize of an ever-increasing social life and band of female fans. I could still enjoy all the distractions off the pitch and drag myself back up the football ladder – a philosophy which came up trumps on a Tuesday night against Peterborough, in front of a watching Jim Smith. Their centre-half Bill Green didn't know what day it was after I smashed him all around the park. I got two goals, cracked the bar twice and hit the post, a five-star performance fuelled by pie, chips and beans, washed down with three pints of lager in the Moonraker pub in Solihull at lunchtime. I didn't know Smith was in the crowd until a reporter from the *Argus* jumped me for a quote after the 4–1 victory. 'I'm glad he saw me destroy Peterborough,' I told him. 'He should never have let me go.' The papers accused Smith of dropping an almighty clanger by letting me slip through the net, bumping up my transfer value to six figures. But Smith hadn't been interested in me when he had ventured to Fellows Park seeking out a cure for his strikerless strugglers. He had his beady eyes trained on Alan Buckley, who'd hit more than 100 goals in 200-plus games for Walsall.

Buckley liked playing alongside me, but there wasn't any love lost between us. He wasn't the bravest player on the planet, and I saw him put the brakes on a few times when the ball was there to be won. He was seven years older than me and a short arse, but he had quick little feet, great technique at that level and was an excellent finisher. Not for the last time in my career, the forward alongside me reaped the benefits of my all-action displays, stealing the goals and headlines after I'd out-muscled the defence. We went on an unbeaten charge of 11 matches, climbing towards the fringes of the promotion race, as Buckley fired five goals in eight games by my side. But he was gone by the end of October, the club-record £175,000 solution for rock-bottom Birmingham's impotency. After his departure, Walsall went limp-dicked, seeing out 1978 and welcoming in the new year with just two wins in 10 matches, freefalling back towards the deadwood.

The Third Division was more kick and rush than the higher echelons, but that suited my battering-ram style. You couldn't out-skill teams down here, as brute force and ignorance won games. It was a case of standing your ground and battling until the end, real sink-or-swim stuff, just like playing for the Stanley Star XI as a kid.

Despite our alarming dip in results, I was still oozing confidence, Billy Big Bollocks kidding himself that he was untouchable. That theory was soon proved wrong as I was painfully put in my place on the banks of the River Severn. Playing at the picturesque and compact Gay Meadow was the nearest thing we had to a derby match, and nearly 8,000 punters had squeezed into the ground to cheer on champions-elect Shrewsbury. They were a good side, getting to the sixth round of the FA Cup that year, before losing a replay to Wolves, which was better than my debut in the famous old competition, bowing out tamely against Torquay. We nicked a point, but the Shrewsbury rearguard nearly broke me in two. Shrews defender Carleton Leonard absolutely mullered me in the first half for having the audacity to score. He crashed straight through the ball, before crunching my ankle for afters. I could have screamed, it hurt so much. Most players would have been frantically spinning fingers in front of their chests, pleading for a stretcher and an early withdrawal, but I couldn't do that, no matter how much agony I was in, as I didn't want to lose face. At half-time I rolled back my sock and winced at a black-and-blue ankle swollen to the size of a football. But I went back on and limped around like a lame horse that desperately needed shooting, knowing full well this was one battle I was never going to win. I might have thrived on a tough-guy image – which was ludicrous at the age of 20 – but I still had a long way to go if I wanted to catch up with the seriously hard bastards on the circuit.

One of my best mates, Ian Atkins, was playing for Shrewsbury. Ian was born and bred in Sheldon, bang next door to Solihull. He was a couple of years older than me, another local boy done good on the football scene, and we'd have a few beers in the Sheldon pub on a Saturday night. Ian played right across the park during his career – sweeper, midfield and in attack – and was a grafter, who in the future, when he was at Sunderland, would be handed the North-East Player of the Year award by Kevin Keegan. Ian was an unassuming, serious character, but he loved his football and we hit it off straight away. He was also the ultimate practical joker, and you needed eyes in the back of your arse if you didn't want to become his latest victim. One Sunday, we got back to our mate Peanut's house at 3am, pissed up, cradling kebabs. Peanut was holding a christening party the next day and there was a buffet feast laid out on the kitchen table. It was covered in silver foil, keeping it fresh for Aunty Betty and Uncle Reggie to tuck into when they returned from the church. We put a porn video on for a laugh while we ate the kebabs, before heading home for a few hours' kip ahead of the christening. After the ceremony the next day, we filed back to the house with the family, who started demolishing salmon sandwiches and sausages on sticks in the living room. Then Ackers announced to the room, 'Everyone's sitting comfortably, Peanut. I think it's time to put the christening video on.' The remote control wasn't working, so Peanut pressed the button on the VCR, only to be greeted by a room full of horrified stares when he swivelled round. The TV wasn't showing a replay of his baby being dipped in the church font, but some bloke getting wet with a scrawny blonde. The only person smiling was Ackers, who was standing at the back of the room waving the remote batteries at Peanut. He'd swiped them after putting the porn tape back in the video player. I'd never seen so many ham sarnies, paper plates and false teeth hit the floor all at the same time.

I was still fooling myself into thinking that I could play Third Division football in my sleep, while doing the twilight rounds away from Fellows Park. Every Thursday night I would go and watch Gaz and Jim train with their Sunday team, before jumping into the back of a car and getting whisked off to a disco for nine or 10 pints. I had another steady girlfriend then, Denise, a lovely brunette, who turned every head walking into a bar. But she wasn't enough to satisfy my constant cravings for attention, and I was also getting adept at 'dropping the shoulder', which had nothing to do with beating a defender down the line. If I wasn't already out with my brothers, I'd kiss Denise goodnight at 11pm, before changing into my shirt, strides and shoes to meet them at a nightclub. More often than not, I'd end up going back to some random bird's house. Trawling for women gave me an even bigger adrenaline rush than playing football. Walsall might have been losing every week, but in my head I was scoring victories every night. My pulling technique had a 95 per cent success rate – which I'm often reminded was better than my shooting – but it was nothing short of scandalous. I was never one for eye-balling a girl at the bar for hours, buying them drinks all night and all that buttering them up bullshit. I was straight in, like a ravenous bull rampaging through a china shop, using the cheek of the devil to snare my prey. It was outrageous, but effective. I would patrol the club like a kid in a candy store, picking out whatever sweet little thing I fancied tasting, before ruthlessly moving in for the kill, telling them what we were going to do, and where we were going to do it.

'When we get in luv, I'm going to look after you downstairs, then all hell is going to break loose.'

Alternatively, I could be really classy and ask: 'So, how many times do you want to cum tonight, darling?'

I swear on my life, I never got slapped, and was only told to fuck off a few times. After firing the opening shot, I settled them down with half a lager, nothing more. If we were still standing there dithering next to an empty glass after 15 minutes, I would let them get on with it. Unless it was a sure thing, I wouldn't waste my time, as I'd rather be necking another six pints. Most of them were decent-looking girls, but I had my fair share of howlers too when the beer goggles were strapped on at the end of a night out; the fat and pig-ugly ones. I was getting so blitzed at that time I sometimes didn't know if I'd been with a girl or not, so I used to give my moustache a quick lick in the morning to find out if I'd done the deed.

There was only one exception to my half-pint rule, and that was Christine Houghton, a Miss UK finalist who had split up with my Birmingham team-mate Kevin Dillon. Christine was a beautiful creature with a mane of curly, jet black hair. She had been on the TV looking a million dollars in a swimsuit, making the top seven in the competition heats. Gaz had fancied his chances, wining and dining her for months without even getting a feel of her tits, but that wasn't for me. I spotted her in the Aero Club, a knocking shop next to Birmingham Airport, just after 1am, standing at the bar drinking with male company.

I just said 'hello' and strolled past, not thinking anything of it. A little bit later, she was on her lonesome, so I zoomed back in and asked her what was up. 'He was a right dickhead,' she replied. Game on, filthy banter and half a pint please, barman. But I pushed the boat out for this very special lady, putting £1 petrol money in her mini so we could drive back to her pad in Sutton Coldfield. I paid for it, though. I didn't get in until 5am and had to be up and fresh in three hours to drive Denise, my sister Lisa and her fella to a wedding in Wales. Know-it-all Lisa had my number. She knew what time I had crawled back through the front door and started baiting me with awkward questions in front of Denise. I could see a big smile on her face in the mirror, but I just stared straight down the road ahead, doing my best to keep quiet and disguise an aching shoulder.

February got off to a good start, with me bagging goals in successive games alongside my new strike-partner, Terry Austin, to seal wins over Peterborough and Blackpool, lifting Walsall back into mid-table. By the end of the month, a thick blanket of snow had covered the Midlands and a massive home match against promotion-chasing Swansea was under threat from the weather. I was desperate for the game to be on against the Welsh side's team of ex-Liverpool all-stars. Walsall put out a successful SOS to fans to help clear the pitch, packing the snow into high banks on the side of the playing area. The Swans were well on their way to flying through the divisions to reach the loftiest perch in the land for the first time in their history. They had ex-Anfield great John Toshack and the Reds' record-appearance holder Ian Callaghan hoping to clip our wings that day. But I didn't care about them, as I had another Liverpool legend in my sights – tough-nut Tommy Smith, who was marshalling their defence. This was my chance to finally test myself against somebody with pedigree hardman status, and boost my own reputation as somebody who could dish out the rough stuff on the pitch.

Smith was built like Fred Flintstone and had a Frankenstein head, covered in battle scars. I'd heard all the myths, how the great Liverpool manager Bill Shankly had claimed his destroyer 'hadn't been born, but quarried', as well as how the Scouse mums would put a picture of his fearsome mug above the fireplace to scare their kids away so they didn't burn themselves. Smith was 34 at this point and playing centre-back, directly in my firing line. He never looked flustered and wasn't going to be physically intimidated by anyone. But it wasn't long before I scorched the Anfield Iron. The ball went down the touchline and he was favourite to get there first all day long, but as a forward you've got to chase it, or the fans will slag you off for being lazy. Smith beat me to the loose ball, took a touch and shaped to send it zipping back down the wing. I slid in to put the block on, clattering straight through the ex-Kop enforcer with the full weight of my body, dumping him in a pile of snow. It was a right picture, the so-called hardest man on the planet, with his head and shoulders completely buried in a frozen mound at the side of the pitch. The old bugger got up with an avalanche of snow falling off his body, an emotionless look on his ugly face, but hell-bent on gaining revenge. His eyesight must have been on the blink in the twilight of his career, though, which unfortunately spelt serious trouble for Terry Austin, who had long hair like me, but minus the moustache. Two minutes later, bosh! Smith sliced through Terry on the touchline, leaving four stud marks down his leg. Terry knew that tackle had my name written on it and tried to have a pop at me afterwards, but I found his moaning hilarious.

We took a point off Swansea, but a disastrous run followed, winning just two of our last 19 games, and I couldn't hit a field full of cows' arses with an orchestra of banjos in any of them, ending the season with seven goals. We finished third from bottom, eight points from safety, which was a gaping chasm at a time when you only got two points for a win.

Relegation hit hard and I couldn't believe I had tumbled from the top flight to the Fourth Division in just nine months. It was so difficult to swallow and I tried to brush it off by telling myself I was just unlucky. In truth I was heartbroken, nursing my bruised pride. After all, this wasn't part of the plan.

But I still had nobody to spill my guts out to about the bitter disappointment of relegation, and especially not Dad, who only ever wanted to talk about the good, never the bad. Birmingham had gone down too, which didn't give me any satisfaction, but in my insular football head a vicious circle was swirling around. I should have stayed at St Andrew's as I could have made a difference there, helping to keep them up. I still had the desire to play with the best, so what was I doing at Walsall surrounded by mediocre players? What could I do to make it all better by myself? All I did was drink a few more beers and shut out the reality of my rapidly increasing shortcomings, plus the embarrassment of preparing for basement-league football. I would get through this by cocooning myself in a drunken summer haze.

6. FIGHTING WITH FELLOWS

ourth Division football delivered a much tougher breed of opponent – the fans, as Walsall's boo-boys singled me out for special treatment. The Saddlers signalled their intention to bounce back at the first attempt by returning Birmingham's £175,000 for Alan Buckley, paving the way for the local hero to become player-manager at Fellows Park. It was an inspired move, as we set the pace in pursuit of a top-four promotion finish, starting the season with a 13-game unbeaten run.

We never bashed our way up the league, but tried to play football, with the focal point being the triumvirate of strikers – Buckley, Don Penn and yours truly. The three of us were too hot to handle at that level, with Penn blasting 25 goals and Buckley netting 16, including four penalties. But guess who was the only one of the trio not to make it into the end-of-season PFA Team of the Year? I only managed seven goals, but hit the woodwork 14 times. And believe me, I kept count, as good as scratching those near misses onto my shared bedroom wall.

Being the poor relation of the three in the goalscoring department was a heavy millstone around my neck. And I was forced to drag it around the pitch every week, as the fans started to turn on me. When the team was announced over the loudspeaker before kick-off, my name would be greeted by a loud chorus of boos. I didn't hide away from it and made a point of being in the centre circle at that time, standing tall and letting out an exaggerated laugh, just to show the mugs I didn't care.

It started when we played Lincoln at home in the middle of September. We were seven games in and I still hadn't found the net, an unhelpful statistic which generated negative rumblings every time I got close to the ball. But I knew I was doing an important job for the team, leading the line and making openings for the other two. I worked the channels, laying the ball back or crossing it into the danger area myself, while Buckley and Penn were goal-hangers who only worked inside the box. Then I'd be back in my own penalty area, defending corners and free-kicks. The lads at the back loved me, as they knew I'd stick my head in where it hurts to clear the ball, while Buckley and Penn stood on the halfway line, hands on hips, waiting for the ball to come back to them.

It would have been nice to get in the box more and have a few shots, but that wasn't my role. But some fans never see that. As a frontman you are just judged on goals, and all I would hear was, 'Give it up McDonough, you useless donkey', or, 'Look at that twat McDonough, he's got the No.9 on his back and he can't score a goal', while I was putting in an honest shift to win the game. You expect it from the away fans, but not your own supporters, and I'd be thinking, 'How dare these fucking idiots question what I'm doing for the team.'

All I was bothered about was my team-mates appreciating me, which one of them would always demonstrate by shouting me a pint after the game. I was more worried about my family, who would get it in the ear, too. Jim and Keith had to pull my old man out of so many scraps as he fought my corner on the terraces, hitting back verbally or threatening physical violence. But I really didn't care what some fat beer-swilling numpty who had found his bravery in the bottom of a pint glass had to say. He was the gormless git standing in front of a factory conveyor-belt all week, packing 40,000 soapboxes, not me. And I took great pleasure in putting them back in their places. I'd look my antagonist straight in the eyes when I was waiting for the ball to be thrown down the line. 'Fair dos mate, you can call me a wanker,' I'd say with a smile on my face, ready to flick the ball on. 'But how much did you pay to get in today? Remember, you're paying my wages. Thanks, pal.' You could see the little cogs whirling around in their thick heads, but they never had a comeback.

Buckley knew I was copping flak off the crowd, but he also realised that my unsung role was key to the team's success. Following another scornful 90 minutes at Fellows Park, he told me, 'Don't worry about goals, Roy. I know what job you do, and you're the first name on the teamsheet.' If my efforts were good enough for the gaffer, then the fans could just fuck right off.

I powered home a far-post header against Lincoln in a 3–0 win, my first goal in 27 matches, which momentarily shut up my detractors. My goalscoring became almost prolific by my standards as I managed another one three games later, against Lincoln again, on 3 October, 1979.

The trip to Sincil Bank would herald a landmark in my career – my first professional red card, 13 days short of my 21st birthday. But I didn't go it alone. The referee was weirdy-beardy Trelford Mills, who wasn't an official I was particularly fond of. He sent our midfielder Ian Paul off for the most innocuous challenge and I went mental at the utter injustice. Now, if I'd been 30 yards away it wouldn't have happened, but I was right in the referee's earshot, so I started throwing fucks at him. And being arrogance personified, like most of the fuckers, he seized the chance to steal all the attention for himself, pushing his red card in my face before it had even gone back in his pocket.

He was well pleased with himself, as I'd been on his back for most of the game. He knew he had cost me half-a-week's wages in club disciplinary fines, as well as a ban. But fuck him and the money, I was the same with all referees. It was a tactic, part of the game, and you had to use it. Some of them were weaker than others and you could gain an advantage by pressing the right buttons and intimidating them. It could mean getting a crucial 50/50 decision in your team's favour – which could be anything from winning a penalty to convincing the referee to disallow a goal and saving your side a point away from home. I was so annoying, worse than a school kid, and I'd be right in their faces from the starting whistle: 'What are you doing, ref? You've got that fucking wrong, ref. Can't you do better than that, ref?'

But there was no dominating Mills. He was like a bloody school teacher ruling over his pupils and had this whole, 'How dare you question me', attitude. But most of them were like that. And I had every right to query their decisions. I was the professional footballer who knew how to play the game. All they did was make it 10 times harder through their sheer incompetence. There was a cage around the players' tunnel at Lincoln, and as I took the walk of shame their fired-up fans ran up to it and started spitting at me through the rusting old wire. With green-and-white slime sliding down my face and shirt, I turned towards the animals on the other side of the cage, shaping to throw a punch. The dimwits all took a flinching step back, forgetting they were being protected by a metal fence. I just chuckled, not even wiping the disgusting gob off my cheek, and walked into the dressing room, where a shocked Ian heard my studs tapping on the concrete. 'What the fuck are you doing here?' he asked. I just put my arm round him and smiled. And the nine lads left on the pitch weren't going to be robbed by card-happy Mills and clung on for a draw.

A one-match ban was no big deal and it gave me a bonus ball Saturday of all-day boozing. I'd stepped up my drinking education by finding a willing tutor in our goalkeeper Ron Green. I loved Ron as he was always up for a laugh. He was carrying a bit of weight, but was a good goalie and he could get away with being smashed in the week as he didn't have to train as hard as the rest of us. I would run Ron home in my motor at 2pm after training and we'd stop off at the Broadway Pub, in Stechford, with the aim of having a swift couple. But it could easily spill over into a nine-hour session.

It was a football pub, with most of the punters following Aston Villa, Birmingham or Walsall. We enjoyed mixing in that crowd, as it made us feel comfortable. There were never any judgemental fingers pointed at us for being professional foot-ballers out on the piss, they just left us to sup in peace. I was drinking every Thursday with my brothers and hitting a club, as well as having a few beers on a Friday before the match. But I could easily play against the Fourth Division's muppet defenders after a skinful, so it wasn't a problem. After the match I would get completely trashed, and on Sunday I'd be straight back on it. I enjoyed Ron's company the most as he was a monster drinker who could get his gloves around 20 pints on a Saturday night. I've seen him sink four beers in a 15-minute race against the last bell, just because he wanted to get as many down his neck as he could. I wasn't that bad, only knocking back nine or 10 pints. But I was on my best behav-iour, being the designated driver. It sounds shocking now, but I really didn't think the drinking was doing my body any harm. I was just socialising and having fun. But the alcohol must have been taking a hold upstairs, sloshing around and poisoning my mind, as increasingly darker mood swings and uncontrollable acts of aggression began to contaminate my football.

Alan Buckley decided to haul me off at a frozen Halifax just before extra-time in an FA Cup second round, second replay. It was the last game before Christmas, but Buckley was fooling himself if he thought I would be showing him any festive cheer. I went absolutely barmy. The only way we were going to win was if I remained on the pitch and smashed their back four. My parents had travelled to the ramshackle Shay on a treach-erous icy night to watch me play, and he had the nerve to take me off. I started rummaging around the dugout, grabbing kit boxes, sock balls and discarded tracksuits, before throwing them on the pitch at Buckley. He was still playing and I was screaming, 'Take me off you little fucker! I'll bloody kill you!' They had to stop the game as I continued hurling whatever I could find in Buckley's direction. The referee sprinted over and had a word, asking me very politely to calm down, so he could get the match finished and we could all go home. When Halifax got the second of their two extra-time goals to seal a third round spot, I jumped up and down cheering, before grabbing the soggy sponge out of the physio's bucket and chucking it across the pitch, just so Buckley knew I was still fuming.

He never said a word to me in the changing room after the game, and all the players stripped in silence as they knew what was coming. I gave him both barrels: 'See you, you little cunt. I'll never kick another football for you again.' But I was getting emotional, holding back tears, and my voice was going all over the place, high-pitched and squeaky. I didn't bother changing or getting on the team coach. I found my folks in the players' bar and got a lift home with them. Buckley never hauled me over the coals, or fined me for my outburst, because he knew he needed me to win promotion.

Neither of us ever apologised, but I did play for him and he picked me, which was about the only thaw in our 'Cold War'. He got his No.2, Bert Johnson, who was like Grandad out of *Only Fools and Horses*, to have a quiet word, telling me I couldn't behave like that again. But there was no rapport off the pitch, or much of one on it for that matter. If Buckley scored a goal, I wouldn't go mad celebrating with him. He might get a token pat, but if it was one of the other lads hitting the net I'd grab them like they were my missus.

Buckley just wasn't my sort of bloke. I thought he was Charlie Big Potatoes, especially when he would get changed in a room by himself. He was in his late twenties – very young for a player-manager – but rarely socialised with the lads and didn't care whether people liked him or not. But he would occasionally appear in the bar after the game and shout us a beer, so he wasn't all bad.

Buckley had a piss-easy job managing that Walsall team, as it picked itself. There wasn't any such thing as squad rotation and you could expect to see the same starting XI most weeks. The elder statesmen like Brian Caswell, Tony Macken and David Serella led the team. They were Buckley's generals and had us running like clockwork. We were motoring in the league and sparkling in second, near the top of the tree at Christmas, sandwiched between Portsmouth and Huddersfield, with Newport in the last promotion place. A 1–0 defeat at Stockport was our only setback in nine games going into Boxing Day. I'd managed goals in wins over Port Vale and Peterborough, as well as earning us a point in a 1–1 draw with promotion rivals Portsmouth, watched by a best-of-the-season 8,000 crowd at Fellows Park. But I could have been scoring hat-tricks every week and the fans would still have found an excuse to have a pop at me. We'd only lost two league games all season, were well on course for promotion and I was earning my corn in the team. The fans might not have wanted to acknowledge my part in that success, but I'd tolerated their vocal criticism all season and was growing sick of it.

The usual crap was flying around Fellows Park against Doncaster on Boxing Day: 'Get off McDonough, you useless piece of shit'. I cracked a belter into the top corner from the right channel for our first goal in a 3–1 win, putting my laces straight through the ball from 25 yards. The main stand was chock-a-block with fans going crazy in celebration, and I was determined to give them something back for battering me. I darted over to the running track, raised both my arms in the air and shouted, 'See you lot – fuck off!' The other players were trying to congratulate me, but I ignored them, jogging past to the other stand on the halfway line, to greet the rest of my fan club with a double one-fingered salute, before going back to the centre circle to restart the match. I thought, 'I got pissed on Thursday night and can still play in this shit league on one leg. You've given it to me, now take it back.' I enjoyed abusing those wankers more than scoring the goal. The other lads were pleased for me, but Buckley never said a dicky bird.

Going into 1980 we were in cruise control, losing just once in 18 games and leading the pack. I registered my seventh and final goal of the campaign in a March win over Halifax, and also managed to pick up another red card. Bashing about defenders for a living has its penalties, and I had totted up enough yellow cards for a two-match suspension. It's an occupational hazard. So, coming into the business end of the season, Walsall arranged a reserve-team friendly against Notts County to sharpen up my match fitness. I didn't need to play in the stiffs, I was fit as a flea, and to make matters worse I was made to play centre-half, which gave me the right hump. I didn't need any provocation, but one of their Scottish lads was trying to put it about as I picked him up at corners, pushing me and pulling my shirt. Then he left a cheeky elbow in, so I smacked him straight across the mooey. Off I trotted again for an early soak, and the watching Walsall chairman Ken Wheldon told Buckley he wanted me out of the club.

Walsall had one hand on the Fourth Division championship trophy when the club dropped an almighty ricket. With four games remaining, the club announced it was paying for an end-of-season trip to Magaluf to celebrate promotion. With the flights booked, the players had their beach towels rolled out and flip-flops on, handing Huddersfield the title by two points. We did the hard part, drawing 1–1 at Huddersfield in front of 17,233 fans, thanks to Don Penn's goal, before another stalemate with Bradford. Next up was a perilous trip to Wigan, who still had a slim chance of promotion, and they tonked us 3–0 among chaotic scenes at crumbling Springfield Park. The referee took us all off the pitch for 10 minutes as violence broke out around the ground. A massive lump of concrete was launched at the players from one of the stands, supporters were trading blows on the terraces and one fan ran towards the opposition spectators armed with a flag stick and starting hitting people round the head with it.

We were all glad to get out of there in one piece, but there was no respite for me in the last game of the season at home to Newport, as John Aldridge scored twice to seal the Welsh side's promotion in a 4–2 victory. We had been the best team all season but had switched off, dreaming of Spanish sunshine, tossing away the championship in the process.

To say the Fellows Park faithful weren't happy was an understatement and, predictably, they vented their frustrations on me. My Boxing Day antics obviously hadn't been enough to silence my detractors, so it was time to sort this out man-to-man. The main instigator was this ugly black-haired bloke with big ears who stood on the halfway line. If I was over that side of the pitch, he would be calling me names and swearing at me without fail. I'd let him get away with it all season, but not this time. The game had been halted for an injury and he'd started firing off the usual volley of insults. So I barked back, 'What do you want, you piece of shit?', then started stomping towards him. I wanted to get in the stand and sort this fucker out. I would let him throw the first punch, then I was going to give him a good hiding. I didn't care if all the other fans joined in and kicked the shit out of me, I was going to have this mouthy prick.

Buckley could see my eyes had gone and I was eager to do some serious damage – he knew the danger signs by then. He raced after me and tried to reach up and grab my shoulder as I approached the wall of the stand. I shrugged him off before taking another stride forward, but he didn't give up and successfully wrestled me away. Buckley must have been a strong little bugger, because if he hadn't stopped me I would have ripped that fan apart with my bare hands. Years later, when I saw Manchester United's Eric Cantona launch his kung-fu kick attack on a Crystal Palace fan, I raised a toast to the Frenchman. How dare some idiot hurl insults about his wife and family, just because he thinks he is protected by some invisible shield on the other side of the wall. Cantona was built like a brick shithouse and was fit as a butcher's dog. These mugs would never shout the odds in real life, down the pub or out in the car park, not in a million years, because they would get murdered. So I thought it was fantastic when I saw him get his own back, and I'd love to shake Cantona's hand.

We were jetting straight out to Spain after the game. I was sat in the players' bar having a goodbye beer with Mum, Jim, Gaz, Lindsay and Denise, when I realised after an hour that Dad was missing. I would get Mum and the girls complimentary tickets in the directors' box, but Dad couldn't be trusted to keep his mouth shut, so he was exiled to the stands. But where was the old rascal? I could see Alan Buckley and the chairman Ken Wheldon talking in the corner of the room and looking at me, so I went over and asked what was up. Buckley told me Dad had been arrested, but not to worry because scrap-dealer Ken had bailed him out. The ground was crawling with Old Bill because games against the Welsh were always volatile and, true to form, Dad had been up to his old tricks, getting into rows with home fans who were slagging me off, as well as abusing the Newport lads on the other side of the police-lined partition. Apparently one of the women coppers had ordered Dad to wind his neck in, but he just told her to 'fuck off' and carried on goading the away fans. He was quickly surrounded, cuffed and dragged out of the stand and into a meat wagon, before being whisked off to a cell at Walsall nick.

I spotted him hanging around sheepishly outside the door of the bar and went and grabbed him, knowing Mum would go bonkers if she knew the truth. I ripped straight into him and he just stared at the floor like a soppy kid. But I got him out of jail, too, by telling Mum he had been helping to resuscitate some bloke at the back of the stand who had taken a funny turn.

We flew out to Magaluf that evening for a week of utter carnage. Ron Green was permanently pissed as a newt, and one night he climbed out of the swimming pool in his trunks and walked straight through a pane-glass door, which he thought was open. He just carried on straight to the bar, bought a drink and came back to sit with us, laughing and covered in blood, with shards of broken glass hanging out of his body. Then the drinking really started to get out of hand, with me and Ron swinging from balcony to balcony on metal fire poles eight floors up at 5am, banging on people's windows to wake them up, and nearly getting kicked out of the hotel. One small slip and it would have been goodnight.

This holiday also served me another first in life's lessons. All the boys were getting on my case, as I was the only one who hadn't got his leg over on the trip. But I wasn't bothered, as

I was more interested in drinking the place dry. There were four girls from Burnley at the hotel, and this petite 19-year-old blonde had taken a shine to me, necking me by the pool. But I was so hammered I didn't even remember getting tongue-tied with her. All the lads were ribbing me, branding me a 'gay boy' and 'bender', so I put another notch on the bed post on the last night, safe in the knowledge she had a boyfriend back in England, so there would be no comebacks with Denise. But when I got home something was seriously wrong with my weepy waterworks. I rang the club doctor, and he told me to head to Ward 19 at Birmingham Hospital and follow the yellow line all the way to the clap clinic. I was mortified, standing in the middle of a room full of dirty old reprobates sitting there itching and scratching. The nurse shoved a small umbrella-like instrument down the middle of my chap and did a smear test. It turned out that I'd caught gonorrhoea. That meant having a needle full of penicillin shot into my arse cheek to clear up the problem. But the injection didn't agree with me. It ended up giving me an allergic reaction and I was covered from head to toe in a scaly rash like a crocodile.

If there was a silver lining running through this murky dose, at least I knew where to send Denise after having to come clean. When I returned to Ward 19 with her, it was occupied by bank manager types, clutching briefcases, which made me feel better second time round. Denise got the green light and I couldn't believe she hadn't packed me in, saving herself a lot of future heartache.

My contract expired that summer, and I was called in to meet Alan Buckley at the ground, just before pre-season training got underway. I had no worries, despite what had gone on between us at Halifax in the FA Cup, because he had already spelt out how important I was to the team. He put a contract on the table for me to sign, but he had cut my wages by £100 a week.

'What's that all about, Alan?' I said.

'Well, you didn't score enough goals, Roy,' he replied.

I was livid. 'That's not what you said during the season when

I was working my nuts off for you. Stick it up your arse!' I said, before leaving his office.

I didn't bother showing up at the ground for a few days, until middleman Bert Johnson got me to sign a week-to-week deal, which meant I could play for a move elsewhere and Walsall could still command a fee for my services. And I was only around for a few weeks at the start of the new Third Division season.

I was in the starting line-up, but we only managed a solitary win against Burnley in our first four games, before Buckley started putting me in and out of the side. He had dismissed me as a troublemaker, a rebel he couldn't control, and was playing games to force me through the exit door. I'd got off the mark against Blackpool in the League Cup, before firing another goal against the same opposition in a draw at the end of September. But the last straw came in the next game at Rotherham. When I arrived at Millmoor, Buckley told me I had been relegated to the bench. I stormed out of the changing room before I had a chance to wreck the place, then ambled up the side of the pitch trying to click my head back into gear. Fans were sauntering on to the terraces and I hid away from detection by having a chat with one of the girls working at the burger bar. After 20 minutes, Grandad Johnson found me, trying to persuade me to put kit on, but I told him to get stuffed. I returned to the changing room when I was ready, pulling my shirt, shorts and socks on in complete silence, before brooding through another defeat, unused on the bench.

I would never play for Walsall again, and Buckley and the fans would be pleased to see me disappear. But the joke was on them, as I was heading back to the big time and the glamour and glitz of London's trendy King's Road. England's greatest striker was about to tell Fleet Street's finest that he wanted me to spearhead his team's attack, and I would also be handed the task of trying to give the Dutch masters of Total Football a good clogging.

7. BRIDGE OF DESPAIR

As Geoff Hurst stepped through the Stamford Bridge lift door with his arm around my shoulders I was blinded by the hot bulbs of paparazzi flash lights. 'I've finally got him,' smiled the striker, who had won England the World Cup with his hat-trick against the Germans at Wembley. 'I've known Roy for a while now and seen him play. He deserves to be playing at a higher level than he has been, which is why I have brought him to Chelsea.'

It was all bollocks. Hurst had never seen me kick a ball in his life. But I was back in the big time and couldn't care less what he said, as the man was a legend and a room full of reporters were scribbling down every word for the national newspapers. I was getting the Hollywood red carpet treatment and it felt great after the long-running battles I had endured at Fellows Park. But once the cameras stopped, I didn't see Hurst at all for another two months, and he turned out to be the worst manager I ever signed for.

I'd been on borrowed time at Walsall since turning down their reduced contract, and had gone on a one-man strike after the Rotherham insult. Desperate to get rid, they sent me down the M5, halfway between Birmingham and the south coast, for a transfer summit with Bournemouth manager David Webb. I reminded the old grump that I had scored against him for

Birmingham when he was at the heart of QPR's rearguard a few years before, but he swatted away the remark and said he didn't remember it. So why was he offering me a fat £15,000 signing-on fee over a service station breakfast table to join him at Bournemouth then?

I told Webby I'd get back to him, which I never did, as I wasn't prepared to drop straight back into the Fourth Division, having just scrapped my way out of it. I was tempted, as things had gone into complete meltdown at Fellows Park, but a surprise phone call would change everything. It was Ron Suart on the blower, the former Chelsea manager, who was now scouting for the west London giants. I thought it was a wind-up at first, but Ron was the real deal and said he had been monitoring my progress at Walsall over the last few seasons. He also told me he was driving Chelsea No.2 Bobby Gould up to Walsall on Saturday to seal the deal, so I had to be playing. There was no first-team game at the weekend, and Alan Buckley nearly fell off his chair when I went on a charm offensive and volunteered to play in a reserve-team friendly against Notts County. Fair play to Buckley, he must have known I had something in the pipeline, but he played me and I scored two goals, which convinced Gould to invite me down to the bright lights of Chelsea for contract talks. I jumped in the Dolomite Sprint with my brother Keith and we bombed down the M6 and M1 on the Monday morning.

When I arrived at Stamford Bridge it just blew my mind, driving through the towering gates at the ground and seeing the high stands reaching for the London skyline. I was the archetypal local yokel, a Solihull boy born and bred, who lived in the shadow of a big city like Birmingham, but was much more comfortable living the life of a simple townie. I'd only ever been to London to play football in the Combination, stepping on and off a team bus. But here I was, just off the famous King's Road, with its elegant five-storey Georgian buildings, chests puffed out proudly behind black metal railings, and the swanky boutiques of celebrity fashion. I'd never seen anything like this and it was frying my brain. I was out of my league, and had no idea how I would be able to afford to feather a nest among such splendour.

Fortunately, Chelsea had put together a highly lucrative contract offer, with accommodation thrown in. I'd never dreamed of being at a massive club like this, playing in the capital city. Fuck the Walsall fans, and Buckley, thinking I wasn't good enough for them. I was bouncing back and, in my little heart, returning to the level I deserved to be gracing. For the first time since leaving Birmingham, my ambition was flooding back. I'd been given a second crack at one of the big boys, and this time I was determined to make it work. Hurst wanted me in his team and I couldn't have wished for a better teacher to continue my education as a striker with. The amazing financial package included a three-and-a-half-year contract, starting at £450 a week, but raising £100 a season. They'd also throw in a £10,000 lump sum every year, and promised to upgrade my shared bedroom with Gaz to a ritzy hotel suite near the ground for the first six months. I was completely made up, ready to sign on the dotted line, but I decided to play the game a bit first and told Hurst I would go home and discuss the move with my family. Hurst shook my hand on leaving, but it didn't feel right. It was limp, not the firm grip I expected from such an icon. My sixth sense kicked in, trying to warn me that all wasn't well, but I ignored the danger signs.

This was a very different Chelsea side from that of the golden generation of 10 years earlier, when SW6 idols Peter Bonetti, David Webb, Ron Harris and Peter Osgood won the FA Cup and European Cup Winners' Cup in successive years, seeing off Leeds and Real Madrid respectively. Financial hardship, increased by the burden of redeveloping Stamford Bridge, with its famous Shed full of hooligans falling to pieces, had dumped the club in the Second Division. And when I returned to London on the Thursday, the cash-laden goalposts had been moved. The Chelsea chairman couldn't understand why they were offering me so much money when I was on a weekly contract at Walsall, so they knocked me on the original deal. In a take-it-or-leave-it address, I was told the offer had been changed to

£450 a week, going up £50 a season, with a single £10,000 signing-on payment. Lording it up at a plush hotel had evaporated too, as I would now be the special guest of a married couple living in the glamorous surroundings of a council estate in Hayes, close to the club's Harlington training ground. I was gobsmacked. Chelsea were taking the piss, but I still had to sign. My family were buzzing about the move and I couldn't face going back to Fellows Park. So Chelsea agreed a £30,000 fee with Walsall, and Hurst took me up in the lift to smile and face the media at the end of September 1980.

Chelsea were jostling with London rivals West Ham for promotion. Frontman Colin Lee smashed eight goals in seven games in October, including a hat-trick in a 6–0 drubbing of Newcastle, helping Hurst win the Manager of the Month award. But I was back in familiar territory, playing in the Combination for the nearly team. The reserve-team coach Brian Eastick had appeared in the office on my first day at the club, with the obligatory stopwatch swinging around his neck. Hurst told him, 'Here's the new striker. He plays for you up front on Saturday.' Eastick looked horrified. His Chelsea twos were top of the league and the last thing he wanted was some village idiot from Solihull forced upon him, breaking up his perfect little team. He didn't fancy me from day one, and the feeling was mutual. To me, he was a 'Clipboard Charlie', somebody who had never made his mark on the game as a professional player, so he relied on absorbing FA coaching manuals to hone his skills. I found his training sessions boring and very routine driven. Especially on windy days when we would be ordered to attack high balls pumped into the box, which would be blown off course, or just hung around in the air. You didn't need a chest full of coaching badges to realise that it would have been better to concentrate on ground work in such blustery conditions. But Eastick would stubbornly stick to what he had planned for the day's session. It was an approach I found frustrating, and mostly quite pointless.

The Harlington pitches were sandwiched between the M4 and Heathrow Airport, and the thing I liked most about training was seeing Concorde fly overhead. It didn't matter if I was running or playing five-a-side, I would down tools, stand still and gawp upwards, until that sleek metal bird had disappeared from view into the clouds.

The second-class stiffs at Chelsea still travelled around the country in first-class style on the posh team coach. When the pampered senior lads played away, they took a chef on the coach with them. On one trip back from a second-string match at Cardiff, Mr Cordon Bleu had started stocking the fridge early in preparation for the first team, so we all scoffed complimentary prawn cocktails on the way home from Wales.

But these were the only highlights of my first few months at Chelsea. I didn't bond with any of the first-team players, only ever exchanging token pleasantries with Mike Fillery, Dennis Rofe, Clive Walker and Graham Wilkins, who were decent lads. But I hadn't seen or spoken to the manager since signing and it felt like I was invisible to him. There was little sanctuary to be found in my very basic accommodation either, as being home alone for the first time tested my resolve to the limits. I was put up by a married couple in their early thirties, who were getting two for the price of one, as they liked having a Chelsea footballer staying with them and were fellow Brummies.

To get over the disappointment of the club pulling the plug on my luxury hotel room, I tried to find consolation in the possibility that my landlady could be fit, an older Mrs Robinson sort. But when I arrived at the three-bed council house in Hayes with my bags, I was greeted by a woman in her curlers, wearing stretched nylon pants pulled up right under her tits to hide her gut. She was like a cross between Hilda Ogden and Simon Cowell, but nowhere near as attractive. The husband was a builder and they had a couple of shy kids, a girl of 12 and a five-year-old boy, plus a white fluffy Sealyham Terrier. I had a tiny box room with a rickety old wardrobe and matching wonky bedside table, and it was freezing as there was no heating in the house. The food wasn't gourmet either – a small piece of meat, served with a dollop of mash and a few spoonfuls of vegetables. But

Fridays were special, as we'd have fish and chips soaked in salt and vinegar fetched from the van.

One morning, the wife called up and said she was leaving my breakfast outside the door, as she was taking the kids to school. I wasn't in any rush to move, as it was too early for training. In my private little slab of the Middlesex Arctic, I could see the icy breath in front of my face, so I burrowed under the covers to try and keep warm. Then I heard a crunch . . . crunch . . . crunch . . . coming from the other side of the door. Breakfast was finished, as the dog was eating my Cornflakes and toast. When I got back from training in the afternoon, the dog was bouncing off the walls like a maniac. It looked a dead cert for a place at Crufts, as it kept lapping the living room at high speed, round the back of the settee and TV stand, before jumping over an armchair. Hearing the racket created by the crazed canine, the wife rushed in and asked, 'What's happening?' She then picked up the dog and shoved its furry fanny straight in my face, adding, 'Do you think she's on heat?' Now, I bet you wouldn't get that from the concierge of a five-star hotel on the Fulham Broadway.

The husband did his best to help me settle in. He handed over a brown envelope of cash to his missus on a Friday night, before keeping back £100 for his weekend drinking money. I'd tag along with him on a Friday for a few beers and frames of snooker just to get out of the house, while he'd pot 10 pints down his cakehole. But being an almost Chelsea footballer was far from glamorous, and I was finding London life increasingly hard. I hadn't seen the manager for weeks and I wasn't getting anywhere near first-team action, despite netting regularly in the reserves. I still hadn't made any new mates and didn't socialise with the other players outside of the club. I went to the Christmas party in some hotel near the ground, going along with a couple of girls from the Stamford Bridge office, but it failed to break the ice. I got completely hammered by myself, and all I could remember about that night was centre-half Micky Droy driving off pissed and wiping out a row of wing mirrors on parked cars as he struggled to find second gear.

I must have seen every movie to hit the big screen during my sorry existence at Chelsea, as I'd go to the afternoon matinee on a daily basis after clocking off from training. I would slump in a chair in the deserted cinema like a zombie with four other saddos, not really even taking the film in, which was a bonus as I'd return to watch the same flick over and over again. It was just a way of killing time – I must have seen *The Empire Strikes Back*, *Smokey and the Bandit 2* and *Any Which Way You Can* at least three times each – before I trod wearily back to the council house, had dinner and went to bed. It's a good job I was only a social drinker – I was never one to sink cans indoors – otherwise I would have drowned myself in my bedroom. But I did seek out a drink to escape my digs on some midweek evenings. I floated around Hayes and Uxbridge in my motor, but I struggled to find any friendly faces in the local pubs. Punters stared at me like I was Darth Vader stepping off his spaceship when I beamed into a boozer and asked for a beer. To them I was an alien, an outsider with a funny accent who didn't speak the lingo. It was intimidating and I could never satisfy my need to share a laugh and a drink, and I'd do well to polish off a solitary pint before fleeing home.

It was a lonely life, and I wasn't strong enough to overcome the suffocating homesickness. Sometimes I'd find respite in a phone box with a pocket full of coins, blubbing like a baby to Mum and telling her that I'd had enough. I didn't want to be a footballer anymore and just wanted to come home and do a normal job like my brothers. But she'd always find the right words to talk me around and I'd stick it out, until the next time I was overwhelmed enough by abandonment to seriously consider packing in the game.

If we had a midweek reserve fixture, I would drive back to Solihull on the Tuesday night after the game, have Wednesday at home and head back to London in the early hours of Thursday morning. I'd do anything to get out of London, rub shoulders with family and friends, and put a smile back on my face. I'd have a drink with my brothers and it would release the tension, giving me the Dutch courage to face going back to Hayes. All my mates were dead proud of me being at Chelsea and would excitedly interrogate me about life at Stamford Bridge. I should have had a bigger nose than Pinocchio after reeling off hundreds of lies about how exciting life was in London, but I had to keep up the false pretence of being the great footballer.

Denise was another victim of my bravado. I bought her a £500 diamond ring from Birmingham's jewellery quarter and splashed out the same amount of cash on her dress for our engagement party at Old Silhillians cricket club. She looked stunning, but I had no intention of marrying her. I just wanted to throw a big show-off party and surround myself with my family, friends and old team-mates from Birmingham and Walsall. Denise didn't deserve that. But, unfortunately, she was a timid little thing who wouldn't say boo to a goose and I trampled all over her.

The trips home more often than not ended in a messy night of drinking with my brothers at Cinders nightclub, which resulted in my first and last punch-up on the dance floor. A drunken idiot was taking the piss out of my mate Alan, a great dancer who was jigging around with two girls. We'd asked his group of mates at the bar to have a word with him as we didn't want any trouble, but this bloke kept on mimicking Alan, who eventually cracked and told him to, 'Piss off.' This prat went to slap Alan, but I let go of my pint, which shattered on the floor, and cracked the plonker in the face before he connected. It was sheer instinct, like being back on the pitch. This twat was taking liberties with my mate and, before I knew it, the autopilot had clicked into gear and I was on top of the guy bashing his ears in. One of his gang ran towards me to smash a glass jug against the back of my head, but Keith flattened him. Then my other brother, Jim, also jumped in, and we were all fighting at the disco like a scene out of a wild west film. Gaz, the biggest scrapper of us all, just stood at the bar giggling, as he had a girl on each arm and wasn't prepared to ruin his chances. We were popular faces at the club, so we didn't get touched as we helped the bouncers kick out the troublemakers. The prat who started the ruck then decided to splatter the manager's nose across his face, so I kneed him in the head and pushed him out the door.

A few weeks later, I was having a quiet drink in a pub with Ian Atkins and our girlfriends, when 14 angry men surrounded me at the bar. The biggest one was shouting the odds about his brother, who was in hospital with a fractured skull, broken ribs and a busted nose, after the doormen had smashed his head through a window outside. Now, I'm generally no fighter off the pitch, and this was extremely uncomfortable, especially with the girls in tow. But Jim had always told me to throw my shoulders back and front it out when the odds were against you, as it made people think twice about their actions if you showed no fear.

'Your brother threw the first punch after numerous warnings, and I didn't put him in hospital. Go away and find out what happened. If you find out it was me that did all this to him, then I'll quite happily meet you anywhere and we can sort it out properly,' I said.

I could see the big lump twitching. He obviously didn't fancy it, despite having 13 mates backing him up, as he looked at the pints I had just bought in both of my hands.

'Well, that's easy to say when you're holding two glasses,' he grunted.

So I rested the pints gently on the bar and replied, 'I've never used a glass in my life, pal, because I don't need to.'

With that, they all rocked back and walked out of the pub and I never heard another thing about it.

Chelsea had come down with the Christmas lights after a poor festive period and were floundering. They hadn't won a game, or scored a goal, in seven outings since the beginning of December, and I believed they were crying out for somebody like me to lead the line and help lift them back up the table. But my only first-team run-out at Stamford Bridge was in a friendly against the Dutch side DS'79. This was no meaningless kickabout, it was a well-oiled publicity exercise designed to lift Chelsea's plummeting profile – as Holland's World Cup Final stars Robbie Rensenbrink and Johan Cruyff would be playing for the visitors. The TV stations and newspapers were full of the story that Cruyff was going to join Chelsea after the match, and the Dutch master's appearance attracted a 15,000 crowd to the Bridge who braved monsoon conditions to see one of the world's greatest footballers in the flesh. But Cruyff wouldn't get the chance to crucify me. I'd be up the other end of the pitch, trying to transfer my consistent Combination scoring form into the first team, showing Geoff Hurst and Bobby Gould they had a miracle worker who could heal Chelsea's biblical drought in front of goal. Or so I thought.

'Roy, left-side centre-half, next to Micky Nutton,' Hurst informed me in the dressing room.

Great, I hadn't played centre-back for 18 months, since an emergency defending stint at Walsall. And to make the task easier, I was handed a man-to-man job on Rensenbrink, who had only played in two World Cup Finals against West Germany and Argentina. That'll brush away the cobwebs. But I needn't have worried, as neither of the Dutch superstars over-exerted themselves. Brazilian great Pelé put Rensenbrink in his top 125 all-time players, which is some accolade, and he was renowned for being cocky on the pitch, telling goalkeepers where he was going to put the ball before he fired it past them. But the cultured striker never said a word to me, probably dismissing me as a kid, and barely broke sweat. The bits he did do were different class – the first touch, movement and vision, when he picked out little holes in the defence with his intricate passes. Cruyff was 33 by then, but he was still from another planet. The Stamford Bridge playing surface was like a drenched farmer's field, but he still danced across the spray and mud, killing the ball instantly and skipping past challenges, when he fancied turning it on. Cruyff made everything look so simple, and even in his twilight years was the most technically gifted player I had ever faced. His team-mates were hitting him with 30-yard passes and he would instantly pick up the flight of the ball. He was like a coach on the pitch, always talking and pointing, as he instructed the players around him where to run and caressed the ball into their paths first time as it dropped out of the grey sky.

Cruyff played behind the front two, so I had to occasionally abandon Rensenbrink to put a challenge in and I was well chuffed that I managed to tackle him twice, although I missed him the other 39 times. I just wish I'd asked a snapper to get some photo evidence of me trying to get a foot near the great Dutchman. We won 4–2 and I was feeling pretty pleased with myself afterwards. That was until Hurst burst my balloon: 'We had a bad 10 minutes out there – when you gave the ball away.'

The first team were still finding goals and wins hard to come by at the start of February, with No.1 strikers Colin Lee and Clive Walker incapable of hitting a barn door with a football from six yards. Walker hadn't pocketed a goal bonus in 10 games, while Lee had only gone one better in that dreadful run. But I was still being kept on a tight leash in the reserves, despite putting in my best performance, a two-goal salvo, a strike against the woodwork and two assists in a 5–1 demolition job of Hereford. I'd run the show from start to finish and the 400 fans swallowed whole by Stamford Bridge had started singing my name.

Dad was excited after the match. 'They've got to play you now, son. All the punters are saying it. You're playing the best football of your career.'

Well, of course I was, in the bloody Combination. The last time I played at this level, I was a fresh-faced pup at Birmingham. I'd been kicked all across the park in the Third and Fourth Divisions before arriving at Chelsea, so I was a much tougher and wiser player, at the ripe old age of 22. The Combination was a league I could have played in wearing a blindfold. But I'd taken a step up, to take a step back.

On the Monday, I was last in the shower after training, Billy No Mates as usual, when Geoff Hurst and Bobby Gould strolled in naked with their towels slung over their shoulders. It was a rare meeting, as the first and reserve teams were kept separate in their preparations. So, I thought, that's handy, as they must have heard about the rout against Hereford.

'How did it go at the weekend, big fella?' asked Hurst.

Was he having a laugh? The manager of the club must have known how well I'd played.

'I got two, made two and hit the bar,' was my puzzled reply.

'Did you really?' Gould sneered sarcastically at my honest match appraisal.

I couldn't believe it, neither of them had a clue. As I stood there covered in soap suds, dazed and confused, the picture started to become clearer as the hot shower steam evaporated after a rinse. The first team might have been going through a major goalscoring malfunction, but I was never going to get my shot at fixing it, as Hurst and Gould clearly weren't aware about my rich vein of form in the seconds. Surely, the reserve-team boss Brian Eastick was giving them glowing reports about my progress. But I had my doubts, as I felt like I didn't even exist at the club.

What I did know was that the last five months in London had been a complete waste of time – the homesickness, surviving hypothermia in a freezing council house, cutting down the booze and staying away from the birds. I was going nowhere fast here and was full of rage. But this was Chelsea, I couldn't go around bashing down doors like I would have done at Walsall.

I needed to remain calm and seek out advice, so I arranged an appointment with Gould. He sat behind his office desk, with his black hair and Wolfman eyebrows meeting in the middle, and asked, 'Problem, Roy?'

I politely replied: 'Yes, I don't know what I've got to do to get in the first team. The senior strikers can't score goals and I'm hitting them for fun in the reserves, but still can't get a game. What would you do?'

Gould stood up and pointed out of his window to the Stamford Bridge pitch. 'When I couldn't get a game, I'd go and run 16 half laps to get rid of the frustration and clear my head,' he smiled.

'So, that's your advice on winning a place in the team – to run laps?' I choked.

'Yep,' he grinned, thinking I was a smart arse.

I went into his office hungrier for success than I'd been since making my Birmingham debut, but retreated overcome with self doubt and an overwhelming desire to chuck my boots in the builder's skip outside my digs.

A few days later, I felt really honoured, as I received a special audience with Hurst, who told me other clubs were making enquiries about me. It wasn't the news I was hoping for, so I decided to get out of London. I drove straight back to Hayes and picked up the meagre belongings I had collected during my friendless incarceration, before returning to Stamford Bridge to collect my boots. Then I headed to the office to say goodbye to the girls, before scanning a map of the UK pinned above a set of battered old filing cabinets.

Doncaster wanted me again, and so did one of the Bristol teams, but the nearest club that showed interest in me was Colchester, one of Jim Smith's old sides. It could have been just down the road from Timbuktu for all I knew. But it was only 60 miles away – an hour's drive with my foot down – offering a fast escape route. I asked one of the office dollies to ring Colchester's manager and tell him I was on my way for talks. As I got into my car at Stamford Bridge for the last time, Dennis Rofe called after me.

'Where are you heading with your boots and bags, Roy?'

'I'm out of here, Dennis. My face doesn't fit and I need to play, so I'm off to Colchester, wherever that is,' I laughed.

Then the full-back gave me my only lesson worth learning in five months at Chelsea: 'When you get there, if you don't really fancy it, ask for silly money. If they give it to you, then sign.'

It was sound advice and I decided there and then that my football career was going to be following a different path. I was going to play for the wages and signing-on fees, to fund my social life and a renewed chase for female conquests. Fuck ambition – where had that got me? It was lower division party time.

8. GIMME SHELTER

I zoomed up the A12 in a total blur, just relieved to escape Chelsea and the isolation of London. It took me a couple of hours to find Layer Road, taking a detour around the town's zoo and pulling up at the Army garrison, before finally parking the Dolomite Sprint outside a destination that could have doubled up as a test site for the military bomb squad. Funnily enough, though, I wasn't offered a tour of this crumbling football temple's inner sanctum, which was shielded from sight by the high brickwork walls of the car park. I was shoe-horned straight into a tiny office to meet smiling manager Bobby Roberts and his Lurch-like No.2 Ray Harford, who were both squeezed in behind a small table. Roberts was a true Scotsman, who liked a wee dram and had played in Leicester's 1–0 FA Cup Final defeat against Manchester City in 1969. He was doing his best to sell the club to me, but I found myself looking around the peeling, faded wallpaper and chipped skirting boards. It certainly wasn't the deluxe grand designs of Stamford Bridge's interiors – it was the arsehole end of the world.

If I'd been thinking straight, I might have turned round and gone back to London, or headed on up the road to speak with Lincoln. And I wasn't interested in the manager's patter either, I just wanted to get down to the nitty-gritty – how much was he willing to pay me to play at this Dog and Duck dive? Colchester were offering a two-and-a-half-year contract of £200 a week, plus a £9,000 signing-on payment. Remembering Dennis Rofe's advice, I said it wasn't enough and told him to get the calculator out to see if he could come up with any better sums, while I retreated to the car and listened to Led Zeppelin on the chunky eight-track cassette player. I returned to the claustrophobic office to be greeted by improved terms, £250 a week, plus a £12,000 down payment. It was hardly 'silly money' and it would be a big drop from my Chelsea wages, but the carrot of guaranteed first-team football sealed the deal. I should have demanded a pay-off from Chelsea for the remainder of my contract, threatening not to leave unless I was financially rewarded for walking away from three more years of a lucrative Stamford Bridge deal, but I was so desperate to leave London behind that I never asked for a bean.

Colchester also agreed to put me up in the nearby Marks Tey hotel until the end of the season. As I collected the keys to my room, I picked up the local rag from reception and it suddenly occurred to me that I had just signed away the next two and a half years of my life without even knowing what division Colchester were in. A quick glance at the league table soon answered that question – near the bottom of the Third Division. So what? In my head, any serious football career was over now. I wouldn't just go through the motions, as I didn't want to let my family down any more than I already had by slumping back to this level, but just as important now would be having a wild time off the pitch.

Colchester desperately wanted to escape getting sucked into the relegation zone and, after shelling out £15,000 for my signature, paid £25,000 for Ipswich midfielder Roger Osborne. Roger had cemented his place in Portman Road folklore by scoring the winner against Arsenal in the 1978 FA Cup Final at Wembley, famously fainting after celebrating. He must have wanted to repeat the trick after running out alongside me at Layer Road for a home bow against Burnley in February 1981. No wonder I never got a tour – it was like arriving in war-torn

Beirut. I didn't know whether to go out for a stretch or dart back inside the tunnel to take cover. The pitch was like a car park, hard and bumpy. It wasn't cut or spiked, but just had the life rolled out of it by a groundsman on two bob a week. As I conducted a 360-degree scan of my new football home in complete bewilderment, all I could think was, 'What the fuck am I doing here?'

A small bank of concrete steps behind one of the goals had giant weeds growing up through its cracks. There was also a ragged old net at the back of it – like a massive spider's web – to stop wayward shots flying into some old boy's garden. If any balls ever decapitated his prized roses or petunias he would start a revenge bonfire during games and there would be choking smoke wafting across the pitch. The other end wasn't much better. It was covered, but the frame of the goal was almost cut into the wooden terracing. Apparently, the terracing had been constructed by German POWs during the Second World War, who had sawn up their beds for materials by the look of things. Mocking visiting fans would bounce up and down on those wooden planks singing, 'Layer Road is falling down, falling down, falling down . . .' to the tune of the London Bridge nursery rhyme. And you needed an umbrella to take shelter underneath one of the other stands – not because rain leaked through, but if a ball thundered against the iron roof you would get covered in a shower of rust.

I should have seen what was coming after getting changed. At Chelsea, we had pristine shirts with our numbers printed on them hanging on pegs, polished boots and clean towels waiting for us in the dressing room. Colchester, in contrast, was more Sunday League. The scabby kit was dumped in a pile on the floor, with all the players scrapping for a pair of socks without any holes in them and a shirt without rips. They took a picture of me in my Colchester strip for the evening paper, and I looked like a tramp fresh off a park bench.

I soon got over the culture shock with a debut goal, showing Burnley's tough-guy defender Vince Overson who was boss by soaring above him to help my new club register a sorely needed

2–1 success. In the club bar after the game, the locals greeted the new hero in town with congratulatory backslaps and hand-shakes – which was an amazing feeling after months of solitary confinement and first-team exile at Chelsea. And Dad was there, too, standing by the beer pumps with a face like thunder.

'What the fuck have you done?' he grunted, equally impressed by my new home.

I just walked past him and headed straight to the bar to get my own drink. He might have been disappointed seeing his son playing at a craphole like Layer Road, especially after knowing what I was capable of doing at a higher level, but I thought, 'Fuck you. Where were you when I needed guidance? Stuck on my own in a cold council flat in London, not knowing what to do. How dare you be so fucking proud. You can just fuck off, Dad'.

After I'd wet my whistle, we drove back to the Midlands in complete silence. I dropped him off at home, then went out on the piss with my brothers and mates all weekend, driving back to Colchester for training at 6.30am on Monday, which became a weekly ritual. I got a phone call in my hotel room after training from Ron Suart, who had engineered my move to Chelsea. He congratulated me on a goalscoring debut, but also rang to apologise about the way I had been treated at Stamford Bridge, confirming my suspicion that personal agendas had hindered my progress at the club. I really appreciated the phone call and thanked Ron for his honesty in filling in the blanks of my Chelsea nightmare.

Life at the Marks Tey hotel was great. Steak was on the menu every night, cooked in a multitude of different ways and coated with special sauces that my commoner's mouth had never experienced before, accompanied by a couple of beers – all courtesy of Colchester United. But the football wasn't going as well as my feast of culinary freebies. The U's were dropping like a stone towards Division Four, with only three wins in my first 10 games. The new hero in town had soon faded back into obscurity as I hadn't managed to add to a cracking debut goal. But beer and birds now meant more to me than a bag of wind. I was out on the piss on Monday, Tuesday, Wednesday, Thursday and Saturday nights now, followed by an all-day session back in the Midlands on a Sunday, with a brief half-time break for Mum's smouldering roast. In my mind, I was remaining professional by staying in the hotel on the Friday before a game, although I'd still drink 12 pints on a Thursday and might have one or two at the hotel bar on a Friday night – just to be sociable with the staff.

One of the employees I got on famously with was the chef, Armando Signorelli. He was an Italian football nut who cooked all the club's pre-match meals and also weaned me off the heavy steaks and on to his native creamy pastas. With the season moving towards a grim end, my free bed and board at the hotel was due to expire. So Armando offered me a room at his house in Stanway, five minutes from Layer Road, with the blessing of his lovely wife Angela, who worked as a receptionist at the Rose and Crown pub. They were in their forties, but had never been able to have kids, so they decided to adopt a big 22-year-old baby and mothered me like surrogate parents. And just like with all new arrivals, there were plenty of teething troubles.

Armando would double up as my minder, driving into Colchester to rescue me in the early hours. He'd frequently find me in a drunken heap outside a nightclub, barely remembering my name, let alone where I lived. While Angela, who turned a blind eye to girls being sneaked back to my room, offered relationship counselling. She spent hours on the phone consoling a distraught Denise as our sham engagement dissolved after I arrived in Essex, and the two of them became good friends. I must have been the tenant from hell, but if it wasn't for Armando and Angela, I would never have survived. They were friendly faces to return to every night – the complete opposite of what I had experienced at Chelsea – while I built up a portfolio of good-time buddies I could knock around town with. And I was a terrible influence, getting them both embroiled in my drinking marathons. I would drag Armando over to the Rose and Crown in the evening to meet Angela, and persuade her to lock the doors, get behind the bar and carry on serving until 5am, knowing full well that Armando would have to be at the hotel to fire up the frying pans two hours later. The Signorellis were so patient putting up with my drunken antics, but never once threatened to kick me out. There was only one strict rule I had to observe under their roof, which Armando ensured I obeyed. The second night I was there, he gently placed his 'safety net' on the dinner table – a shotgun he kept under his bed.

'You mess with my woman, and I'll blow your bollocks off,' he smiled. Just for once, I toed the line.

On the pitch, things were deteriorating faster than my doomed relationship with Denise. Colchester fell through the Third Division trapdoor – with Sheffield United, Blackpool and Hull for company – just two points adrift of Alan Buckley's Walsall survivors. We signed our own death warrant, with just one win in the last nine games. But I did manage one personal victory, shutting up Barnsley's mouth-almighty centre-back Mick McCarthy, without paying the consequences.

Playing at the back with his future Republic of Ireland No.2, Ian Evans, he was shouting all the odds at Oakwell and giving it the big 'I am' in front of his team-mates. Mick was an imposing character and I wouldn't have wanted to meet him in a dark alley for a scrap, as he might have taken me to the cleaners. But this was football, where nothing scared me, and he was giving me earache. I growled over his annoying rants.

'Oi, mate, forget all the verbal. Let's see how much bottle you've really got by sticking your head in with me for an hour and a half.'

It was all bravado, of course, but it paid off, as he didn't want a head-smacking contest. Once the big, hard Yorkshireman knew I meant business, he kept his gob zipped shut, even though his team won 3–0 and he had every right to rub it in my face.

My second goal in 12 starts, sidefooted from all of five yards, earned us a miserable 1–0 win against Carlisle on the final day of the season. Already damned to the basement, only 1,400 gloomy souls bothered turning up at Layer Road to cheer us down. It was the second time in three years I had sunk to the bottom of the pile. I still remembered how painfully it had bitten me at Walsall, but we had found a quick cure by bouncing straight back then. It wouldn't be that easy this time. Not because Colchester weren't as good a club, or didn't have some decent players, but because I had lost my self-respect. It didn't register that I was drinking a beer or 10 more than I should have been, approaching kick-off. And going down certainly didn't hurt anywhere near as much second time round. I was cheating my family, club, team-mates and the fans paying their cash to come through the turnstiles. But, most importantly, I was cheating myself. I still believed I could breeze through the Third Division with a gut full of beer, so Fourth Division football would be easier, allowing me to indulge in even more late nights, lagers and ladies.

At Fellows Park three years before, I had been mortally wounded by relegation, but drinking plasters had covered those scars. I'd been at Chelsea in February – a club down on its luck, but still one of the biggest and most glamorous in the country. Three months down the line, I was at tin-pot Colchester staring into the abyss again – not knowing then just how big an impact this club would have on my life. But my downward spiral didn't bother me one bit. All I was concerned about was pleasing myself. Nothing else mattered any more.

9. WIN OR LOSE, ON THE BOOZE

I couldn't wait for the new fixtures to be printed – so I could map out my drinking. Intricate planning revolved around whether we were playing on a Friday night or Saturday afternoon, and how many hundreds of miles away we would be. Calculating what time the team coach would get home and plunging back into my social life was now more important than playing football. I needed to slap my money down on a pub bar before the last bell rang, then head to a Colchester night-club to buy some lucky lady half a pint of lager.

The biggest obstacle to my partying was the league we were playing in. They might as well have renamed it the 'Fourth Division North' as most of the away trips were to khazis like Darlington, Halifax and Rochdale. But the players never let these long slogs dampen their spirits – it just gave us more drinking time. The 1981/82 season had started well, so we deserved a few beers for our efforts. Going into November, Colchester were in the thick of the promotion hunt, having won 10 of our first 15 matches. We'd reached the giddy heights of the League Cup third round – with yours truly claiming a brace against Cambridge – before bowing out at Tranmere. Even more surprisingly, I'd packed my shooting boots for most of the league games, banging in seven goals in a nine-match run, including a couple of tap-ins at Hull. If you'd put both goals together, the distance I scored from would still have been no more than three yards out, but that was the way my luck was going for once. At Walsall, these chances would have clipped a post or smacked the bar, but they were hitting the back of the net at Colchester. So I felt fully within my rights to celebrate as often as possible.

Without initially intending to, I was earning a reputation in the team for being a serious drinker. The lads would say to me, 'Blimey, big fella. You can get it down your neck.' So I hit it even harder because of the macho bullshit which dominates changing rooms; the competition and the desire to be No.1 – 'no fucker is going to outdrink me'. The motto was always the same, 'Win or lose, on the booze.' And when you are winning, like we were, the drinking is outrageous.

Parking up at an opposition ground, the most important part of pre-match preparation was collecting a whip from the players. The coach driver was handed the cash and would find an off-licence during the game, buying three cases of the strongest lager possible for the return journey. That's 72 cans. The manager didn't have a problem with it, as he wanted to keep us all onside. And if we got a positive result, the happy gaffer would reward us with some extra drinking money, forking out for another three cases. That's a grand total of 144 tins. And not the little fuckers, but the biggest, tallest cans we could find.

But the players would already have been comfortably numbed before stepping foot on the coach, having obeyed the strict 'Six by Six' rule. A Saturday match would finish at 4.45pm and it was a rule of the team that you had to get in the bar as fast as you could and slosh down six pints before departing at 6pm. If you'd picked up a knock during the game it was very tough, as the physio would be strapping your ankle in the changing room until 5.30pm, but there was no leniency afforded to the lame, and you would still be expected to sink half-a-dozen pints like everyone else.

It goes without saying that I never moved as quickly on a

football pitch as I did getting off it, making sure I was showered, changed and up the ramp by 5.05pm. Of course, nobody was ever going to be left behind if they didn't drink their full quota. It was just peer pressure, the usual keeping-face exercise in front of the other lads. And I didn't need any encouragement to lead the party. I was determined to be top dog, making sure I lived up to my image of drinking club chairman.

Six solid hours of motorway boozing would be poured into empty stomachs. There was no fish and chips fetched on to the bus, because it stopped us drinking. With no toilets on the coaches, knots were tied in bursting bladders. You had to hold your piss until the driver pulled over on some dark hard shoulder in the middle of nowhere – a line of players making room for more beer by watering the bushes in the freezing rain.

I sat at the back with the other naughty schoolboys, leading the noisy banter and playing drinking games like Spoof, where you had to guess how many coins were in your team-mates' hands. If you lost, you had to quickly drink two or three fingers of beer, or down the whole lot. I was a dab hand at this game, hardly ever losing, but I would still manage to work my way through 16 cans.

You had to keep going, and woe betide anybody who fell asleep, as they would wake up with cigars – which some of the lads smoked on the coach – up their nostrils, ashtrays emptied on their heads, Biro moustaches, or a new hairstyle. It was utter chaos all the way to Colchester, unless you were one of the frowned-upon dullards, sitting at the front reading their books. They got the shit ripped out of them, and being a boring bastard wasn't for me.

I'd get off the coach at Layer Road still clutching a can of Special Brew, with another one nestling in the pocket of my tracksuit bottoms, before getting in my car and driving to the pub. Most people wouldn't be in a fit state to find their car, let alone struggle into the seat, after drinking such vast amounts in a short space of time. I'm not excusing my behaviour, because I know it was wrong and dangerous, but I'd built up such a strong tolerance to alcohol that I never felt shit-faced getting off the coach. God knows how, but I just felt super-merry, and ready to let the good times roll. But that was me, I loved playing the fool – as I craved the attention of my team-mates – and being the most drunken idiot in the squad got me all the adulation I needed.

There were also two different factions at Layer Road before training. All the married and sensible players were gathered in the home changing room, while the rest of us herded ourselves into the away team's quarters. No prizes for guessing where I got kitted up. But one of the most senior pros at the club changed with us misfits. Long-serving goalkeeper Mike Walker was 36, which was 13 years my senior. He was over 6ft tall, with a strong build and looked like Jimmy Savile with his bleached white hair. But Mike was a self-centred sod and thought he was Mr Important. To prove his point, he would turn up for training every day in a full suit, complete with a ponsy hanky hanging out of the breast pocket. The rest of us would roll up in scruffy jeans or ragged tracksuit bottoms, before Mike strolled in proudly wearing his jacket, trousers, shirt and tie. I'd just stand there taking the piss.

'Fuck me, Mike, this is Colchester United, not fucking Manchester United.'

But he wouldn't take the bait. One day, as that minging herringbone suit hung there on the wall, I thought, 'I can't have this'. Making sure I got out of the shower first after training, I grabbed the shirt, tie and jacket off the peg and pulled it over my soaking wet body. I stood there in the mirror admiring myself, top-half suited, but nothing on underneath apart from a pair of football boots, with water still dripping down my legs. Mike exited the shower with a towel wrapped around his waist, a calm expression turning to sheer horror in a split second. He saw the smirk on my face and went to throttle me.

I ran out of the door and he chased me down the tunnel on to the muddy Layer Road pitch screaming blue murder, while my bare cock and bollocks flapped around the bottom of his tie. I was shouting back, 'Catch me if you can, old man', and all the other boys, who had been alerted by the commotion, were leaning on the dugouts cheering us on. I was getting a stitch from laughing so much, and Mike was a fit old boy, eventually rugby tackling me to the ground and giving me a hard dig in the ribs for good measure. His suit was ruined as we rolled around wrestling on the mucky pitch, but I think he saw the funny side – about a month later. And he still carried on wearing a suit every day.

Colchester went into 1982 still going great guns at the top of the table, and I was having my best season ever in front of goal. I got on the scoresheet again to earn us a point in a Boxing Day clash at Bournemouth, which was my 10th goal in all competitions before the turn of the year. My preparation still could have been a lot better, as I was going through the motions on the training ground, during the mundane team programme of fitness work and five-a-sides. But I was still turning up for the games. Scrapping hard for a win on a Saturday afternoon – no matter what shape I was in – was something I could never lose enthusiasm for.

One thing I did take pleasure from at Colchester was the one-on-one training, which always brought the best out of me. The assistant manager, Ray Harford, had been a decent centre-half in the lower divisions and was a first-rate coach. He knew exactly how a forward would react when the ball was played into him and, from his own experience, how the defender would respond to win back possession. Ray would take me off alone for 45 minutes for a sharpening-up session, passing on his wisdom and making me more aware about getting the best out of my marker. I always listened to Ray's advice, as he took a special interest in improving my game – which never happened once at a 'big club' like Chelsea. Ray went on to become one of the top coaches in the game, and I know he rated me. When he moved to Fulham a few years later as manager, I was informed that he was considering taking me to the Second Division club as his targetman. But he never went through with it, as he knew I was a drinker. He banned me from saunas and exercise bikes at Colchester, running me ragged instead to squeeze the juice out of my sweating body.

Ray hated alcohol and its related sins, which was never so apparent than when we played a practical joke on a team trip to Spain. He fell fast asleep in a chair at the airport, so we bought a bottle of duty-free whisky, unscrewed the cap and placed it under his mouth as if he was drinking it. The moment was captured on camera and the picture pinned on the changing room wall one morning before training. Everyone was sniggering when Ray arrived, but he failed to see the funny side, tearing the picture off the wall in anger and making us all pay for it on the running track.

I even managed to make a pig's ear of the only sensible thing I tried to do at Colchester – safeguarding my future by getting a first foot on the property ladder. More than happy as a lodger with the Signorellis, I bought myself a brand new three-bed semi-detached house in a quiet cul-de-sac in Great Cornard, just over the Suffolk border. I had the place fully furnished, ready for our striker, Ian Allinson, to move into, which would cover the £15,000 mortgage. But he blew it out at the last minute to move in with his girlfriend, so I hurriedly found another tenant, who did a bunk after three months, costing me more than £1,000 in lost rent. I think the place must have been built on a graveyard, as it was definitely cursed. I flogged it at a small loss after three years, without spending one night under its roof. I hadn't made any mortgage payments for nearly six months – cancelling the standing orders to boost my beer money – and was summoned to the bank for a hearing. My debts were mounting and I had a drawer full of bills, totting up to a good few grand. At the bank hearing, a familiar-looking blonde was chewing my ear off about being an irresponsible footballer and telling me that I would have to sell the house, or it would be repossessed. Then it clicked. A few months before, the bank worker had taken centre stage around a mate's house, putting on a girl-on-girl show with her married pal. How ironic. I'd knocked the bollocks out of her that night and now she was knocking the bollocks out of me.

My regular drinking buddies, David Moss and Steve Wright, got more use out of that house in one weekend than I did in three years. Steve was one of our defenders, and his father, Peter, had been a popular winger at Colchester during the Fifties and Sixties. And Dave was an ace face around town, as his old man was a well-known businessman in the furniture trade. A couple of girls they had met on holiday were coming to pay a visit, but they had nowhere to conduct their fun and games. Seeing as Dave and Steve had shown me the party ropes when I landed in Colchester, I thought it was only fair to return the favour and gave them the keys to my pad so they could shag away to their hearts' content. The totty turned up on a Thursday, just 24 hours ahead of our match against table-topping Wigan at home. But I wanted to tag along, so we headed out to Suffolk for the busy market day in Sudbury, where I wouldn't stick out so much. I managed to polish off 10 pints of Guinness before getting in the car to drive the boys and girls home late in the afternoon. As I pulled into a pub car park for pint number 11 on the way back, a Mini slid into the side of my motor, ripping the wing out. The first thing I did was run in the pub and order another pint to steady my nerves after the impact, not realising that two cars behind the Mini was an off-duty bobby, who had called in the incident. Ten minutes later, a police van turned up.

'Excuse me sir, have you been drinking?' asked the cop, staring at the glass in my hand.

'Fucking hell, mate – that car has just smashed into me and I'm a bit shaken up. Give me a break,' I replied.

But he wanted his pound of flesh, and I knew I was facing a long overdue drink-driving ban as he pulled out a breathalyser. He screwed the bag into the machine, handed it over and asked me to blow into it, before leaning into the van to grab the paperwork for a clear-cut collar. Well, fortune favours the brave, so instead of taking deep breaths to inflate the bag, I exhaled in short and sharp bursts while he still had his head in the van.

Turning round, the puzzled policeman took back his device and studied the light indicators on the side.

'You're fine sir, thanks for your cooperation,' he said, staring at me in total disbelief.

I was just as shocked as he was, but gave him a cheeky smile and a wink before Armando arrived and ferried us back to Colchester.

I got a call the next day from Ian Phillips, another footballer who was at Peterborough but lived in the town and knew a few of the local constabulary. 'Watch your back, Roy,' he warned me. 'The cops can't believe you've beaten the bag test, as they know you were absolutely bollocksed. I'm marking your card – they're looking for you now.'

When the Mini smashed into us, I felt I had remained pretty calm. But me and Steve were definitely suffering from delayed shock that Friday night against Wigan, as neither of us could stop shaking in the changing room at half-time, studs rattling against the cold floor. I really could have done with another beer before going back on the pitch.

Steve was a quality lad and we'd hit it off in pre-season, drinking ourselves silly in Norway after a friendly with Kongsvinger, about 60 miles from Oslo. We were staying in a hostel, as it was mega-expensive over there, and the club had given us an allowance for the week. But it was £7 a pint in Norway and we exhausted the club funds on the first night, breaking the midnight curfew and getting back at 4.30am with a couple of Nordic delights. We were banging the backsides off these two girls, while our defender Phil Coleman was asleep next door. When the girls left, we found a discarded tampon on the floor. We thought it would be hilarious to drop the string of the tampon down Phil's forehead and nose, resting the body against his mouth, so when he was snoring it was blowing in and out of his gob. Well, it tickled us.

I'd got my drinking bearings by then and was in my element at Colchester, widening the socialising net by inviting out-of-town players down for a session. Twenty miles up the road, Ipswich Town were flying in the First Division title race under

Bobby Robson's shrewd stewardship. The Suffolk side had a team of household names, many of whom were top international stars, but they still loved getting their hands around a pint glass and needed a watering hole away from Portman Road. I was happy to provide shelter for the Ipswich boys, taking them to the Andromeda nightclub under the cover of darkness, or getting them involved in the mayhem of our Wednesday all-dayers, as we'd get the day off following a Tuesday night game. Defenders Terry Butcher and Russell Osman were particularly good company as we were all the same age. Russell was a good-looking boy, and a swarm of girls would leave their numbers on bits of paper under the wipers of his sponsored Merc outside the Andromeda, which provided us with a regular source of female company. On another occasion, Terry and Russell joined me at the Headgate pub in Colchester the day before they were due to report for England duty. We were drunk as skunks, and I loved getting pissed with Terry, as I would wipe the floor with him playing Spoof. He was absolutely useless and didn't know when to give up. And this time he was made to pay the ultimate price – a forfeit know as 'The Pirate'. Russell had already been forced to do press-ups in his pants on the grotty pub carpet. But Terry's punishment was to run a lap of the bar – around the tables, stools and punters – completely naked, hopping on one leg with a hand covering his right eye. And fair play to him, just like the great player he was on the pitch, the future England captain led by example – doing the circuit three times.

One of the most eagerly awaited dates on the football calendar is FA Cup third round weekend, when the minnows are paired against the big boys. Colchester pulled out a plum draw in January, an away match against Geordie giants Newcastle – after a blood-and-guts battle much closer to home had earned us a trip to the north east. We had seen off Brentford in a Layer Road replay after scrapping to a draw at Griffin Park, following a 20-man brawl, with plenty of fists hitting their targets. We scared the life out of them in the punch-up, and I had my own unorthodox duel with Bees midfielder Terry Hurlock during the match. Everyone knew Terry's reputation – the Brentford fans called him 'Animal' and he was supposed to be the toughest bastard in the world, and the first one in if a row kicked off. He looked like a big gypsy who had fallen off the back of a caravan, with massive hooped earrings and a huge fuzzy mane of black curly hair. He never fazed me, as it was that same old mentality, if Terry was tough then I had to try and be as tough as him. But Terry wasn't just some thug who earned his money kicking lumps out of people, he could play the game as well. At one point during the match, we tried to outmuscle each other in the centre of the park and Terry came out on top, knocking me off balance. But as I headed towards the deck, I shoved my left hand up his shorts and grabbed hold of his sweaty bollocks, pulling him to the ground with me. Terry had tears in his eyes as the pain increased during that slow motion fall together, but he never hunted me down afterwards, as a mutual respect had been won. I still had black springy hairs under my fingernails as I shielded the ball by the corner flag to waste time right at the death. Brentford centre-half Jim McNichol was trying to force me out of the way, pushing and pulling, as I held him off. Then I decided to step aside, sending Jim into the corner flag at full pelt, which bent in two, then pinged back up and hit him smack in the face. I was pissing my pants, and even the Brentford fans were laughing along at their own player's comical misfortune.

You don't play at many better grounds than St James' Park, and it definitely gave me an extra spring in my step. The voices inside my head were fighting to be heard above the deafening noise of the passionate Geordie coliseum, telling me that this was the level I deserved to be playing at, not slumming it at Layer Road. I had to get out there and silence the noisy fuckers by showing I still had what it takes. We started off well, but fell behind to a first-half goal from Newcastle forward Imre Varadi. Steve Wignall scrambled in an equaliser after the break, before the chance to take a famous scalp fell at my feet. I broke into the box and rounded goalkeeper Kevin Carr, but the ball was lacking half a yard of pace as I rolled it towards the unprotected net, giving Magpies defender Steve Carney enough time to slide my shot off the line to safety. The voices went quiet, drowned out by Geordie jeers.

The sold-out Layer Road replay was on a Monday night under floodlights. On the Saturday we drew at home with Bury in the league, so I drove back to the Midlands, which resulted in scandalous preparation for such a high-profile match. I demolished 18 snakebites with my brothers and pals when I got back, before shaking off a hangover watching Jim and Gaz play for their Sunday team, Trojan, over at the park. Usually, I'd be standing there screaming like a maniac – just like Dad used to – but I had to be careful as I'd got sent off 'guesting' for the team a few weeks before, offering up Gaz's name when I got my marching orders. After the game, it was all down the pub, before getting home late for mum's roast dinner, then we headed out on the lash again. The boozers all closed by 10.30pm in those days, so we took up residence in a Birmingham curry house for a late tipple, turning in at 4am.

After five hours' kip and still groggy from alcohol, I drove back to Colchester for the match, which was an end-to-end belter. The ground was bursting at the seams, with 8,000 fans packed inside tiny Layer Road. We gave the Geordies another decent account of ourselves, but fell just short as they edged through 4–3 in extra-time. I didn't have a single clear-cut chance and my major highlight was watching Newcastle's young winger Chris Waddle, who was fresh out of the sausage factory. Waddle was untouchable that night, flying up and down the line aided by an aerodynamic mullet, and getting one of the goals. He was so strong on the ball, which was glued to his feet as he rode challenge after challenge. He was what I would call a brave player, somebody who never hid during the game, but was always in the thick of it, demanding the ball, desperate to be involved. Waddle was a few years younger than me, making his first tentative steps at a big club, and seeing him work his magic with such enthusiasm made me realise just how far I had fallen.

Dad and Gaz were getting the drinks in after the game, offering me heartfelt commiserations for being so unlucky. The old man told me a scout had been on the phone before he drove down, making out that Everton, Manchester City and Sheffield Wednesday were all keen on me. But I couldn't listen to it and ran off to the toilets to escape the watching eyes of a packed bar. I was hit by a tidal wave of emotion and the realisation that I should have been doing so much better for myself – if only I could get my shit together and knock the booze on the head. But I knew deep down that I couldn't, and really didn't want to. I loved to drink, and this was my level now. I had accepted that. My problems were more deep-rooted than just giving up beer. I was growing increasingly bitter and twisted inside, believing the game had cheated me. My rebellious streak was growing worse, and I was teetering on the edge of being out of control. Standing over the washbasin, I frantically splashed my face with water, terrified a fan would come in for a piss and discover the hardman centre-forward crying his eyes out.

League leaders Sheffield United visited Layer Road on the first Saturday in February, with Colchester still seeking win No.1 of 1982. The club bought Cambridge striker John Lyons for £25,000 to reignite our own promotion drive. The Welshman was joining a deadly frontline, with Ian Allinson and Kevin Bremner registering 21 league goals apiece by the end of the season – another two forwards to benefit from my combative shifts at the Fourth Division coalface. This was the Yorkshire club's first experience of life in the basement, and we made sure the culture shock continued in front of the *Match of the Day* cameras, blunting the Blades 5–2. Lyons got the ball rolling with a debut goal, before I challenged goalkeeper Keith Waugh and headed past the flapper from the penalty spot. Their central defender, Stewart Houston, was another soft touch who didn't have the stomach to fight me, making it easy for Allinson, twice, and Bremner to pick up the pieces and finish the job. After the final whistle, I motored straight back to the Midlands to watch *Match of the Day* with all the family. It was the first time I had been on TV and it was nice to hear the commentator John Motson saying positive things about me: 'Roy's a good player at this level and is working his way back up', and, 'A lot of people in the game admire Roy because he's as brave as they come'. It was a brilliant moment seeing the pride spread across my family's faces as they listened to Motson's words.

We only won three of our next 17 matches going into April, and I reverted to type, managing a solitary goal in a draw at Peterborough. Bobby Roberts got his P45 and Ipswich's Northern Ireland international defender Allan Hunter was drafted in as player-manager. But our promotion hopes had long been extinguished. Sheffield United had taken full advantage of the new three points for a win rule, amassing 96 as champions. We finished sixth, but still a massive 16 points short of promotion, which was a disgrace with the firepower at our disposal.

A ginger lining did break through the gloomy end-of-season clouds hanging over Layer Road in the form of an ugly, freckle-covered carrot-crunching apprentice from Great Cornard. Perry Groves broke into the team as a 16-year-old, and his youthful exuberance certainly gave the place a lift, helping us win three of our last six matches. I even managed to chip in with another two goals, taking my final tally to a respectable total of 16. Perry was seven years younger than me, but I took an instant shine to him as it was like staring into a mirror of the past. He was teetotal and completely dedicated to making it as a professional footballer, just like I had been at his age at Birmingham.

Grovesy was my boot boy and took great pride in working that polish and brush around my footwear to the highest standard, the same as I had with Trevor Francis. He was a terrific athlete and had an enormous long throw, which could be as dangerous as a corner. But Grovesy's two biggest assets were blistering pace that meant he would have been able to beat the Road Runner in a 100-metre sprint, plus huge self belief. He was a mouthy git for such a young spunk, never afraid to put the senior lads in their places on the pitch, screaming at them to get the ball to his feet if they kept pumping it over his head. But I didn't mind that confidence, as I could see he had something special about him from day one. He was devoted and lived a healthy life off the pitch, and I wanted to help him stay that way. I'd lived both sides of the story, and I didn't want his promising career sliding into the gutter, like mine had. Grovesy was very direct when he burst on to the scene and played straight down the middle as a striker. Eventually, his lightning pace was shifted out to the wing, where he could murder the full-back, but his decision-making was crap. So I'd give him advice, and the most important thing I told him was to keep things simple. Once he'd beaten his man, he only had three options: to whip the ball into the near post, far post or edge of the box, depending on where the defenders had been dragged by the frontmen to open up gaps. Hypocritical as it sounds, I also told him to steer clear of the booze and not to worry about his puppy love girlfriend as, despite being pale and ginger, there would be plenty of birds sniffing around in the future. I just wanted him to focus on his football, escape Colchester and make something of his ability.

For all his bravado, Grovesy was still a naive teenager with a lot to learn. On his first overnight trip to Blackpool, he got on to the coach with a bag that his mum had clearly packed for him. I couldn't believe it, a fucking bag – all I took away with me was the tracksuit I was sitting in, with a toothbrush and shaving razor in one of the pockets, plus my matchday suit. Once Grovesy had left the coach to get a snack for the journey from the Layer Road tuck shop, it was open season. I yanked everything out of his bag and found a horrible pair of green-and-white striped pyjamas, the sort of thing my grandad had slept in. I put them on, over my clothes, pulled up tightly around the crotch with my nuts poking through the bottoms and the waistband riding high around my chest. Grovesy got back on the coach munching a bag of crisps to a chorus of horn blasts from a laughing driver, finding me plastered in green and white like a giant grinning spearmint.

'For fuck's sake, the cunt's got my jim-jams on,' he said.

I couldn't believe my ears and battered him for it, 'You wanker. Does mummy call them your jim-jams?'

Everyone was pissing themselves, and I wore those Winceyette specials for five hours, all the way to Bloomfield Road, before checking into reception at the team hotel still wearing them. But it was a great lesson for Grovesy – don't ever give anybody enough rope to hang you with. He was in the big boy's world of professional football now, and if he didn't get wise fast he would get slaughtered.

10. SUICIDE ISN'T PAINLESS

As Allan Hunter began his first full campaign in charge of Colchester, the pressure to win promotion was back on. But the focus on players improving their technique and expressing themselves, championed by former first-team coach Ray Harford, was crushed by his replacement, Cyril Lea, who boosted our ex-Ipswich contingent. The Welshman's training regime was all about fitness, with the balls padlocked in the cupboard. On his first day, Lea summoned us all to a meeting and chalked on a blackboard behind him in big white letters: FOOTBALL IS ALL ABOUT RUNNING. We had some gifted ball players at the club, who I knew from experience would be stagnated by these methods. So I told Lea from the outset that he was talking crap, adding, 'Football is about keeping possession – the other team can't hurt you if you keep the ball.'

He just looked at me and said, 'Run, run, run', which was his answer to everything.

If your shooting or passing was off target, it wasn't practice that was going to make it perfect, but a long, hard slog of a run. The only time we got close to a football was when Lea thumped the balls into all four corners of the ground, ordering us to run after them. But I would look like Seb Coe when it came to following his daily routine – making sure I had a bunch of cripples for company. My running party consisted of Hunter, who was approaching 40, with the years taking their toll on his legs; his old Ipswich defensive partner Kevin 'Shot to Bits' Beattie, who was in his thirties and only managed four games all season; plus Mike Walker, who was 36 going on 56. I always finished streets ahead, no matter how much I had drunk the night before. And that's what I call using your football brain.

We topped the table after starting the 1982/83 season with a seven-match unbeaten burst. I won us three points on the opening day against Halifax, and John Lyons was on fire, netting four times. October's League Cup second round brought First Division Southampton to Layer Road for a goalless first leg. But I could have had five goals, were it not for the brilliance of England goalkeeper Peter Shilton – and a linesman who should have gone to Specsavers.

I had Shilton's number early doors. For a muscle-bound bloke, he didn't like physical contact, and I had him down as a coward. A few years later, when he let Maradona punch the ball into the net at the 1986 World Cup, it only confirmed my view of that night. Shilton had *carte blanche* to go straight through the Argie when he came out like Superman – knees, elbows and everything – as goalkeepers always get away with it. If it had been me in goal, I'd have made sure Maradona left the field on a stretcher. He wouldn't have dumped the whole England team on their backsides with his stunning second solo goal – he'd have been lying in a hospital bed by then.

Shilton might not have been the bravest, but he was first class at pulling off top-drawer saves. He denied me four certain goals at Layer Road – including a stinging close-range half-volley from a corner – throwing himself left and right with amazing agility to palm goalbound efforts to safety. The only time I did beat him, I headed back across goal and the ball hit the inside of the post before crossing the line, but it was hurriedly cleared and the referee waved away my frenzied protests. The next day in the paper, a picture showed that it was a good yard over and I had been robbed of a memorable winner.

We lost the return at the Dell 4–2 after a gutsy display, but I won my personal battle, scaring Southampton's young centre-half Mark Wright to death. He couldn't get near me and I won every header, taking him right out of the game. He hadn't played in the first match, and I was determined to find out how brave he was. Every time he tried to breathe down my neck, I'd shout to the lads, 'Fuck this tosser. I fancy a row. Stick the ball in here and I'm going to smash this cunt'. Wright looked traumatised, but he should have been grateful for the education. It wasn't the last time he came off second best facing me, and I'd like to say thanks for the full set of crystal decanters I've collected over the years for winning Man of the Match awards against him.

Footballers have so much time on their hands after going to work for just two hours training a day, and finding things to do away from the club was my biggest problem, as a low boredom threshold always led to a pub door. I started training a Colchester Sunday League side on a Wednesday night to keep out of trouble, and would also pop along to Layer Road to watch the reserves play. One Tuesday night, the stiffs were up against Tiptree United, who had one of our former players, Geoff Harrop, turning out for them. Sitting in the directors' box next to the gaffer, John Lyons and Steve Wright kept me away from the bar for 90 minutes. But it was a nothing game, unexpectedly brightened up by four attractive young ladies, all aged about 19, gliding along the side of the pitch and parking their pert backsides in the seats right next to us. They were full-on football groupies and one of them was a little smasher, with dark hair and a pretty face. It was Harrop's ex-fiancée, Jackie, and she had caught my naughty eye, which hadn't gone unnoticed by the boss. I clocked Allan Hunter's stare and chuckled, before he laughed back and nodded without saying a word. I knew what that sign meant – the challenge had been set – and I replied, 'Seven days'. Hunter nodded again and smiled.

I had a new girlfriend at the time, Wendy, who worked as a barmaid in the Lexden Sun. She was a redhead, which I found fascinating as it was undiscovered territory for me. I'd laughed her into bed following a similar bet with some of the lads, because I was curious to find out if the collars and cuffs matched. Anyway, the following night I went to the Andromeda and there was Jackie, dancing away with her entourage. We did it three times that night on her parents' lounge floor, and the next day I went straight into Hunter's office and held my hand out. Finally, he had something to say. 'No way,' and handed me a fiver, while shaking his head. He couldn't believe I'd come up trumps in little more than 24 hours. I was well pleased with myself, as it was another big buzz to win a bet against a team-mate, let alone the manager, especially when it involved the opposite sex. It was just a bit of fun at the time, and I didn't have a clue that it was the beginning of an up-and-down, here, there and everywhere relationship with Miss Jackie Parker.

Having a laugh was the last thing on my mind at the end of October – when I broke the Bury left-back's leg at Gigg Lane in a 1–0 defeat. It was a complete accident – vindicated by the referee's refusal to show a card, despite loud vocal encouragement from the crowd – as both of us had slid in honestly to contest the ball. It was awful hearing the sickening snap and seeing his shin buckle, and the genuine horror of the incident left me distraught. After the game, I was walking off holding the ball, and a bunch of angry Bury fans ran over to the wall and started flobbing at me. But I hadn't done anything wrong. I was the innocent party for once and didn't deserve the flak, so I hurled the ball at them as hard as I could, earning a yellow card in the tunnel. I got out of Gigg Lane as quickly as possible, not even bothering to have a drink. Back in Colchester, I was still full of remorse and wrote a letter to the defender, explaining how gutted I was and that I genuinely hoped he healed quickly and was playing again soon. I could never have imagined then, though, that my life was about to be rocked by an even greater tragedy.

One of my best drinking pals at the club, John Lyons, was getting a lot of unwarranted stick off the supporters. I knew it was getting to him, and he had my sympathy because I'd got the badge, T-shirt and duvet cover for taking abuse from some of my own 'fans' at Walsall. I didn't understand it, as he had started the season well, getting seven goals in the first few months, which is a decent return for any striker. The big problem was that he'd replaced benched crowd favourite Kevin Bremner in the team. Kevin, or 'Mad Max', as he was known, had been signed from the Highland League's Keith FC, but had a shocking touch and equally poor appreciation of the game. Lyonsy was a much better player technically, but didn't chase lost causes for 90 minutes, which Bremner did, and the punters love all that. He had no control when he was running after the ball at full pelt, and he must have wiped out 15 advertising boards after putting on the brakes too late. But what the fans didn't realise was that Bremner had refused to sign a new contract and wanted to quit Colchester to up his pay packet, and poor old Lyonsy got the shitty end of the stick for it.

We beat Chester 1–0 at home on a Tuesday night, and after having a few drinks at the club I headed with Lyonsy to the Rose and Crown to meet Angela and Armando, where we could get served until 5am. I was always attracted to people who wanted fun out of life and we became thick as thieves. Lyonsy was a natural entertainer, a hilarious storyteller who could have been a comedian if he hadn't been a footballer. He had that rare ability to hold the attention of a room full of people, who would silently hang on his every word before pissing themselves at an immaculately delivered punchline. We always had a rest day after a midweek match, but John rang me in the middle of the night, well 9.30am, and asked if I wanted to meet up. As I struggled to come to terms with seeing daylight through one half-opened eye so early, I said, 'Do me a favour, John, I've only had four hours' kip. I'm fucked. I'll meet you later at the snooker club in town.'

We had a beer for breakfast, in the Colchester Billiards and Snooker club on the High Street at 11.30am, before going to his place in nearby Layer de la Haye in the afternoon. His parents were coming down from Wales for a visit at the weekend and there were tins of paint everywhere, as he was planning on decorating before they arrived. There was also a large loop of black cable on the floor, left over from sorting out his TV aerial. After a few more beers made us feel braver, we talked a girl we knew, who was only ever a phone call away, into joining us for an experimental threesome. It was a new buzz for me, but it all went wrong when she got cold feet and stormed out halfway through the act.

That created an awkward atmosphere, so we drove to the Lexden Sun for a few more drinks. As the punters started drifting in at 6.30pm, Lyonsy was in his element, back in the comedy routine and cracking up all the regulars. But something wasn't right. As I stood there watching, his mouth was giggling but his eyes were blank, completely absorbed in gauging his audience's reaction, and I started to wonder what was going on inside the poor bloke's head. Last orders meant a shift of venue to the Andromeda for another three hours at the bar, before Lyonsy dropped me off at 2.30am. Forty-five minutes later, the police smashed down his front door to find him hanging from the aerial cable at the top of the stairs. As well as the crowd stuff, I knew he'd been having problems with his regular girlfriend in Cambridge, but you don't expect somebody to kill themselves over a few bird troubles. Lyonsy had rung his girlfriend just after 3am to spell out what he was planning. The police were informed immediately, but it was too late to prevent him from taking his life on Thursday, 11 November, 1982, three days after his 26th birthday.

I was put in the grim picture after arriving for training, feeling rough but ready to run it off. Turning up last, as usual, it was deathly silent as I approached the changing room. Mike Walker, Steve Foley and Steve Wright just sat there without saying a word, and one of the young kids, Wayne Ward, was so pale he looked like he'd seen a ghost. This was supposed to be the laughing and joking room, and I thought, 'What's up with you miserable bastards?'. Then one of the most senior players, Micky Cook, ushered me to the manager's office, where I was gently told the devastating news about Lyonsy.

I couldn't believe what I was hearing and felt my legs failing underneath me as I broke down in tears in front of Allan Hunter. It was only a few hours ago that we'd been partying together, and this didn't add up. The police paid a visit to ask a few questions, as I was the last person to see Lyonsy alive. They also asked me if I would ID his body in the morgue, as his family were hundreds of miles away in Wrexham. But I couldn't do that, not in a million years, and said no. Training was cancelled and everyone sent home. I needed a drink, so once I was finished helping the police with their enquiries, I went to the snooker club with Phil Coleman. Everyone there knew what had happened as it was the top news item on Anglia TV. People were trying to console me, offering to buy me a drink, but I didn't want their sympathy, however well meant. Just for once, I wanted to be left alone, to drown my sorrows and make some sense of this terrible mess. As I stared into the bottom of a pint glass, I was beating myself up inside my head, wondering how I hadn't noticed something serious was wrong. In hindsight, there were so many tell-tale signs. Lyonsy had a Renault, which he took great care of, but a few months earlier he had turned up at training with a broken window. When I asked him what had happened, he said, 'Oh, some idiot clipped me, that's all.' It turned out that he'd tried to do himself in by driving into something, but had failed, temporarily putting off the inevitable. And after a game, he would shrug off the fans' criticism with a typical quip, 'Fuck me, if things don't get better, Roy, I'll have to hang myself'. If I'd heard him say that once, I'd heard it 15 times, which should have set the alarm bells off. What upset me the most was that, even though Lyonsy was one of my best mates, he had obviously felt he couldn't confide in me. However, I shouldn't have been surprised, as footballers never discuss their true feelings with each other, for fear of being ridiculed around the club.

I returned to the ground on Friday morning for a light training session, ahead of an overnight stay at Tranmere. I hadn't slept a wink and Allan Hunter was amazed to see me there at all, but despite everything that had happened Colchester still needed a result to keep in touch with the leading pack. I'd only just turned 24 myself, and nothing as serious as that had ever invaded my carefree lifestyle, so the boss must have been concerned about my mental state. The bus was leaving for Prenton Park at 2pm, and he asked me if I could play. I really wasn't with it, but I'd already made my mind up. I said I'd play, as I wanted to do it for Lyonsy, but only on the condition that I got to wear his No.9 shirt. Hunter agreed, and I sat slumped at the back of the bus on my own in a complete daze. All the lads were distraught, and we might as well have travelled to the game by mobile library, as it was the quietest six-hour coach journey of my life. I'd always play the goat before kick-off, clowning around and being a general nuisance, but on this occasion I never said a word before the game started.

I slipped on Lyonsy's shirt – which didn't feel weird at all, as I just wanted to do the best I could for him – and pulled on a black armband. The Tranmere announcer paid tribute to Lyonsy over the loudspeaker system and the referee got both sets of players around the centre circle for a minute's silence before the game, which the fans observed impeccably. That minute went on for an eternity, as I stared downwards through moist eyes at the white chalk and green blades of grass between my boots. It was all hitting me again and Hunter stood close by my side for support. When the whistle went, he just patted me on the shoulder. That was it, time to get playing. And what a start it was – it couldn't have been more perfect if it had been scripted by Hollywood's finest. We broke straight away, won a corner and I stretched my neck muscles to the limit to head the ball past goalkeeper Nigel Adkins after just 45 seconds. I was never usually a massive celebrator of goals – if I scored, I scored – but this time I went crazy, running around like a wildman. I didn't look up at the sky, or wonder whether Lyonsy was with me in spirit at the time, despite it being one hell of a coincidence, as I'm not at all religious. The release, though, was unbelievable, and I just thought, 'That one's for you Lyonsy. Get in there, mate'.

But the distressing events of the previous few days finally

caught up with me on 30 minutes, as delayed shock kicked in and I collapsed on all fours in front of the dugouts. My stomach was empty as I hadn't eaten for two days, but I was heaving my guts up with disgusting green bile spilling out of my mouth. Cyril Lea dashed on to the pitch and poured kaolin and morphine down my neck from a big bottle, which got me back on my feet. I started retching in the centre circle again ahead of the break, but was determined to come out for the second half and managed another 20 minutes before I had to come off. I was physically and emotionally shattered and just sat there on the bench, half-comatose, as the lads rounded off a 4–2 win. After the game, the boss told me to take as much time off as I needed, so Dad and Gaz drove me back from Tranmere to the Midlands for a few days.

It wasn't long before I was back behind the wheel, driving Phil Coleman and Cyril Lea to Lyonsy's funeral in Wrexham. When we arrived, the church was absolutely packed. There must have been 400 people there, which says something about the stature of the man. After the ceremony, I was introduced to his family, who surrounded me and made such a fuss. They all thanked me for what I'd done – wearing his shirt at Tranmere and getting a goal – and I was just blown away by their warmth. I didn't feel worthy of their affection as I was just a dickhead footballer who had let his career go down the swanny, and the whole experience was so humbling. The waterworks soon started pumping again and I could have filled the Welsh valleys with my tears. But football never stops and I had to start focusing on the next match, which was coming up in a few days. I kept Lyonsy's No.9 shirt and I've never forgotten him, as the bloke was a blinder. It's not something you're supposed to admit as a tough-guy footballer, but as a pal and as a man, I absolutely loved him.

After the funeral, his girlfriend in Cambridge kept calling me. I was still living with the Signorellis, and they got me to invite her down so we could all have a drink for Lyonsy. She visited on a Friday and we did the rounds, returning home at silly o'clock as usual. During the night, I found the poor girl hugging the bottom of the bathroom sink with her underwear on full display. But I thought, fair play girl, get it out of your system, and cleaned both her and the bathroom up, before putting her back in the spare room. On Saturday, the four of us got pissed up again. When we got back to the house, Armando and Angela went straight to bed, so I sat talking in the living room with Lyonsy's ex-missus. Out of nowhere, she put her hand on my knee and went for a kiss. I backed off straight away, saying, 'Sorry luv, that's never going to happen.' I may have been a player with the ladies, a man with very few morals who would have muffed a dead dog when he was drunk, but you don't mess about with a mate's bird, especially when he's just killed himself, and I didn't see her again after that.

A few weeks later, I was having an afternoon pint in Colchester's Six Bells, which was just across the road from a flat I'd taken on to use as a shagging palace. I was talking to a few of the lads about football, when some geezer at the end of the bar piped up.

'Footballers are you?' he said. 'What about that wanker Lyons. Shame he didn't top himself six months earlier, he could have saved us £25,000.'

I tried to rewind, 'What did you say, pal?'

He replied, 'Shame he didn't do it six months before and save us a few grand.'

I smashed my fists on to the bar, and as I turned to land one on the idiot the barman grabbed at my arm and I slipped off the stool on to the floor. The gobby fucker was terrified and left the bar in a rush, but that's typical of a small-minded football fan.

Rain or shine, I was always last one on the training pitch and last one off it – unless it was Christmas Eve. Then I'd always be first to leave, so I didn't miss out on any drinking time, and in 1982 I ran straight from Colchester's Army Barracks, where we had been training, and into town to get my fill of festive cheer. I jogged into a pub at 2pm on that Friday and finally crawled into my pit completely plastered after a 14-hour bender.

Most people sleep it off with a Christmas Day lie in, before waking up to the sound of presents being unwrapped and the delicious odour of a gravy-covered turkey dinner. But we were playing at Peterborough on the Monday, 24 hours after Boxing Day, so Allan Hunter hauled us in for Christmas morning training. I was a total shambles when I limped to the ground, with multi-coloured party popper strands in my hair, red lipstick kiss marks on my cheek and the Embassy nightclub doorman's entry stamp still printed on the back of my hand. The boss wasn't happy watching me stumble through the session, but he still picked me and he must have been really pissed off when I only lasted 34 minutes of a blood-and-thunder festive cracker. Posh's centre-halves, Neil Firm and Trevor Slack, were more interested in kicking me than the ball. It was the same old story and I was getting no protection from the referee, John Key. I still felt like a bag of shit from Christmas Eve and wasn't putting up with that treatment for 90 minutes, so I waited for a chance to readdress the situation. The ball was played into my feet and I knew Firm would fly through the back of my legs, but on this occasion he slid under me. Milking his challenge, I threw myself down on top of his body, knees-a-blazing, driving one in his rib cage and the other into his chin, opening up his face in the process. I was straight off, with my team-mate Micky Packer not far behind, in a heated 2–1 defeat. But I didn't feel an ounce of remorse. And why should I have? You reap what you sow on the pitch, and I'd happily earned that red card fair and square by doing the fucker properly.

Allan Hunter dropped a bombshell in February when he announced that he was quitting Layer Road as he didn't believe he was cut out for management, handing over the reins to his No.2, the 'Running Man', Cyril Lea. That wasn't a great appointment for me, as we didn't like each other and he was determined to clamp down on my boozing. He would drive around Colchester midweek scanning the pub car parks for my motor so he could discipline me the next day. But the physio, Charlie Simpson, who liked me as he knew I did a good job for the team no matter what I got up to in my spare time, tipped me off. So I left my car at home and drove Wendy's motor to the pub so Lea would never find me.

I'd managed seven league goals by the end of February, but with injuries ravaging the squad I was becoming less of a targetman and more of a utility player, plugging the gaps in midfield and defence. I didn't mind and never caused a fuss, though. We were still closing in on the fourth promotion spot and as long as I was helping the team I was more than happy. Cyril Lea then had the brainwave that I could do a solid job as a defensive midfielder, protecting the two centre-halves, so he arranged for me to give the role a try in a reserve match at Tiptree United. One of our ex-players, Paul Dyer, was playing in midfield for the opposition and wanted to prove a point after being released. A strong challenge went in on Dyer, whose instant reaction was to grab our lad and start punching him freely in the face. I marched over and dragged Dyer away. He took a few swipes at me, clipping me on the chin, but no big deal, and Lea came round the corner of the stand to see me performing the perfect holding role – on an opponent's throat. Then Dyer booted me in the shin, which hurt, so I flattened him with a right hook. We both got sent off, so I followed Dyer into the showers, inviting him to finish off what he'd started, but he didn't have the bottle. I'd picked up another ban from a meaningless match, and Lea was fuming. But the Tiptree manager helped smooth things over by ringing the Colchester boss to plead my case, explaining I was provoked into the whole confrontation by defending a team-mate who was taking a pasting.

Being the ultimate team player backfired when the walking wounded were all fit again. Lea dumped me on the bench, which had never happened to me at Colchester before. He just smiled at me and said, 'You can play anywhere Roy – that's why you're the perfect sub.' We finished sixth again, missing out on going up by just two points to Scunthorpe, who joined Port Vale, Hull and Wimbledon in Division Three. I managed one more goal at the end of April, against Bristol City from the bench, having replaced Micky Cook in the right-back berth at the break – and it was probably my best ever from a football perspective. I headed clear a corner to Ian Allinson – who swapped one-twos with strike-partner Tony Adcock – and carried on running the entire length of the Layer Road pitch, before collecting the return pass, rounding the goalkeeper and slotting home. I was red-faced and blowing out of my backside, but it was definitely worth it.

I celebrated my athleticism by draining tangy snakebites in the Andromeda until 3am, before deciding to drive back to the Midlands. I'd just started a six-month driving ban for tallying up too many speeding points. I was driving on Gaz's licence and borrowing his Austin Maxi, but I was so sloshed I could barely get my key in the door. I woke up staring into the red brake lights of a lorry on the M6 after falling asleep at the wheel. I quickly swerved into the contraflow at the last second to avoid hitting the juggernaut and crashed through a queue of plastic bollards, which went flying over the roof of the car. Severely shaken, and still not sober, I carried on to Solihull ultra carefully, with my eyes wide open.

I couldn't sleep once I was stretched out across the safety of a stationary bed, just tossing and turning restlessly, trying to get my head round how I was still alive. It was as if somebody had been telling me to calm my jets, as I couldn't keep going on like this. Maybe it was John Lyons sending a warning from the other side, but I didn't believe in all that guardian angel stuff so I instantly dismissed that theory. Eventually I crashed out and, after waking up in one piece, I clicked straight back into living the life of a lunatic and prepared to pack my beer bucket for a new challenge by the seaside.

11. NO I DON'T LIKE TO BE BESIDE THE SEASIDE

John Fashanu had the balls to stick his head in a giant goldfish bowl full of eels and wade through snake pits on TV reality show *I'm A Celebrity . . . Get Me Out Of Here!*. But when it came down to a straight fight for a contract at Southend, I proved a much tougher proposition than any Bushtucker Trial.

My Colchester deal had expired, but manager Cyril Lea wanted me to stay – as a perennial bench warmer – and offered terms to match. He valued my services at £190 a week, a £60 drop in wages, and there was no chance of a signing-on fee to pour down my throat. I found the offer insulting, after having slogged my guts out for Colchester, playing in nearly every position, to try and get the club where it deserved to be. This was a case of Alan Buckley syndrome all over again, and my response was exactly the same as it had been at Walsall. I treated Lea and his crummy offer with the contempt it deserved and drove straight to the Midlands, never to have a conversation with him again.

I was available on a free transfer now, and 15 clubs called during the summer, all courting my signature. Bristol City were in again, plus Cardiff and Swansea, who were all a major step up. But home – now Colchester – was very much where my heart belonged and I needed a new employer within a commutable distance. Being Mr Soppy Bollocks, I'd convinced myself I was in love with flame-haired barmaid Wendy, so the easiest option was to follow my football compass 40 miles south to the coast and sign for Colchester's Essex rivals Southend.

I held talks with the manager, Dave Smith, a little baldy Scotsman, who showed me round Roots Hall and tried to win me over with his ambitions for the season. Joining Southend was still a step up – they were in the Third Division for starters – and the Shrimpers had a larger fanbase and ground than Colchester.

The only thing concerning me was the man in charge, who struck me as a right odd bod. Smith seemed nervous during our conversation and tapped a pen repeatedly against his office desk, before he finally pressed down too hard and it flew over his shoulder, hitting the wall. He just carried on talking as if it hadn't happened, drumming his fingers instead, before relaxing and offering his hand to verbally shake on a one-year £350-a-week deal. I took his hand, smiling, thinking I'd just agreed to sign for Mr Magoo. There was no signing-on fee, but it was a pay rise and would allow me to remain shacked up with Wendy. It was job done in my eyes.

But Smith was told to clear out the drawers of that desk he was so fond of tapping on before I got chance to put pen to paper. And his successor Peter Morris – another ex-Ipswich player taking a turn on the local managerial merry-go-round – told me I had to convince him I was worth the agreed deal by going on trial at Roots Hall during pre-season. I wasn't best pleased by this development, but swallowed it, as I was desperate to stay in Colchester.

Running across Southend's hot summer sands, past small fishing boats bobbing around gently in the sea and wooden beach huts painted in a rainbow of colours, I got a first glimpse of my contract rival, John Fashanu. We were similar players, whose main job was to lead the line as the focal point of the attack, both 6ft 1in tall, the same weight and dominant in the air. Southend were only ever going to need one of us. The only real difference was our ages. I was nearly 25, four years older than Fash, which meant I had been around the block a lot more times. Fashanu hadn't played 10 league games at his last club, Norwich, while I had nearly reached 200 appearances, making me much more street-wise. I also believed I was technically better than him with the ball on the floor, which wasn't hard, as Fash couldn't trap his foot in a door. But the real deal-breaker came down to my raw aggression, which he never had a hope of matching, and I blew him out of the seaside water. During the training sessions and practice matches I attacked every ball with a snarl on my face as if my life depended on it. Poor Fash couldn't equal that level of ferocity and ended up looking like a lanky plank. The final hurdle in sealing the deal couldn't have been simpler, putting on a good show in a pre-season friendly against Japan's national team at Roots Hall. Everyone knows that the tallest Japanese bloke is only about 5ft 2in high, so I had a field day, winning every header without even jumping, pushing Fashanu out of Roots Hall in the process.

The 1983/84 season stuttered into life lethargically, with three draws and two defeats, including my first goal in Southend colours in a 4–1 disaster at Preston. I turned Lion-tamer in the next game, clawing out another goal as the Shrimpers beat Millwall 3-2 at Roots Hall to get up and running at the sixth attempt.

Things were never dull at topsy-turvy Southend, with plenty of goals flying in the net, but unfortunately for us it was at both ends. A bizarre 6–4 defeat in lashing rain at Plough Lane condemned us to an early League Cup exit at the hands of Wimbledon's route-one giants, before we ended September on a deadly high, as pocket dynamo Steve Phillips fired a Friday night treble in a 6–1 triumph at Scunthorpe's Old Showground. The players were over the moon on the coach and shared a crate of beer for every goal which had dented the busted Iron, returning to Essex about 3am.

I went home and had a few hours' kip, but woke up still very much in the party mood, heading over to the snooker club for the most important meal of the day – a Saturday morning pint. As we didn't have a match that day, I'd promised my mate Joe O'Sullivan, the manager of non-league Chelmsford City, that I'd present the Man of the Match award at the end of his game. So after a few more beers in the snooker hall, I drove the 25 miles down the A12 to Chelmsford's New Writtle Street home, which was next door to Essex Cricket Club's County Ground. I didn't see much of the game, as I was preoccupied with exhausting the beer pumps in the bar under the main stand, having a joke with the punters and getting increasingly stewed. Being the guest of honour, I made sure I looked the part, getting fully suited and booted, before having one too many and wrapping my tie around my head. After the game, the star man, Adrian Owers, came into the bar to collect the award, but I stole his thunder. I leant my body against the back wall and drank a pint of lager in seven seconds standing on my head – without spilling a drop – before springing back upright to milk the applause of an appreciative audience. Although, I'm not sure Adrian was clapping along. Then it was time to bid the drinking gallery goodbye and get back in the car with a snooker pal, Ian, who had tagged along for the afternoon. On the way back up the A12, I kept drifting over to the hard shoulder, and Ian was repeatedly pushing the wheel to nudge me back on course. I drove home using one eye, as I was so far gone I couldn't see through two.

The goals were still flying in all over the place as far as Southend were concerned, and we ended October with a 6–0 demolition of Brentford at Roots Hall. But none of the goal dust was falling my way, as I only forced two efforts over the line in the next 14 games, against Leyton Orient and Lincoln. More worryingly for the mid-table Shrimpers, was that we were shipping goals left, right and centre as 1983 faded away, including a 5–0 annihilation at Sheffield United and a 4–0 drubbing at Plymouth. But it was a 5–1 Boxing Day drowning across the Thames at bogey team Gillingham where I was pitted against my toughest opponent ever.

I always came off a poor second best against the Kent side and, on this occasion, I was greeted by a mute central defender. He had a face with more lumps and bumps than a knobbly old potato. Steve Bruce was as hard a bastard as they come and never spoke a word throughout the whole game. As we contested the ball you could hear the bones cracking as our heads continually smashed together, splitting Brucey's ear. He never said a thing, despite all the pain being dished out and the blood splattering around, and when that happened you knew the fella was the real deal. Even at Gillingham, Bruce was a far better player than people gave him credit for. He wasn't just about heading the ball and hoofing it clear, as he had an excellent touch and was an accurate passer. Just for once, the boot was on the other foot after that game. I usually thrived on owning my marker for 90 minutes, but I had to bite the bullet this time, as this was a centre-half who I had to respect, signified by a big, firm handshake at the final whistle. Bruce was one of the best ever at that level, and my one regret is that I didn't get to play against him later in his career, when he deservedly reached the top flight with Norwich and Manchester United. I'd have bought the bloke a beer after the game and told him straight to his face that, compared to all the other defenders I'd fought over the years, he was just different class.

As well as keeping me close to Wendy, joining Southend had the added bonus of teaming up with a great bunch of lads. I'd been convinced to try my luck at Roots Hall by some of the Southend players after bumping into them on a boys only summer holiday on the Greek island of Ios. Eight of us had drunk one beach bar dry, emptying two 6ft-high fridges full of cans of Lowenbrau, with the beaming owner sending a little boy off on his bicycle to bring in reinforcements from the supermarket. When I turned up for training on my first day at Roots Hall, I got a standing ovation in the changing room. The Southend players were delighted to see me, as they knew there was a serious social secretary taking up the reins.

We had a nice drinking party. Both of the goalkeepers liked

a pint, Mervyn Cawston and John Keeley, as well as the left-back Steve Yates and Greig Shepherd, a Scottish striker who was good with the girls and had arrived at the same time as me. After home matches I'd usually remain in the players' bar right to the death, before driving back up the A12 to Colchester for extended hours. But one night I followed one of the players home with a barmaid from the ground. She wasn't shy and he was shagging away and getting his cock sucked, while I stood there watching, before he shot his bolt and ordered me to take over. Now, I wasn't completely comfortable with this sort of thing – yet – and the only previous time I'd attempted a three-some with one girl had been the disaster at John Lyons's place. I looked at this blonde, thinking, 'What are you doing, luv?' But she was extremely keen, on bended knee waiting for me, and I had to go through with it, otherwise I'd never have lived it down back at the club. So I started to kiss her before climbing on top. My team-mate was obviously enjoying it, as he leaned against the door giving a running commentary, 'Go on, big fella, give it to her properly. She loves it'. But I never finished the job – I just couldn't in those circumstances.

I was fully expecting to get slaughtered by the players on Monday morning for my inadequate performance, and I did, but for something completely different. They were taking the piss out of me for kissing the barmaid after she had given my partner in grime a blowjob – 'Morning cock lips', and, 'Did that bird taste nice, Roy? Bit salty was she?' But it hadn't even occurred to me at the time, as I was too busy dealing with the pressure to think about where her mouth had been.

My time at Southend would be shortlived for two reasons – I wasn't sure about the gaffer, Peter Morris, and I was sick of the sight of his No.2, Colin Harper. I'm sure Morris felt I had been forced upon him, even though I'd gone through the head-to-head with John Fashanu for a year's contract.

Morris knew I wasn't settled at Southend, and at Christmas he went out and bought another striker, Trevor Whymark, from Grimsby. Once Trevor was at the club, Morris started exploring the possibility of playing me at centre-half, which didn't appeal to me at all as a regular position, so I knew my days were numbered at Roots Hall. Another club was tapping me up at the same time, which I'm sure the manager was aware of, so I decided to chuck it in after only four league goals in 22 games. But not before I had settled a long-festering score.

I didn't like Morris's sidekick, Colin Harper, from day one. He would never look anyone straight in the eye when he talked to them and he was always looking Wendy up and down in the bar after matches. That alone made me not want to be at the club anymore, no matter how well I got on with the other players.

At the beginning of 1984 I played my last game for Southend, a 2–2 draw at home to Hull. But I knew it wouldn't be long before I packed my bags again, so my chances of putting Harper in his place were running out. During the week, I was training with the lads, playing a five-a-side match on the concrete car park at the back of the main stand. Harper was running round like Billy the Chirp, shouting out his coaching instructions, but the players who shared my dislike of him knew what was coming. They started rolling passes in short when I was near Harper, as they knew I wanted to crunch him. But he kept pulling out when I got too close for comfort. However, he was too slow bottling it one last time, jumping up and catching me in the balls and ribs with his knees, which made my eyes water. So I grabbed his shirt, punched him in the face and watched him hit the deck like a sack of spuds. He lay there fishing for sympathy, but everyone was laughing at him. The most disappointing thing was that I didn't catch him properly, not anywhere near as hard as I had wanted to, although it was probably just as well as I'd have done him some serious damage. It still felt really good, though, as I'd been desperate to give him a slap for months, but the manager was understandably far from pleased. Morris phoned me that afternoon to have a pop, but I knew he didn't want me and I didn't care about his opinions on giving his lapdog a long overdue dig. I left him in no doubt whatsoever that I was quitting Southend.

It was totally reckless on my part, as there was no concrete move to another club signed and sealed. But I didn't give a shit about what happened next. I just wanted to see the back of Southend as quickly as possible – even if it meant leaving Wendy behind.

12. LOVE AT FIRST PINT

L eaving Southend guided me towards one of the biggest loves of my life, Stella. The rocket-fuel strength lager, not another woman. Known universally as 'Wife Beater', as it brings out the monster in most men, it had the complete opposite effect on me. I spent 10 months in a fuzzy, blissful blur, desperate to share my new-found happiness with every member of the opposite sex I could get my grubby hands on.

A few days after decking Colin Harper, I was playing snooker in Colchester. I was closing in on my first-ever 50 break, for which the club would later reward me with a small trophy from behind the bar. I was leaning over the table, with my cue arm cranked back ready to strike, when a tannoy message blurted around the club, 'Gerry Francis on the phone for Roy; Gerry Francis on the phone for Roy'. The barman, Tony, knew how desperate I was to get that first big break, and I thought he was trying to shatter my concentration with the finishing line in sight. Then it started again, 'Gerry Francis is on the phone, Roy – REALLY!'

Letting out a frustrated grunt, I put the cue down and strolled over to the public payphone, which was inside a head booth, hanging on the wall. 'Hello, Roy,' said a voice. 'This is Gerry Francis, the Exeter City manager – I know you're unhappy at Southend, and I wondered if you'd sign for us?' I couldn't believe my ears. How the hell did Gerry Francis, a former England captain, know how to reach me at the snooker club? I had a rough idea where Exeter was – somewhere south of Bristol – as I'd gone there as a kid on one of Dad's summer cricket tours. I knew they were in the Third Division – although I didn't know where in the league table. Francis offered me £400 a week, which was a raise, but I insisted on a £15,000 signing-on bonus, which would clear a few debts and keep me in beer tokens for the next 12 months. The £15,000 was the only stumbling block, but I gave Francis my word that if he came back with the money, I would drive down for a medical and sign straight away.

I carefully lined up the cue ball again, then there was another announcement, 'Roy, Millwall are on the phone; Roy, Millwall are on the phone'. This time I was greeted by hushed Irish tones, the sort usually reserved for delivering absolution from behind the screen of a Catholic confession box. If it was a priest waiting to hear my list of sins, then it was going to be a very long and expensive phone call. But it wasn't a man of the cloth, it was Theo Foley, George Graham's No.2 at the Den. My old Colchester team-mate, Kevin Bremner, had signed for the Lions and had given Foley the snooker club number to track me down. It turned out that Graham wanted somebody who could put it about up front and had been impressed when I'd scored against Millwall earlier in the season. I really did fancy going there. It wasn't far away, and I knew that Millwall's notoriously volatile fans would love me as one of their own, a forceful centre-forward who would fight the opposition for them. And they would have got me too, if Graham hadn't played silly buggers. I asked Foley if he wanted to sign me three times, and he kept repeating, 'George wants to talk to you'. I didn't want to play childish mind games and wasn't going to drop my whole world for George Graham. I told Foley that I'd promised Gerry Francis I would join Exeter if he could stump up the cash I wanted, but thanked him for the interest.

What another great piece of business that was from

'Rudderless Roy', acting as his own blundering agent, yet again. Millwall won promotion to the Second Division the following season, after signing none other than John bloody Fashanu. And another 12 months down the line, Graham and His Holiness, Theo Foley, were holding Saturday mass at one of football's biggest places of worship, Highbury, as they guided Arsenal to a glorious period of success. Who knows what might have happened if I'd just gone and spoken to them?

Joining Exeter would mean leaving behind the main reason I had been hanging around Colchester all along – Wendy. But I was more relaxed about that now, with any lingering insecurities about our relationship long gone. We'd spent a lot of time together over those last few months and I felt settled in my head. Whatever happened, wherever I was, it was me and Wendy all the way, and we would stick together. Heading to Devon would be good for my family, who rarely made the long-winded trip through the maze of roads that led to Roots Hall, instead opting to attend away games up north within easier reach of Solihull. But Exeter was directly connected to Birmingham by the M5, allowing them to slide straight down to St James Park to watch me play. All I had to worry about was getting my football head screwed back on and earning a few quid by escaping Southend.

I was back at the snooker table a third time, ready to finally bust the 50 barrier, when there was a third announcement. Gerry Francis had got me the £15,000, which would be paid in two instalments over a two-year deal, and he had agreed a £5,000 transfer fee with Southend. So it was game on, literally, as I finally cracked that cue ball and went on to complete a 57 break, picking up my little plastic trinket before getting a round in to celebrate the move to Exeter.

What an idiot I was! In terms of football, Exeter was the worst in a long line of career mistakes. I quit a mid-table club at the start of January, just because I didn't like the people in charge, to saddle up with a sorry old mob in the Third Division drop zone. Francis also stitched me right up by promising the local rag, 'Roy is the man who will save us from relegation.'

No pressure then, Gerry. I didn't score another goal before the end of the season.

When I spoke to Gerry Francis on the phone, I visualised the bloke who could have posed as a Page Seven Fella in the papers, stripped to his shorts and showing off a ripped torso. The same guy with the fish-shaped hairstyle and matching sideburns, a cultured midfielder who I'd watched on TV and played against as a kid, when I scored at QPR for Birmingham. I'd thought to myself, 'Yeah, I can up sticks to Exeter and play for a man like that'. But what greeted me at St James Park completely shattered the illusion. Player-manager Francis, now in his early thirties, was a disaster area. He was receding, a couple of stone overweight and breathing through his rear-end during matches. Now my body wasn't where it should have been because of the boozing, but I was always strong and never had a belly poking through my shirt. The other reason I stayed in half-decent shape was because, no matter how much I hated it, I did all the running I was asked to in training. Francis didn't. While all the players were lapping the pitch to sweat the beer out, he was standing with his No.2, Malcolm Musgrove, playing keepy-uppy, before putting the ball down and doing a couple of token six-yard shuttle runs. But as a player-manager you can't behave like that in front of the players, and it didn't take me long to work out why Exeter were struggling so badly – nobody respected the manager. Francis had everyone's utmost respect for being an ex-England captain, but for being a tub of lard and not doing the running when we all were he got zero.

I felt Francis's general commitment to the club was shabby, despite being well paid by the chairman for being a big name. He sucked a lot of us into the club from hundreds of miles away on the strength of his past glories, but he never bothered moving to Exeter himself. That just gave us a free pass to run wild around the city, because the boss was never there to catch us out. He had a club-sponsored Saab Turbo, which he must have done about 500,000 miles in, commuting from his Surrey home every day. Unless you're doing 120mph, it's a good three-hour drive, and he turned up to training knackered every day, looking like a bag of shit. He was still trying to manage the team while on the pitch as a midfielder too. But he couldn't issue any instructions as he was puffing and panting too heavily to speak, and there was never any chance of him tracking back and helping out.

We were getting smashed about all over the park in one home game and trudged off to the changing room at half-time resigned to another defeat. Francis just sat there with his bloated red head bowed. The players were waiting for a rousing speech to lift their spirits, but were forced to sit in silence for a couple of minutes. Then two blokes burst in wearing long raincoats, one tall, the other a little Arthur Daley lookalike wearing a trilby. The bigger one started holding court and giving out a team talk, while Arthur Daley circled the room with a white paper bag handing out boiled sweets to the players. I was as lost for words as Francis. As I trotted out stunned for the second half, I asked one of the lads, 'Who the bloody hell were those two?'

'Oh, that's the manager's dad and one of his mates,' he replied.

Years later, when Francis became the Spurs manager, he was being touted as a possible candidate for the England job. Who was he going to take to the World Cup as his No.2, his old man and Arthur Daley?

Exeter was a sleepy but lovely little city. The football ground was a shocker. It was just as poor as Layer Road, with crappy open terraces and weird grass banks cut into the front of one of the stands, but at least the pitch was decent. The training ground was great, though, as it was just across the road from a big, busy pub, the Cat and Fiddle, where I spent most of my lunchtimes, afternoons and evenings.

But I'd never seen so many hairdryers in one place as I did in the Exeter changing room. Usually the hardest thing about joining any new club isn't sorting out the wages or contract length, it's taking your clothes off for the first time in front of

25 strange blokes. The first thing they do is look at the size of your cock, to see if you're a threat. But I needn't have worried about my winkle holding up, as the Exeter boys were more worried about their barnets. The dressing room was like a poodle parlour, with all the players bringing their own hair-dryers to training and refusing to go to the pub before they had curled their mops. I was a wash-and-go-to-the-pub-with-wet-hair man and would call them all 'nancy-boys', but they just carried on blow-drying away. My flatmate, goalkeeper Len Bond, wouldn't even go to the newsagents to fetch the morning paper without giving his hair a good blast. What a bunch of tarts!

The Southend jungle drums had reached Devon before my arrival – my reputation as a lover of beer and birds filtering through into the changing room. So the serious drinkers at the club wanted to test me out, to see if the reality lived up to the myth. And I've never been one to disappoint. On the first Tuesday after my debut, a 2–1 home defeat to Bristol Rovers, I was escorted to the Clifton pub by forwards Steve Neville and Ray Pratt, defenders Martyn Rogers and Keith Viney, plus Len Bond. It was a cracking boozer with a pool table, which was always lively with locals. The landlord was Exeter's record goalscorer, Tony Kellow, who was one of the record drinkers, too.

'Here's the new boy, here's the big boy – what are you drinking?' Tony excitedly called out.

I scanned the pumps and something new zoomed into view – Stella Artois. It was only 1.30pm, and this was obviously potent shit, weighing in at 5.2 per cent alcohol content, but I wanted to make my mark and show the other players who was boss of the bar. Tony started pulling the pint, saying, 'Fucking hell boys, looks like we've got one here.' The taste was chemical and strong, like drinking a bottle of Domestos, relegating the likes of Heineken and Carlsberg to piss water. And I liked it, making a 10-pint debut and sticking with it for the next 10 months. I was floating into the most cloudy period of my career, spending most nights fucked out of my brains – with 18 pints of Stella my personal record. I never gave my body a chance to clean out the pipes, relentlessly topping up the tank, and I can't remember half of the time I spent in Exeter. The high street banks didn't help either, with their instant hole-in-the-wall cash machines popping up everywhere. These new inventions might as well have been printing off beer vouchers, because that's all I was using my cash for.

There were so many pubs to test out, and I'd be in one most lunchtimes, afternoons and evenings. More often that not, it was the Cat and Fiddle, due to its close proximity to the training ground. I'd have at least 12 pints with the lads on a Monday and 10 more on a Tuesday if we didn't have an evening game. If we did have a match, then Wednesday was a day off and I'd spend it at the bar, easily finishing 16 pints of Stella. Drinking on Thursdays was frowned upon as it was so close to the weekend match, so I'd only have seven or eight, and Fridays were strictly out of bounds, although I'd have a quick couple somewhere. Then I would play the game on Saturday, get smashed out of my head after the final whistle and keep on drinking through Sunday, before the week started all over again. Looking on the bright side, I don't think I suffered too many hangovers, as I was never sober long enough to get one.

Exeter's other great charm as a city was that it had a university – stacked full of crumpet without a pot to piss in. All you had to do was flash a tenner and you were home and dry. You could say it was the girls who benefited most from my move to Exeter, as I got my leg over with half of them. Wendy caught the train down every now and then to stay for a week, but the desperation to remain by her side that I had previously felt was on the wane. At Southend, I would go back to Colchester most nights and climb into bed with Wendy. My drinking hadn't got any worse and, apart from the threesome with a barmaid, I'd been pretty much on my best behaviour. But putting 300 miles between us had changed things and we were growing apart in more ways than one. My boozing was heavier than ever, and playing football had never been less important to me. I played 16 games for Exeter that season without scoring a single goal or featuring on the winning side.

I didn't give a fuck about scoring for Exeter, as all my efforts were focused on scoring in the bedroom. Leading a promiscuous lifestyle was an irresistible addiction. The sex was on tap in Exeter and I was turning into the Third Division's answer to Michael Douglas. I was lining up different girls for every night of the week, who would be labelled the Monday Girls, Tuesday Girls, Wednesday Girls etc . . . I still wasn't chasing women around bars and didn't need to. You soon got to know which bits of skirt were regularly doing the rounds – who was out because they wanted a couple of drinks and a good rogering at the end of the night.

One girl, Bev, who I wasn't attracted to that much, sat on the doorstep of the flat for three hours waiting for me to return from the pub one afternoon. I was about to tell her to hop it, when I noticed she had this big Fresh Fruit Daily bag. When I peered inside it, there was a bottle of wine, a white basque and thong, plus a pair of high heels. Fair play, I thought, and I told her to go home, get changed and I'd be round for a session in 30 minutes, after I'd been to the football ground to put in a letter to the FA answering a disciplinary charge. And there was another little treat who had a thing for our skipper. I'd go round to hers and give her one, while she looked at his picture framed proudly in red-and-white stripes on the bedside table.

At the same time, I had this other lass who wouldn't stop stalking me, no matter how hard I tried to shake her off. One night, she was waiting outside my flat in her car as I went inside with another girl. When I went to training next morning, she was still there, asleep in her motor. I crept past quietly, thinking no more of it, but when I got back home she was lying in my bed with all her naughty gear on. She'd climbed in through an open window and waited all those hours for me. Now, I admired that kind of dedication, so I gave her the reward of her dreams.

Nobody, however, could ever top Teresa, who invited an entire team of Exeter's merry men to empty their quivers in 24 hours. Some of the players had an hour's commute to

Exeter, so I told them they could kip at my flat after a Tuesday night game and we'd hit the town. We ended up in the Warehouse, a glorified pub turned nightclub, by the quayside. It turned out to be an oddly barren night, so we just got more and more lashed. That was until the clock struck 1am and a gift from God appeared. There was a basement disco, mostly full of teenage students, and a miracle floated up the stairs on the arm of apprentice Mike Lane. This blonde manifestation was in her early twenties and dressed up as Robin Hood, with a green velvet outfit and fishnet stockings, little boots and a feathered cap. My eyes were popping out of my head, and I barked above the music, 'Laney, come here.'

I got a lager and vodka and orange in for the pair of them, before persuading Mike to disappear. Forty-five minutes after meeting us, good old Teresa was giving one of the players head in the middle of the back seat, while I was driving him home to his future wife. 'Go on big 'un, keep going round the block', he kept saying. After a few laps – knowing I'd sunk about 14 pints and had six passengers, which was a policeman's dream – I kicked him out before he had finished, despite Teresa's best efforts. When we got back to the flat, she really came into a league of her own, taking on four of us – one at either end and one in each hand – while everyone tried out different areas and angles for an hour or so. Eventually, we all crashed out, two of the boys in the lounge, and Teresa sandwiched between me and one of the other lads in bed – all naked, of course, and reeking of booze.

In the morning, we left her there and went to training. The lad who hadn't gone the distance was already bragging about getting a nosh in the car, but soon shut up when he heard what had happened after. Well, all the boys wanted to get involved now, so after training I went straight to the Cat and Fiddle and phoned the flat. No answer. Four new faces followed me home anyway, and Teresa was still there, ready for round two. She'd already picked up the phone, hanging up on Wendy, which took some explaining later on, so didn't answer it a second time. Before we got going again, Teresa asked me if I'd get her a few groceries from the corner shop. So I popped across the road and bought a bottle of baby oil, a carton of strawberry yoghurt and the biggest cucumber I could find. As I handed the money over to the suspicious young girl at the counter, she looked at me as if to say, 'What the fuck are you up to?'

Back at the flat, I told the boys I would get things going, which I did, ensuring I had yoghurt dripping off my grinning face when they came through the door to get involved. I left them to it and went down the pub, but Teresa wasn't finished. She still needed two more players for a whole team, and came back for a third evening stint, all shampooed and smelling lovely, wearing a tight black leather mini-skirt. So I recruited two eager volunteers by phone to complete Teresa's fantasy football XI.

A few years later, I returned to Exeter for an old team-mate's wedding. The venue for the ceremony had two receptions going on at the same time, and I couldn't believe my eyes when I spotted Teresa in the opposite one. She looked beautiful on her wedding day – a picture of pure innocence. I just hope her groom had plenty of stamina.

On the pitch, we were so bad that the fans dubbed us 'Gerry and the Pacemakers'. Exeter managed just a solitary victory in 22 league outings following my arrival, a 2–1 home win over Preston at the end of April – and I was suspended for that one. I didn't get any goals, but I did manage to pick up a comical third professional red card, in a 2–1 defeat at Wimbledon in February. It was only my third game for Exeter, and I'd already picked up a booking for moaning at the referee, Derek Brazier, for not giving us a penalty – then I decided to swat an irritating insect. Wimbledon defender Gary Peters couldn't play the game, so he compensated for it by being annoying – picking the ball up and booting it away when it was your throw or free-kick. He was a wind-up merchant and loved giving it all the verbal. It didn't usually bother me, especially if it was somebody half decent dishing it out, but Peters had such little ability that I just couldn't take it from him. He was the sort of bloke I went looking for right at the start of the game, and he probably dined out on this one for ages. I swung a boot at him at the first opportunity following a fracas, but swiped through thin air. The referee's aim wasn't off, though, and he showed me a second yellow card, red card cocktail for intent, and I was off again.

Exeter finished rock bottom – 16 points from safety – and I had my third relegation to the Football League basement firmly in the bag, with Southend sliding into the bottom four to make it a double celebration. But I couldn't care less now, and I wasn't even bothered about being dropped for the final match at Millwall. I'd got wind that Gerry Francis was going to resign after the game at the Den, so I got hammered on the Thursday night, before turning up for training 20 minutes late and barely able to stand up straight during a head tennis session.

I travelled to south London on the coach, but didn't make the squad, so I went straight to the bar and raised a glass to my old Colchester team-mate Kevin Bremner, as I watched through the slat window as he notched a hat-trick for the Lions in a 3–0 success. After the game, all the boys trooped into the bar, demoralised as usual, to find me trolleyed again. 'Fuck Gerry,' I shouted. But Gerry was long gone.

13. WAITING FOR GOD

'd hit rock bottom at Exeter and desperately needed salvation. The God squad was waiting just around the corner, but when they came calling my penance would be leading the line for one of the worst football teams in history.

The summer of the 1984/85 season saw the arrival of Exeter's new boss, but I wouldn't be sticking around long enough to get to know Jim Iley, the former Newcastle midfielder, who must have felt right at home at St James Park. Iley had some interesting – and by that I mean strange – training ideas. He made us run around a giant ring of footballs in blistering heat for 45 minutes, which branded a mark like a crop circle onto the pitch. Then we had to dribble the ball quickly to him, which he then picked up and volleyed into the air, barking at us to run after it and catch it. Then we had to bring it back again – just like a dog fetching a stick for its master.

Head tennis sessions – usually played in a small space to hone technique – were held on a full-size pitch. A net was stretched across the halfway line and we had to smash the ball as hard as possible to reach each other. But the summer's key command was, 'Out of sight.' When Iley shouted those words, you had to vanish super-fast and hide behind something, with the last player in view made to pay a forfeit of press-ups. During one session, a bright apprentice threw himself into a patch of six-foot stinging nettles and couldn't train for two days because he was in so much pain.

I finally got my first Exeter win and goal – netting a far-post big-boy's header – at the 17th time of asking, as we made a rampant start to life in the Fourth Division, nailing visitors Northampton 5–0. But Exeter soon reverted to type, losing 3–0 in the next game at Blackpool, where I surpassed myself with a second red card for the Grecians, following a tussle with their full-back in front of the dugouts. He went down like a big baby under my challenge and kicked out at me. So I aimed a stamp at his shin in retaliation, but only clipped him, with my boot powering into the grass next to his leg. Despite being off target, the referee still ordered me down the tunnel. But I wasn't overly concerned by the dismissal, and it certainly didn't register that I had a disciplinary problem. It was only my fourth sending-off in six years playing regular first-team football and I felt that was completely acceptable.

A handful of games into the new season, it was time to pack my bags again. Iley knew I loved a drink, but he also realised he could make a few quid out of me. The club was skint and most of the lads had been transfer-listed without even knowing it. I only found out when one of the Southend boys rang to say he'd seen my name on the circular of available players that lands on managers' office desks up and down the country. It didn't bother me at all – it was about time I negotiated a fresh bar tab.

One of my new suitors was Cambridge United. They had just been relegated to the Third Division and were bottom of the table, but it was only the start of September and there was plenty of time to climb. Most importantly, it was only 50 miles from Colchester, which meant I could move back in with Wendy, who was still tolerating my antics. I arranged to meet the manager, John Ryan, after a midweek reserve game. The money was OK, £350 a week plus £10,000 in my pocket, and I promised to come back for a medical the next morning with a view to signing a two-year deal. Then I bumped into an old mucker, Danny Greaves – the son of Spurs and England legend Jimmy

– who had been a team-mate of mine at Southend. We ended up in a Cambridge nightclub with some of the other players, and it was the same old bollocks. If they drank 12 pints, I would have to do 14 – beating them, then raising them – to show who was king of the pint glass.

I never made it back to Wendy, who must have been well impressed on what was supposed to be our first night living together again. Instead, I got my head down at one of the players' digs. I turned up for the medical slightly worse for wear, but the examinations were a joke. All they did was play around with my ankles and move the knees a bit, before carting me off to Addenbrooke's Hospital for a few X-rays. There was no fitness or blood test, it was all about identifying wear and tear in the joints, so drinking never came into the equation.

So it was all signed and sealed again before the latest idiotic training regime unearthed a serious problem which had dodged the club doctor's radar. The players were shunted into the back of the club's white transit van for a spin through the country, before being ordered to get out at Newmarket and run 14 miles along the A1303 back to the Abbey Stadium. Always eager to make a favourable early impression, I stayed sat in the back with my arms folded, stubbornly refusing to pound concrete and grass verges in my tennis pumps. So John Ryan and his burly No.2, John Cozens, grabbed my arms and legs, removing me forcibly and throwing me on the ground next to the van. 'See you back at the ground, Roy,' Ryan said, before the two of them drove up and down the road for the rest of the morning, making sure nobody was thumbing a lift or calling a taxi. But I didn't run, I walked and jogged it, taking more than three hours to get back, which was at least an hour longer than the others.

The next morning, I couldn't get out of bed I was in so much pain, and Ryan thought I was taking the piss when I rang him. I drove to Addenbrooke's, bent over the steering wheel like an old lady, where a CAT scan revealed three fractures in my lumbar spine vertebrae. The doctor said it was a long-term injury, which made me rewind the years to when

Walsall goalkeeper Ron Green had landed on my back like a ton of bricks while mopping up a Bradford attack. I'd never had any trouble with it before and must have been getting through games on adrenaline (and drink), but pounding concrete for all those miles had aggravated it. I couldn't have an operation to fix it and I would have to build up the muscle around the spine to protect it. It was my first serious injury. 'Bet you're glad I did that run now, gaffer,' I told Ryan, as my first month at Cambridge was spent on the sidelines – a combination of a red-card hangover from Exeter and rehabilitation.

My delayed debut was a 2–2 October draw at Leyton Orient, and it only took me another four matches to get off the mark, netting the winner in a 2–1 success at Newport County – Cambridge's first victory in 11 Third Division fixtures. If there was any consolation to be found in my latest frying-pan-to-fire move, it was that I had joined a team of record breakers. Cambridge were still bottom of the table and wouldn't budge an inch all season, but we did it in style, clocking up 33 league defeats, which at the time was the most in a season for a Football League club.

Maybe things would have been better if I'd prayed more, following the example of the Abbey's very own sect of dressing-room monks. Cambridge's Holy Trinity was centre-half David Moyes, plus midfielders Alan Comfort and Graham Daniels. I couldn't stomach religion, a scar left over from being the childhood figure of fun for my fellow church-going pupils at St Margaret's School. I could have been a great project for the Cambridge congregation, the biggest of all lost causes in need of redemption. But I was never going to become a disciple, as I resented being surrounded by bible bashers and tested their faith to the maximum. The three of them sat in the changing room with a little black book, discussing their beliefs, when they should have been getting psyched up for a relegation scrap. I would cut out a lurid tabloid newspaper story and stick it on the noticeboard in front of them, saying, 'See that pervert? That's what you lot will end up like. Vicars messing around with the choir boys.' But they just turned the other cheek.

I completely lost the plot with the God Squad after a 3–3 draw at Wigan. My own pre-match build-up might not have been the best, but when I hit that pitch I battled all four corners for my team. Wigan had three vile centre-halves – Tony Kelly, Colin Methven and Steve Walsh – and I'd been fighting and elbowing, the whole kit and caboodle, with all of them. Kelly was a horrible Scouser and he'd been stepping well over the line, cranking up the verbals. So when he played a lazy one up the wing, I smashed straight through the fucker's standing leg on purpose and stretchered him. While he was getting treatment, he called big Walshy over, pointed at me and said, 'Sort that bastard out.'

My eyes were all over the place, and I was pumped up to dish out another bashing: 'Kelly, shut your fucking noise and don't try to get your mate to do your dirty work. As for you, Walshy, give it a try son, and you'll end up fucked like your mate.'

Walsh took the advice and played hard, but fair, for the rest of the match. I was still in a bad temper after the game, sinking a couple of cans on the coach before launching into a fully blown persecution of the Christians. In my mind, they were the biggest part of the problem. They were too nice on the pitch, not nasty enough to win games, so it was like turning up with eight men every week. I battered Moyes first, demanding to know how a giant ginger Jock from Glasgow Celtic could play with absolutely zero aggression, putting all of his energies into bleating on about Jesus instead. Alan Comfort had scored that day, so I gave him a wide berth. But there was no respite for Graham Daniels, who had recently become a father, but was out of contract at the end of the season.

'And you,' I spewed. 'I'm fighting the world for this team and you're doing nothing. Forget all that little black book bollocks. Where is God when we're fighting for our lives and getting beaten every week? He's not giving us much help, is he? You've got no chance of getting a new contract here – who's going to fend for your baby and put food on the plate?'

Daniels just looked up at the roof of the coach, smiled and said three words: 'He will provide.'

I could have baptised him with a can of beer there and then, but I didn't want to waste it. After that, I never bothered saying anything again, and the three of them stuck to their beliefs. Comfort became a vicar and Daniels is one of the head honchos for the Christians in Sport charity. As for Moyes, well most people would say he has been performing miracles for years as manager of cash-strapped Everton.

Like Exeter, Cambridge wasn't your classic football town. Its dreaming spires, cobbled streets and punting rivers were a magnet for middle-aged couples on dirty weekends and university boffins, not the stellar names of the beautiful game. Cambridge had only become a Football League club in 1970, climbing to the giddy heights of the Second Division at the end of the decade. But it was a small club, still playing at a non-league standard ground, which was now paying the ultimate price for punching way above its weight for six seasons – a one-way ticket back to the bottom feeders. We still had a couple of talented players, like young midfielder Andy Sinton who had a lovely left foot, which he would put to work in an England shirt in the future. And there was also Steve Spriggs in the engine room, who was another solid pro.

For a club that was getting battered week in, week out, there weren't too many drinkers around, unless you counted the communion wine. But Spriggs could hold his own at the bar. He was a tiny fella, just 5ft 3in tall, but could drink his own body weight and then some. Spriggsy lived in a caravan at Cherry Hinton, just outside Cambridge. It was proper handy, because if we'd had a few too many, which was more often than not, I'd head back with him and sleep on a camp bed. And I always paid my way, keeping his girlfriend's best mate entertained, which made that caravan rock around the clock.

Most of the other players were lightweights in the drinking stakes, and the Christmas night out was under-the-thumb central. An afternoon session around town transferred to a nightclub and, true to form, I was leading the party, playing the clown and pulling my trousers up and down on the dance floor. But when the clock struck midnight, all the players' wives and girlfriends materialised, dragging their little pumpkins off home. Left on my Jack Jones, I hung on until 2am, before swaying back to my motor. The car park had one of those metal humps, raised about 10in off the ground, which won't go down and let you out until you've paid the fee. I was so sloshed that I couldn't feed the money into the machine's slot, getting out of the car and dropping my coins all over the floor. I couldn't see my hand in front of my face, let alone a few stray 10p pieces in the darkness. There was a queue of other cars building up behind me, impatiently bibbing their horns, so I fell back into the seat, put my foot down hard and hurdled the ramp like the *Dukes of Hazzard*. I don't know how I did it without ripping off the exhaust.

How I got home in one piece after running the A604 gauntlet, a bendy old road directly linking Cambridge and Colchester, is another complete mystery. It was a terrible road, with fields full of trashed motors, abandoned by drink-drivers who'd done a weekend runner. I had no recollection of the journey back when I woke up, marking another disgraceful episode in which I showed no regard for my own safety, or anybody else's for that matter.

Cambridge might as well have pulled the Third Division plug at Christmas as we were pretty much relegated by then. The chairman must have thought so, as he flogged our best striker, Robbie Cooke, to Brentford before the festive decorations had come down. He was still our top-scorer at the end of the season with six league goals. But I finished just behind him, with five of my own (albeit in 32 matches), including a March double against Leyton Orient in a 3–2 home defeat.

The manager, John Ryan, who was closer to 40 than 30, tried to lift the gloom by pulling his defensive boots back on, but successive red cards swiftly ended his playing days again. Unable to exert his fading influence on the pitch, Ryan tried to get inside the players' heads with a new innovative training method. Ordering us to report to the ground at 7am, he promised, 'You lot are going to get a taste of normal peoples' lives. There's going to be no more rolling up at 10am. You're going to clock on at the same time as factory workers – because that's what you will all be doing next year.' But he made himself look a right fool, as it was still pitch black when we got to the ground. Not able to train, we sat in the dressing room waiting for the sun to put in an appearance.

We had gone 17 wretched games without victory since Boxing Day – including 13 defeats – ahead of an April visit to the Den. And my frustrations boiled over after a Millwall mugging. I didn't buy into the whole intimidation myth surrounding the Lions' south London home. I never felt worried when I was on a football pitch and if a supporter did run on to have a go, you would give them a smack if you were half-decent. The only trouble I had was dealing with the thugs in the Millwall team. It was top versus bottom, as George Graham's Lions roared towards the Second Division, but we weren't making life easy for them.

I chested down a pass from full-back Mike Bennett just inside the Millwall half, when my targetman's sixth sense gave me an alarm call. Their centre-half, Dave Cusack, was moving in for the kill, but I could handle him all day long as he was nothing more than a bully, lacking the balls to take me on face-to-face. As I prepared to turn and thread the ball down the line for the overlapping runner, Cusack was all over me like a gorilla. Then a familiar face starting charging towards me, John Fashanu, the big plank, who didn't bother me either. But this wasn't one-on-one, the bastards were ganging up to do me. Cusack clamped me in his grip, giving Fash the green light to crack an elbow across the side of my head, knocking me spark out on the touchline.

Smelling salts soon cleared the stars as I came round covered in snot and gob flobbed on by Millwall's scumbag fans, who got both verbal barrels as I clambered groggily to my feet. Every fucker there was taking liberties with me, the punters and the players, and I was spitting feathers. Then big coward

Cusack stepped over the line again, making no attempt at all to contest the ball, as he thrust his studs straight into the nuts of our winger, Tom Finney.

The final whistle blew, 2–1 to Millwall, 18 games without a Cambridge win, and all the home fans were singing Cusack's name, while he took a bow and clapped them back. But I wasn't having that, ignoring the phony handshakes and making a beeline for the tunnel. When Cusack came round the corner, I grabbed his neck and pinned him against the wall. 'You fucking shithouse,' I shouted at him, furious spittle covering his chin. I didn't bash him, I just put him in his place, so he knew he had done wrong, before shoving him away and hitting the showers.

But the hot spraying water wasn't having a calming effect, as the flash-points of the match replayed in my mind. I couldn't shake Fashanu's behaviour out of my head – he had got away scot-free. I was having a beer with Steve Spriggs in the players' lounge 30 minutes later, when in bowls Fashanu wearing a white suit with a stupid smile on his face.

'Alright, big man,' he said, normal as you like, as if nothing had happened.

But I was still livid, ready to have a ruck with the whole Millwall bar, and lashed out.

'See you, go fuck yourself you big black cunt.'

Heads turned away from pint glasses everywhere, but a highly-restrained Fashanu never said a word. He didn't want a row, which he had every right to after being insulted like that, and he ignored my very personal attack. I interpreted Fash's cool and calm reaction as silent acknowledgement that our score was settled. After all, I was the one who had been purposefully pole-axed unconscious with a smack of his elbow, so I thought he was getting the good end of the deal. But it was a bad choice of words, used in the heat of battle, which I know is not an acceptable excuse. Neither is claiming that it was a much darker and different era of football back then, when racist chants where unfortunately the norm at a lot of football grounds. I should have known better, having been picked on myself as a child, branded the 'smelly kid from the poor family' in the playground. And it is not a choice of words I am proud of now.

Bobby Mimms grasped thin air as I beat the Rotherham goalkeeper from the penalty spot in the second half at Millmoor. That goal sealed Cambridge's first three points in 24 attempts, 18 of which had ended in defeat. There was no great delight in stopping the rot, just the relief that we were only a home game against Bolton away from ending a nightmare campaign. After shipping 95 goals, Cambridge finished bottom of the pile, a massive 26 points from safety and 25 points adrift of the nearest teams, Preston, Leyton Orient and Burnley, who also all made the drop. But I still got to embarrass myself in a Cambridge shirt one last time on home turf.

A few of my mates from the Colchester snooker club played for a Saturday football team called Friday Woods. The manager asked me if I could do a Friday night presentation at their end-of-season party, but I told him I couldn't as I had a game the next day. 'What does that matter? You're already down,' was his reply. True, I thought, so I agreed to show up at 9pm for an hour. The plan was to hand over the awards, have a couple of beers to be sociable, and head straight back to Wendy, retaining some grain of professionalism.

The event was held at Silver Springs, a function suite with chalets, on the way to Clacton, where husbands would rendezvous with their mistresses for a secret bunk-up. I handed over the prizes, but one or two pints turned into a game of Spoof, with none of the lads letting me put my hand in my pocket once for a drink. But this was major league stuff, we weren't playing for one or two finger forfeits, it was a pint of beer or cider in one go, or a big glass of throat-burning Scotch, which I usually steered clear of.

The next thing I remember is Wendy shaking me at 12.30pm on Saturday. She was a nurse by then and had just returned from her night shift. And it's a good job she did, or I would have slept through until Sunday. 'Shit,' I thought. 'I've got to

EARLY DAYS

Seaside fun – me on the left with twin brother Gaz and my sister Lindsay

Lifelong union – Mum and Dad get hitched

Padded up – captain of the cricket team, front row, centre

McDONOUGH STRIKES TO SEE VILLA HOME

MIDLAND INTERMEDIATE LEAGUE

Aston Villa 2, Bristol C. 0

TWO smartly taken goals by young Roy McDonough gave Aston Villa a victory against Bristol City which their second half performance well merited.

Purdie worked hard in midfield but City looked more the dangerous side in the first half.

Jake Findlay did well in goal and he had good support from John Oberton and Billy Wright. Gary McDonough also played soundly in the Villa rearguard but it was his elder brother, Roy, who stole the limelight with two fine goals in the 55th and 70th minutes.

McDonough was quick to hit home a centre from Fagan to open Villa's account and a well-placed shot from 15 yards found the corner of the net for Villa's second goal.

McDonough went close to notching a hat-trick and Peters also was near to increasing Villa's lead as they dominated the closing stages.

Rising Villa star – newspaper cutting of goalscoring for youth team

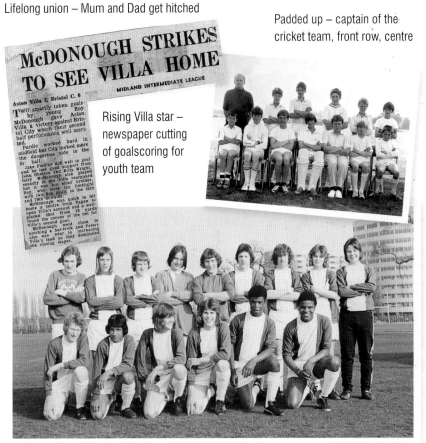

Top of the class – in the Birmingham Schools' team, front row, third left

BIRMINGHAM & WALSALL

Off the mark – national headlines after first (and only) goal for Birmingham

Blue-eyed boy – at Birmingham City, aged 18

McDonough earns point

BIRMINGHAM did their best to spoil Frank McLintock's big night. McLintock, at 37 the oldest player in the First Division, was playing his 610th and final League game before going into management.

McLintock began his career with Leicester 20 years ago and the players of both sides lined up to join in the applause from a sparse crowd.

Rangers' manager Dave Sexton gave McLintock a silver tray on behalf of the club and there were other presents from the patrons' club and a supporter.

Rangers, without skipper Gerry Francis, gave a half-hearted per-

| QPR | 2 |
| Birmingham City | 2 |

By BRIAN SCOVELL

formance. Birmingham were much the more inventive side in the first half and nearly scored in the 14th minute.

The alert Trevor Francis passed to Gary Jones just inside the box, and Rangers goalkeeper Phil Parkes just saw the ball in time in the bright sunlight and tipped it over the bar.

But another long shot out of the sun brought Birmingham their 28th minute goal. Terry Hibbitt squared the ball inside

and skipper Howard Kendall fired a 15-yard shot into the net via Parkes' left hand and the crossbar.

Rangers improved in the second half and equalised in the 53rd minute when left-back Ian Gillard made a run down the left and beat two defenders before his shot was blocked but Don Masson slammed the rebound into the top right-hand corner.

Webb scored Rangers's second goal in the 75th minute with a header from a Thomas cross.

Birmingham's equaliser in the 86th minute was a far-post header by centre-forward Roy McDonough.

Father figure – Birmingham coach Ken Oliver was a big inspiration

On the move – to Walsall for first-team action

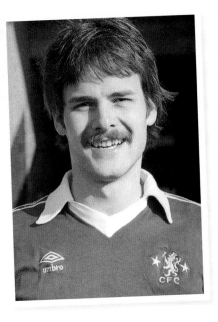

CHELSEA COLCHESTER & SOUTHEND

Thwarted – Southampton's Peter Shilton keeps another one of my goalbound shots out at Colchester in 1982

Bridge too far – life at swanky Chelsea in 1980 was far from glam

Heaven sent – heading a goal at Tranmere after just 45 seconds, wearing my dead pal John Lyons' shirt

On me rising head, son – winning a Southend contract against Japan's national team

Fash Bashing – on my way to beating John Fashanu to a Southend contract in 1983, with manager Peter Morris (right)

EXETER & CAMBRIDGE

Fancy a pint after the game? – Exeter face-off with Northampton's Brian Mundee

He's behind you – Exeter debut against Bristol Rovers

Air sandwich – challenging for the ball at Exeter

Mass stretch – under the watchful eye of Cambridge's God Squad

SOUTHEND AGAIN

I've got your back – standing behind one of my heroes, Bobby Moore (middle row, second right), at Southend

Follow me – training at Southend, watched by Frank Lampard Snr (top, right)

FA Cup clash – Newport's Tony Pulis receives treament at Roots Hall, as I head off the pitch dismissed (right)

Raising the roof – celebrating a Southend goal

Raining goals – scoring past Scunthorpe in a Roots Hall downpour

SOUTHEND GLORY

Rammed home – Derby's Peter Shilton is beaten from the spot as I celebrate in front of him

Giant-killer – the Southend boys pelt me with socks after my penalty beat top-flight Derby in 1987

Goal of the Season – defying gravity to hit an overhead kick winner in a seaside battle with Blackpool in 1989

COLCHESTER

Put it there, pal – signing for best mate Ian Atkins at Colchester

Muppet show – winning a header against a Mickey Mouse Conference defence

Playing dirty – non-league mud bath

Well done – Mario Walsh congratulates me on a goal, but I was the bane of his life

End dance – injured taking a shot against Altrincham

Diving in – header against Wivenhoe in FA Trophy

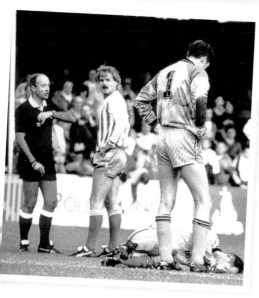

Stitched up – gash in my ankle ends season

What did I do ref? – David Elleray books me against Burton in the FA Cup

COLCHESTER BOSS

Married to the club – with first wife Jackie, the future Colchester chairman's daughter, at Layer Road

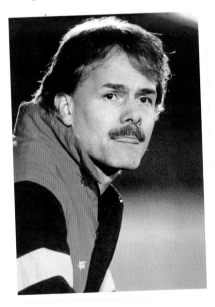

Manager's jacket – a rare night in the dug out through suspension

On me head – celebrating the 1992 Conference title win

Take a bow – picking up the Manager of the Year Trophy in 1992

Wembley bound – crashing home a penalty in our FA Trophy semi-final win over Macclesfield

WEMBLEY '92

Suited and booted – all ready
for the Twin Towers

Nightmare on Wembley
Road – Colchester's
fans give me a Freddy
Krueger makeover

Pitching in together –
on the Wembley turf wi'
a proud Dad, brother Ji'
and nephew Leigh

Marching my troops into battle – walking out at Wembley for the FA Trophy Final

Wembley winners – my triumphant Colchester
FA Trophy-winning team

Ticket to ride – Double winners
on open bus tour of Colchester

The Three Amigos –
celebrating 1992 FA Trophy
win with Paul Roberts and
Dave Martin

Lovely bubbly – soaking in the Wembley bath with FA
Trophy and bottle of plonk

END OF THE ROAD

Iron faced – slumming it at Braintree at the age of 35 (top)
Still got it – pulling on the Canvey Island shirt i 1995, aged 37 (above)

Giving blood for the cause – in the infamous Colchester jailbird kit

Two Chelsea legends – facing Glenn Hoddle in a pre-season friendly

Welcome to hell – shaking hands on the Chelmsford manager's job with chairman Trevor Wright

Red Card Roy – the shirt says it all as I beat two players at 38, for Chelmsford

Ullo Roy! Gotta a new motor? – car salesman in Colchester

ROY OF THE RAVERS

McDonough .. he played away

Twin strikers . . . but soccer cheat McDonough swapped wife Jackie (right) for lookalike best pal Liz

Soccer boss runs off with his wife's lookalike best pal

Jackie . . . she discovered secret calls

SOCCER boss Roy McDonough has kicked his marriage into touch after scoring with his wife's best pal.

The former Colchester United manager left missus Jackie on the sidelines as he tackled blonde lookalike Liz Blacknall, wife of the club's groundsman Dave.

Heartbroken Jackie discovered his two-year fling when she opened their itemised phone bill and found he had made 54 secret calls to mum-of-one Liz, 31.

And she got him to confess after forcing Liz's car off the road for a furious early-hours row. McDonough, 36 – who once turned out for Southend beside Britain's most expensive player Stan Collymore – began his fling with Liz after she and Dave joined him and Jackie on dates.

Jackie, 31, who has now split from Roy and wants a divorce, said last night: "It's my worst nightmare come true. I've lost my husband and best pal in one go."

She went on: "What hurts most is that they lied and deceived me for so long. I can't believe they could be so cruel.

"I just hope Liz thinks it's worth it. Roy's always chased women and I'm sure he won't stop because she's with him."

McDonough – who played for teams including Birmingham City and Chelsea – married Jackie in 1988, two years before his appointment at Colchester.

Once at the Essex club, the pair quickly became firm friends with Liz and husband Dave, 31.

Jackie, who became Colchester's promotions manager but quit this year, said: "Liz was my best friend. We talked about everything – or so I thought. I even gave her £60 to buy a dress at Christmas. She bought a low-

cut strapless one – probably to show herself off to Roy."

McDonough was sacked by Colchester chairman Gordon Parker – his father-in-law – in May last year after the club slumped in the Third Division.

Jackie confronted the pair but both denied any fling, even after she discovered the 54 calls.

Ironically, the truth emerged after desperate Jackie had a fling of her own and the couple angrily split up. Jackie said: "I'd been starved of love and got lonely, feeling under-sexed and

Screamed

"We rarely made love any more and he was always staying out until the early hours.

"I'd always suspected he had affairs and then I discovered he was sleeping with Liz."

neglected. But Roy had accepted my affair and we were going to get back together.

"However in June – six hours after we'd made love and talked about me moving back in – I saw Liz following Roy's car at 1am.

"I chased her, forced her off the road, then screamed at her. Then I went home and shouted at him and he admitted it."

Jackie who now lives at her parents' home, went on: "After this, I just want a divorce – and I shall name her in the petition.

"But I still love Roy. I have done since I was 18."

Liz is staying with friends while husband Dave, 31, looks after their six-year-old son. He would not comment.

McDonough, now a food firm rep and playing semi-professional for Vauxhall Conference League side Dagenham and Redbridge, admitted his romance with Liz. But he said: "Me and Liz is more than a fling. I'm in love. It's a proper relationship.

"Jackie has probably given you most of the true facts, but I'm sure she's covered her backside."

Page Seven Fella – *The Sun* breaks the story about my affair with groundsman's wife Liz

McDagger – looking happy after signing for Dagenham

Tracksuit manager – at Heybridge Swifts in 1998

HAPPY ENDING

Happiest day of my life – marrying my beautiful Liz

Spanish sunshine – drinking a non-alcoholic beer with Liz at a beach bar

Pride of place – Colchester Wembley shirt on wall of my Spanish home

My boy – having a cuddle with Ollie

Boys of '92 reunion – my Double-winning team celebrates its 20th anniversary at Colchester in May 2012

Still got it! Back in Colchester kit for testimonial, aged 53

be at Cambridge, 50 miles away, by 2pm, before the team sheet goes in to the referee.'

Former Chelsea defender, Ken Shellito, had taken over from John Ryan as manager. So I rang the new boss in a panic – buying some time by telling him that I had a flat tyre – and confirmed I would be at the ground before kick-off. Then I showered, shaved and pulled my suit on in a flash. I was in such a blur that looking at myself was like staring in one of those distorted mirrors at the fun fair. I was swaying about all over the shop, which made keeping bloodshot eyes trained on the zig-zags of the A604 at full pelt a right mission.

Senior pros Steve Spriggs and Steve Fallon took one look at me as I tumbled into the dressing room just after 2pm and said, 'What the fuck have you been doing?' Shellito came in for his team talk 10 minutes before kick-off, and I bowed my head pretending to tie my boots up, so he couldn't see my face.

As I stood in the centre circle, nursing a splitting headache and waiting to kick off, I could see two distorted balls at my feet. If I hadn't realised it before, I knew I was in real trouble when the ref blew his whistle to start the game and I nearly fell over rolling the ball two yards to a team-mate. I'd never been that messed up during a game before, and Spriggsy was pleading with me to feign a hamstring injury so they'd take me off. But I couldn't do that and just tried harder to compensate for being pissed. After 25 minutes, I ran after the Bolton centre-back to chase a ball over the top, stubbed my toe on his trailing boot and headbutted the heel of his other foot, closing up my eye with an instant shiner. It was as if somebody was telling me it serves you right, mate. God knows how, but I managed to last an hour of another defeat before getting hauled off.

I felt like complete dog shit and was dreading going to the supporters' end-of-season do after the match – with Player of the Season a toss up between Andy Sinton and the tea lady – which was compulsory for all the players. I felt guilty after such a poor season, especially because the fans had raised

£25,000 themselves to bring me and Alan Comfort to the club. So I tipped back three quick pints to top up the tank again and blot it all out.

What the fuck had I become? Aged nearly 27, I was jumping from one disaster area to another, and I was concentrating most of my best efforts on drinking away the last vestiges of my football career. How many more seasons as a professional footballer could my body tolerate if I carried on down the same punishing route? I wasn't a kid anymore, and it was taking longer and longer to recover from a night on the sauce. Not even Cambridge's bible clutchers had wanted to help turn my life around, which just about said it all. Maybe I was a lost cause and it was impossible to turn back the clock.

As I stood at the Abbey Stadium bar, hypnotised by the DJ's hazy disco traffic lights changing from red to green, I realised the thing that hurt most wasn't just the drinking or womanising, it was losing every ounce of respect I ever had for myself. I should have been hitting my peak by then, flourishing in the company of better players. Instead, I was nose-diving the other way, saddling up with shit teams who were relegated by Christmas. But I couldn't blame Gerry Francis or John Ryan, as the moves were all my choices – nobody forced me into them. One thing I could rely on, though, was good old beer, which never let me down – drinking every day to flush away a never-ending catalogue of disappointments.

Luckily, there was a helping hand not that far away – 70 miles down the road, in fact – thrust in my direction by England's greatest-ever football captain.

14. BOBBY'S ROY

Every time I see that famous picture of a red-shirted Bobby Moore holding the World Cup and being hoisted high by his team-mates, I am filled with immense pride. There is a sense of patriotism, but the main reason is because England's most famous captain believed I was worth paying money for. As a kid, I played at centre-back just as often as I did up front, and Bobby was one of my biggest heroes. My seven-year-old eyes were glued to the TV when England won the World Cup in 1966. And the one thing that has always stuck in my head is how spotless our victorious skipper's shirt was at the end of that historic game. The pitch had been cut-up during the battle against the Germans, but his jersey was completely clean, proving just what a great player Bobby was. He carried himself so well and didn't need to get dirty, as he never dived in or went to ground easily. He was just too good for that. He was a football god to my young eyes, and nothing had changed 19 years later when he put the call out for me to join him at Fourth Division Southend.

Getting tapped up by another club in the lower divisions wasn't a cloak-and-dagger operation – it happened at the bar over a pint. Where else? Towards the end of the 1984/85 season the Southend physio, Buster Footman, was hovering around the Cambridge bar after a game. His shiny bald head soon sidled up next to me, and he just came out with it.

'Do you want to come back?'

Buster knew I wanted to quit the Abbey congregation, but I was apprehensive about re-joining the Shrimpers. After all, it was only two years since I'd left Roots Hall under a black cloud after chinning the No.2, Colin Harper. The Southend experience had been the first falling domino of three disastrous moves, playing for three terrible sides in two seasons, who all got relegated. But there was an irresistible carrot dangling in front of my nose now, and to be fair most Cambridge fans probably believed this particular donkey belonged on a seaside beach. Bobby Moore was the Southend boss now, and that kind of pull was too powerful.

I was in complete awe of the man when I first clapped eyes on him in the flesh at Roots Hall. I was sitting across a table from a living legend, who was talking to me on the same level as if he was any ordinary human being. The first thing he tried to do was sell me the club's ambitious plan to build a state-of-the-art 25,000 all-seater stadium, showing me a detailed plastic model of the ground, which is still about as close as they've ever got to realising that dream. We had a short haggle over the contract, but there really was no need, as I'd have played for Bobby for nothing. All the doubts had evaporated and were replaced by the utmost respect. I loved the bloke from day one and would have done anything for him – if he'd have told me to stick my head in a bucket of shit I'd have done it without hesitation.

I'm not going to pretend that signing for Bobby conjured up some magical cure for my wayward lifestyle, transforming me into the consummate pro, because it didn't. I still liked the girls and enjoyed a good drink, but it did start to give me back my self-respect. We trained on local parks most of the time, and seeing Bobby standing there in his tracksuit every morning – still a perfect physical specimen in his mid-forties – made me try so much harder. I wanted to impress him at every session and be the best player on his team. It was a desire I hadn't felt in years, playing for teams that amounted to little more than

Third Division cannon fodder. But I couldn't let this great man down, and signing for him definitely put a spring back in my step. Maybe I even laid off the beers a little, drinking eight pints, instead of 14, on a Wednesday night.

I definitely tried to improve my diet, attempting to eat proper meals, rather than surviving on a sandwich and bag of crisps floating around a liquid lunch every day. Previously, my only proper dinners had been omelettes or chicken dishes on an away trip, which could have been once a fortnight. Even more importantly, this Bobby Moore-inspired spark stopped me living in the past, forever harking back to long-gone days when I was a teetotal, super-fit young gun aspiring to play at the top level. I'd been living to be drunk for so long, getting smashed to get through the shit times at crap clubs, as an escape from the bad career decisions and relegations which haunted me. It blanked out the mental torture of convincing myself that I was still the kid who scored in the First Division for Birmingham and got a big move to Chelsea.

Boozing also helped me to sleep at night. I hated being on my own, and if I didn't have female company then I would have to drink more so I could switch off behind closed doors. I realised deep down that I should have been coming into my prime, not whirlpooling in the opposite direction in the bottom of a pint glass. I'd been disillusioned for so long, but playing for a football icon who lived up to the hype – not a ghost like Geoff Hurst or a fat Gerry Francis – finally got me out of bed, raring to go. I never turned up pissed for a match on Bobby's watch, not once repeating my disgraceful episodes at Exeter and Cambridge, where I didn't really give a shit. One of my most prized possessions is the Southend programme in which Bobby wrote about me.

'Any aspiring young player should come and watch Roy McDonough on a Saturday afternoon, for the effort, endeavour and work he puts in for his team-mates.'

I can't tell you how proud that made me, and even more so my old man, who kept a tight grip on that programme until the day he died.

Just as influential to me was Southend No.2, Harry Cripps. He started out at West Ham, where he had forged a lifelong friendship with Bobby. But it was at the Hammers' bitter rivals, Millwall, where he made his name, becoming a Lions immortal as a no-nonsense defender. Harry might have been a Millwall hardman, but you'd never have guessed it, as he didn't have a bad bone in his body and was the life and soul of Roots Hall. Bobby liked a joke and had a dry sense of humour, but his right-hand man was the big village idiot. Harry had amazing energy, which he injected into training, making every session enjoyable. He would often do silly things just to make us laugh, like wrestling our goalkeeper, Jim Stannard, to the floor, who would then get Harry in a headlock and rub mud in his hair. Everyone loved Harry, and he was especially good to me. He knew I had ability, but was a boozer whose preparation wasn't as good as it might have been. So before every home game he took me into the gym 20 minutes before kick-off, playing one- and two-touch, controlling the ball and knocking it back, to warm my feet up. That kind of attention always meant something to me. Harry was a diamond.

Another thing that really got me buzzing was playing centre-back alongside Bobby Moore in our eight-a-side training matches. He never ran around much, as he let his brain do all the work for him, and he had an almost supernatural ability to read the game. One of the opposition boys would make a darting forward run and, being a striker normally, I thought I had a pretty good idea where they were heading. I'd follow them, but Bobby would just wander off. 'Gaffer, gaffer, where are you going?', I'd call, trying to work as a pair. But the ball flew towards Bobby like a magnet, allowing him to intercept the pass free of pressure and pass it on nonchalantly, before giving me a telling smile. I'd thought the boss had been completely out of position, and my initial reaction was, 'jammy git'. But if he did it once, he did it 100 times. It was never a gamble, just pure class, which is why the guy was so special.

When we travelled, some opposition fans would give him a standing ovation when he took his place in the dugout. At other grounds, a stand full of supporters would forget about the game and just watch Bobby – one of world football's most instantly recognisable figures, taking centre stage at their theatre of rust.

It goes without saying that I was desperate to buy the man a drink, so I ambushed Bobby at Roots Hall. He never drank pints and said, 'I'll just have a half, please Roy.' I was at the head of a queue of people wanting to shout him a beer, and before long there were nine half pints of lager in front of him. Not being one who liked to see waste, I asked, 'Are you going to drink all of those, boss?'

He beamed back: 'Let me give you some advice, Roy. There will come a day when people won't want to buy you a drink. So never disappoint them, don't let them down. Don't worry, I'll drink them all.'

And he did, every last drop. But Bobby didn't mind the lads having a beer if we did the business for him on the pitch. And we set the all-time drinking record on the Southend coach that season. Jim Stannard's dad ran a pub, so he would always fetch along four cases for an away trip – which was 96 beers. But we took it to another level after a win at Exeter, with Bobby asking me to use my local knowledge and point the driver in the direction of a shop where we could get more supplies. It was quite surreal navigating the supermarket aisles, past the fruit and veg, fish fingers, burgers and ketchup bottles, alongside England's World Cup-winning captain, before we filled up another four plastic bags with beer. But we ran dry an hour short of London and, completely pickled, I escorted a wobbly Bobby across two busy dual carriageways to stock up at a shop on the opposite side of the road. Bobby lived in Eastwood, just outside Southend, and the coach would drop him outside his front door. He gave us a little wave and said, 'Have a good weekend, lads', before we watched him stagger up his drive. The physio, Buster Footman, walked up and down the coach back at Roots Hall, picking up 159 empty beer cans, which was an amazing feat when you consider that not everyone was drinking. It was a total which would never be conquered.

Bobby had paid £15,000 to bring me back to Southend. The wages were a slight improvement on my Cambridge salary, and I had another £10,000 signing-on fee to boost my ailing finances. But I realised that word had spread that I was having a few drinking-related money troubles when I was sprawled across the Roots Hall pitch waiting for treatment during a game. The club doctor was a little Indian chap, who sprinted down from the directors' box if his assistance was needed, with his medical potions stored in a black briefcase. On this occasion he was called into action, and one of the Southend fans called out, 'Better get up and run, McDonough, it's the debt collector.'

The Shrimpers started the 1985/86 season well, but it was a frustrating spell for me. I was mainly being used as a playing sub for the first couple of months, which I wouldn't have tolerated for anybody else but Bobby Moore. And I wasn't too fond of my new strike-partner, Richard Cadette, who I watched grab four goals on his debut in a 5–1 August thumping of Leyton Orient – the club he had just arrived from. He scored 49 league goals in two seasons with us, but he was a lucky fucker. He was young, quick and strong, but wasn't a great finisher. He just got on the end of things in the hope of making some sort of contact, before praying the ball crossed the line. He beat five men for one of his goals against Orient. But not through Maradona-like skill, just sheer flukiness. He trod on the ball, fell over, got up and trampled across a centre-half, knocked the ball against the head of another defender, which bobbled through his legs, fell over someone else and then toe-poked a shot past the goalkeeper. For one of the others, he tried to give it the big shaven-laces finish, but miscued and sent the goalie the wrong way, with his effort dribbling into the goal. Then he raced off to the fans milking the applause, like he had meant it.

I couldn't stand him, and it had nothing to do with jealousy, it was the fact that he only played for himself and never acknowledged the work the other players put in for him. I'd get a smack in the head or clatter the goalkeeper, taking 12 stitches in the shin, to help a team-mate get the winning goal, but Cadette never cared about anybody else, or offered any gratitude. In training, I would tell him, 'You'll be struggling when you haven't got me, pal.' But he just laughed.

Sheffield United paid £120,000 for him after a couple of seasons at Roots Hall – massive money for a Fourth Division club. And I took great delight in watching his career go pear-shaped as he struggled to score goals anywhere else – apart from a spell in the Scottish numpty league with Falkirk – which isn't usually my style at all. Hate to say it, but I told you so.

I didn't get my first goal until the end of October, in my fourth start – an angled header in a 4–2 Essex derby disaster at home to my old club Colchester. And it was a good pal of mine, speed demon Perry Groves, who did the damage, accelerating to a match-winning hat-trick. I knew we were in trouble before kick-off, as whippet Grovesy was up against our left-back Frank Lampard Snr. I couldn't stand the ex-West Ham star, as I believed he wanted Bobby Moore's job. He was 37 by then, with legs shot to pieces, and Grovesy must have been licking his lips in the away team changing room, plotting the premeditated murder of his ageing marker. It was like Lampard was playing in quicksand and he never threatened to get tight as Grovesy got fed the ball on the halfway line and beat him for fun every time. He didn't know whether to stick or twist as he was ravaged by raw pace for all three of the ginger winger's goals.

But just before half-time, Lampard did one of the most embarrassing things I've ever witnessed on a football pitch. Seeing the relentless Groves charging forward again on halfway, he just looked away, turned his back on him and started running towards his own box. You could actually hear the crowd gasp in disbelief as the former England international ran away from his man. I'd never seen anyone else just give up like that – the bloke was completely destroyed.

After the game, Grovesy was in the bar acting the cocky fucker – spinning his hat-trick match ball on his finger for everyone to see. He was still only 20, a fully dedicated lad and not much of a drinker – a point he had proved at Christmas. We had gone clubbing in Colchester and he was mercilessly punished after requesting a 'Snowball'. When he returned from the toilet, he was festively greeted by eight glasses of the yellow muck lined across the bar, decorated with green umbrellas and red cherries, so they looked like Christmas trees. But he couldn't finish them off.

Southend and its famous seafront wasn't all kiss-me-quick hats, slot machines and candy floss – it also had a much darker side, dominated by Essex's criminal underworld. I never upped sticks from Colchester to Southend, as there would have been just too much temptation with all the clubs, pubs and girls. If I'd been there every night of the week, I'd have fucked and drunk myself to death. But we played a lot of Friday-night football under the Roots Hall floodlights, which was always popular with the punters, and gave me an excuse to get on the lash in town after the game.

Our striker, Steve Phillips, introduced me to his mate Kim Webber, who was a big Southend fan and a serious hard bastard. He was a street fighter, not the sort of bloke you fucked about with, who sold second-hand cars for a living. I bought one off him, which blew up. But I didn't take it back, as I didn't want to upset him. I just went to see him again and paid for another motor. Fortunately, Kim enjoyed my company and we became good drinking and shagging buddies, taking girls back to his Westcliff flat overlooking the seafront. Trouble was, I didn't know what world I was getting myself into, and I started doing the dirty with the wrong girl.

We usually ended up in TOTS, the nightclub where all the ace faces hung out. One Friday night, I strolled into the club wearing my leather trousers and felt a granite hand grab my shoulder, spinning me round to face a hard-nosed wideboy of a doorman.

'Mess with her again and I'll break your arms and legs. I'll say no more', he warned.

The friendly words of advice were being offered by John

Moody, the local light-heavyweight boxing champ, who worked the doors around Southend. I didn't know it was one of his birds that I had been dipping my wick with, and I wouldn't be going there again. Having a battle with a grizzly centre-half on a football pitch was one thing, but I wasn't going to start having rucks with boxers and bouncers.

These people were serious headcases, and I found myself going out for drinks with Kim and his cronies more often, in murky seaside bars I didn't even know existed. They were the sort of establishments where you would get a broken glass rammed in your face just for giving a bloke something interpreted as the wrong look. But that was never going to happen in the company I was keeping, a 20-strong gang of men, ranging from their thirties to fifties. They all had horrible facial scars – cut down one cheek, or slashed across their forehead – like it was some sort of membership badge for their club.

I didn't know what they were all into, apart from the iffy cars, and I didn't ask. I was just glad to get out of some of those places in one piece. But these fellas liked the fact I went to war on the pitch – they could identify with me – and took me under their wing. They never tried to get me involved in anything dodgy, it was all about talking football and cracking a few funnies over a beer. But there were plenty of other naughty firms doing the rounds, like the Rettendon boys, who were all found shot dead in a Land Rover a few years later. Pushing their chemical poisons around the Southend nightspots – mainly ecstasy tablets – they hated seeing footballers on their 'manor'. They wanted to be the centre of attention at all times and took particular offence to us getting a few tasty results, as it made us major players with the ladies, too. Fortunately, I had a lot of guardian angels watching over me.

The most magical thing about football is the coincidences that it throws up. And there is no greater generator of the little quirks that all fans adore than the FA Cup. We were handed a home tie with Third Division Newport County in November's draw, giving me an unexpected chance to settle an old score with their midfielder Tony Pulis. In another twist of FA Cup fate, it was exactly a year since Pulis had got right under my skin during a rare away win for Cambridge. And we earned those three points the hard way, as the Newport pitch was more like a battlefield. It was an intimidating match, with some horrendous challenges going in – real leg breakers. The referee was out of his depth and failed to get a grip on the game, and it was amazing that nobody in the Cambridge side got hospitalised. And if the backward Welsh wankers weren't trying to maim us, they were firing poisonous insults at our ears, or even worse, spitting at us, which is just about the worst thing you can do to a fellow pro. I always had a healthy appetite for a penalty-box skirmish, tussling with any fucker that had big enough bollocks to have a pop at me, but Pulis was pathetic, a little fucking squirt, who wasn't man enough to put his studs in with me at full pelt in a 50/50 challenge. Anyone can run around calling names from a distance, and that's all he did, mouthed off. That pissed me right off, as he kept well out of my way when the game was active and escaped getting a clout, despite repeatedly threatening to give me a good hiding at the back of the stand, or out in the car park, after the match. Pulis thought he was Newport's Superman, a midfield enforcer who should be feared. But he was nothing of the sort, and I offered to take him up on his offer after the match, as nothing would have pleased me more than to fill his big gob with a knuckle sandwich. I'd wanted to kill the fucker, but he was nowhere to be seen when I came out of the changing room. There had been a few heated words exchanged in the tunnel, when he had a herd of other Welsh retards to back him up, but he totally bottled going into the players' lounge. So I'd been stewing a long time, waiting to exact revenge.

Before the FA Cup game, Bobby Moore overheard me slagging off Pulis to the other lads in the changing room. 'You alright, big fella? You won't let me down, will you?' he asked. 'Course not, boss,' I replied.

The game was only seven minutes old when a glorious chance to even things up presented itself. Pulis miscontrolled a pass on the halfway line, with the ball bouncing off his shin, up his thigh and onto his chest. I really couldn't believe my luck as he struggled to get it under control. I launched myself through the air like Bruce Lee, striking the ball hard with a flying kick, but making sure I followed through into his chest. As he crumpled on to the grass, I tried to finish the job by messing up his head with my studs, but I was too slow. The referee, Tony Ward, was already whistling anxiously, so I retreated to the changing room without even looking back at the official, knowing full well I was running the taps again.

It was the fifth professional dismissal of my career, but the first of seven red cards I would earn in just five years at Southend. I was gutted that I'd let Bobby Moore down, as we lost the game 1–0. My actions were also going to cost me yet another club fine and a two-game ban. But I owed Pulis and he had needed sorting out – the time was worth the crime.

Spitting at another pro is the lowest of the low. But don't get me wrong, I've spat at players before. Just ask Perry Groves. Grovesy got another treble against us in the Freight Rover Trophy that season, so when we went to Layer Road in the league Bobby asked me to play at the back and do a man-to-man job on him. The first time he got close, I flobbed just past his legs and on to his boots to mark my territory, as if to say, 'Don't you fucking dare come near me.' Grovesy whined, 'What are you doing, Roy? I thought we were mates.' But he could have been a complete stranger. I gave him the cold shoulder, never making eye contact or talking to him during the game. We lost 2–0, but Grovesy was scared to death and never had a single shot. After the game, his old man 'Ginge', who I got on well with, stormed into the bar with Grovesy, fuming about my behaviour. Defending my actions, I said, 'It was just a game, lads. I couldn't let Perry have a sniff for 90 minutes, nothing personal.' Five minutes later, it was all forgotten over handshakes and I got the beers in.

I'd managed to chip in with a few more goals in the league, getting us a draw with Preston and flicking in a scabby header from a throw-in to beat Cambridge, who were still having a terrible time. But Bobby Moore handed me a perilous weekend pass in January, paving the way to the Midlands for a beer and birds build-up to a match at Swindon, who were breezing towards the Fourth Division championship. The game had been switched to a Sunday, and Dad had offered to drive me down from Solihull.

I also got a hot tip from a pal about this sex-mad brunette, whose blonde friend I'd already been through on the Friday night. On the Saturday, I linked up with the girls again, before talking my way into this dark-haired beauty's knickers. But she lost her bloody keys, so I had to break into her flat for a bunk-up. I climbed over the back garden wall at 3am and managed to shin through a small window, ripping my trousers and cutting my knee, while also fending off a concerned neighbour who thought I was burgling the gaff. I swaggered back into my parents' house, at 10am, well pleased with myself, to find Dad eating breakfast. 'Where the hell have you been?' he demanded to know. But I didn't care what he thought about me staying out all night before a match. I'd been living away a long time by then and lived my life how I wanted to. Anyway, I'd only had 10 pints and didn't feel too bad during the drive to Swindon. That feeling didn't last long, though, as my own team-mate, John Gymer, knocked me out as we both contested a Swindon goal-kick, headbutting me straight in the temple. The next thing I knew, I was being dragged along the front of the main stand, with one arm draped around Bobby Moore's shoulder, with the other being supported by Harry Cripps. 'You'll be alright in a minute, Roy,' they assured me. But I could see three cross-bars at one end and wasn't so sure.

I made it through to half-time, gave the smelling salts a long, hard sniff and demanded to go back out because I didn't want to disappoint Bobby. It was down to the player whether or not you carried on back then, not like now when a head injury automatically earns you a two-week break. I had a decent second half, too, going agonisingly close to getting us a point after smacking a meaty header against the bar. Not bad at all, when you consider I finished the match with double vision and a swollen left knee, courtesy of Colin Calderwood's boot.

That sore knee gave me plenty of jip for the remaining four months of the season – but I always played through injuries. Soldiering on didn't do me many favours, though, as the rubbing of my joints produced burning flakes of bone which calcified into a lump on the knee the size of half a golf ball. Once the season was finished, I went under the surgeon's knife for the first time in my career. They had to slice the knee in two to carry out the repairs, before double-folding the skin and giving me 12 blanket stitches. Let's just say it was slightly tender afterwards.

I hobbled on to my next goals in March, against Aldershot and Hereford, as Southend dropped out of the promotion race. But April got off to a fiery start, as I claimed a Welsh sending-off double in a 0–0 draw at Wrexham. The sheep shaggers loved every minute of it, with the home crowd baying for my blood as I walked back to the tunnel with my eyes shut.

Playing against the Welsh teams was always like going to war – they hated us, and we hated them – and their fans gave us the most stick. Wrexham defender Mike Williams had got in on the act too, launching his size 13 boots into my body at every opportunity. And he was getting away with it as the referee put in the usual blindman's shift of watching my back. I'd had enough 10 minutes before half-time and snapped after one boot up the backside too many, turning to snarl and join foreheads with Williams. All of a sudden we had a Racecourse Ground miracle as the match official's vision returned and he dismissed me for threatening behaviour. He thought I was going to headbutt Williams, which is one violent reprisal I never dished out. I might have swung out the odd elbow, but I mainly used my fists on the pitch, because it was fair and gave your target a chance to defend himself. I've been headbutted plenty of times, but it wasn't a weapon of revenge that I ever chose.

My reward was another two-game ban, but I felt that I was justified in feeling hard done by on that occasion. A couple more goals took me to seven for the season, way behind 'Mr Selfish', Richard Cadette, who tripped, miskicked and bobbled his way to 25. But Southend could only finish ninth, 15 points behind the last promotion spot, grasped by Port Vale.

Three games before the end of the season, Bobby Moore resigned. His managerial achievements were never going to come anywhere near mirroring what he did as a player, but he didn't get the credit he deserved at Roots Hall that season. The club was on its uppers and had only pulled in one home gate above 2,000 fans since the turn of the year. The previous season, Southend had just managed to dodge re-election, so coming ninth wasn't a bad turnaround at all. But I always sensed things were not quite right with the managerial set-up. Bobby had been on the wrong end of a few bad business deals, including a nightclub which burnt down, and was definitely at Roots Hall because he needed the money. But I think he was sick of boardroom interference. One day I turned up late, 30 minutes before kick-off, after a car crash on the A12, to see Bobby coming down the stairs from the chairman's office with the team sheet. The club's owner, Vic Jobson, was calling players' names out at him, and Bobby just nodded, unhappily. I've got no doubt in my mind that he was trying to influence Bobby's selection, as chairmen often believe the money they put into a club entitles them to have their say. Unfortunately, that's how most managers survive these days, by brown-nosing the big boss.

Pandering to Jobson, though, must have been the final straw for a proud man like Bobby, and he quit after a 1–0 defeat at Rochdale at the end of April. The weather was atrocious, with heavy rain lashing down throughout a seven-hour journey to Spotland. Stuck in traffic, we nearly missed the kick-off. The physio, Buster Footman, had to sprint the last few miles to the ground to get the team sheet in on time so we didn't get fined.

The pitch was like a swamp, and some bright spark had packed a white kit, which was covered in shit after five minutes. Well, all of us were, apart from the team tart, midfielder Barry Silkman. He didn't have a speck on him as he tiptoed around the pitch like a ballerina. I didn't mind Silkman, but when the shit hit the fan you knew he would let you down. He'd played a few games for Manchester City and thought he was the world's greatest playmaker. Every game he would ping a couple of million-dollar balls to feet, drawing appreciative oohs and ahhs from the crowd. But the other 25 would end up in the fans' laps, obliterating pies and knocking over cups of tea.

Bobby Moore was a gentleman and never slaughtered players, but he could swear with the best of them and he'd be hollering at Silkman to stop prancing around like a five-a-side player and get stuck in. But sunbed slave Silkman wasn't going to get his orange body mucky. This was the player who got ripped by the lads pre-season for walking into the bar after a friendly wearing black leather trousers and white shoes. A bottle of Nivea moisturising cream fell out of his back pocket. And as everyone took the piss, Silkman just picked it up, squeezed a couple of squirts on to his cheeks and started rubbing it in like a bird. But 10 minutes from time he got his comeuppance, as one of the Rochdale lads clipped him, sending him flying into the sticky mud. Bobby Moore raced out of the dugout, celebrating the sight of the big-haired poser covered in shit from head to toe. He was splashing about in the crap as if we had just scored the winning goal. But Silkman had no respect for Bobby and started shouting things out at him on the coach home. He hadn't done a stroke for 90 minutes, yet he was sitting there ridiculing England's finest captain. It wasn't the first time either, as he would take the piss behind his back in training, too. Bobby wasn't tough enough in these situations – and didn't need to be – but it didn't wear with me. I snapped, pushing Silkman's head against the window. Pointing down the front of the coach towards Bobby, I said, 'How dare you speak that way, about that great man there. Keep your fucking gob shut.'

Bobby resigned after the game, moving upstairs as a show-piece addition to the board of directors, but was rarely seen around Roots Hall. Seven years later he was dead, cut down in his prime by bowel cancer on 24 February, 1993, at the age of 51. I heard the news in the snooker club and was gutted, as I adored Bobby. I was with a group of mates, so I kept my emotions inside, but it didn't stop flashbacks flying round my head. There were the complimentary words Bobby had written about me in his Southend programme notes, which made me and my family so proud. Then I remembered a time in the Roots Hall gym when Bobby was yawning during his sit-up routine. I asked him if he was OK, and he replied, 'I'm a terrible sleeper, Roy. Always happy if I can get just four hours in a night.' And that made me wonder if something was wrong back then. I zoomed forward a few years to a night of personal frustration at White Hart Lane, where I had to watch from the bench as Southend lost 1–0 to Spurs in the League Cup. After the game, Bobby stepped out of the lift with Terry Venables, Gary Lineker and Paul Gascoigne. Bobby was flanked by three of the modern game's biggest names, but it was his hand that everybody wanted to shake. It was typical Bobby, and so was what he did next. Seeing me at the other end of the Tottenham bar, he walked past everyone else, shook my hand and put his arm around me warmly, before saying, 'Nice to see you big man, what are you drinking?' It was one of the proudest moments of my life.

The last time I saw Bobby was at Roots Hall after he had been commentating for the TV or radio. He was wearing a flatcap and looked so gaunt, with sunken cheekbones – a pale shadow of the super-fit guy I wanted to bash down doors for. It made me so sad to see him like that, as I knew this great champion was losing the biggest battle of his life. Sure enough, a few months later Bobby was dead – the first member of England's World Cup-winning team to pass away. Until the day I go to my own grave, I will always be so grateful that I got to spend one season so close to such a great, great man.

15. WEBB OF HIGHS

A long-harboured grudge spelt trouble for me as Southend unveiled a face from the past as their new boss. The last time I'd seen David Webb was sitting across an M5 service station breakfast table. I'd blown out his offer of signing for Bournemouth – and seven years later he obviously hadn't forgotten. Webby had been tough as old boots as a player, a defender who wrote his name in Chelsea folklore with a brave winner in the 1970 FA Cup Final replay against Leeds. Now in his early forties, he was still a fearsome sight with a huge block of a head plastered with war wounds, powerful shoulder blades and hands like shovels. He was from the East End of London and rubbed shoulders with some naughty people, even going to the funerals of the notorious Kray twins. But he was more Frank Butcher than Mad Frankie Fraser.

Webby was the used car salesman of football managers, a wheeler-dealer with a great eye for a bargain player. The fans all believed he was a big disciplinarian, who ruled with an iron fist. But he was strangely shy and a terrible communicator who rarely spoke to the players. His No.2, Kevin Lock, orchestrated all the usual banter about the weekend birds and beer, before taking us through the training warm-ups. All Webby wanted to do was play eight-a-side matches. He was obsessed with scoring goals and let the grim veil temporarily slip when he got one, punching the air like a big kid. We soon realised the formula for an easy day was to let Webby score five or six goals in training, then we'd just do a few shuttle runs and knock off early.

As for coaching, I wouldn't have put him in charge of a team of 10-year-olds. He loved shadow play sessions on a full-size pitch, where 11 players would take on a team of stationary dustbins guarding an open net. All he wanted was the centre-halves to hammer the ball up the pitch as hard as they could, and if the ball reached the forwards we would shoot wide of the open goal just to wind him up. His other favourite was kick-off practice. For 45 minutes we would tap the ball across the centre circle, then hit it back to the midfielders, or out wide to the wings, which completely miffed me. I always thought that a decent side only had to kick-off once to win a game.

One thing Webby did demand was complete bravery. If it all went off during a game, his golden rule was, 'One in, all in', as the referee would struggle to see who had landed the punches in a mass ruck, and in those days there were no TV replays to pick out the bones after the match. Webby also took heading the ball very seriously. He pointed to the rivers of old scar tissue running across his forehead and said, 'If you can't win the header against an opponent, head through the back of the player's head to win the ball.'

He also made it clear that he didn't like me very much, and loved putting the boot into me at training. One Friday, I swung out an elbow to protect myself, knowing full well he was gunning for me and might try a mid-air headbutt. But I split his eye open, and he went berserk. Webby tried to kick me at every opportunity, ignoring the fact that we had a match the next day and I was the only player at the club who could do the job in the air for him. The other lads thought it was hilarious, rolling soft little balls into my feet, so the gaffer could launch himself at my legs. But I escaped unscathed and had the last laugh when he plodded into the changing room the next day, nursing three black stitches around his eye.

Webby's greatest strength as a manager was spotting talent,

coarse diamonds plucked from youth teams or found stagnating in reserve and non-league football, who he buffed up into shining gems. During my time at Roots Hall he unearthed the likes of Justin Edinburgh, Spencer Prior, Dean Austin, Chris Powell and Brett Angell, who all went on to play for Premier League clubs.

His Fourth Division class of 1986/87 might have been rougher around the edges, but it was still a fine vintage. Southend were known as the Cockney Mafia then, a team mostly recruited from Essex and London. We never feared anybody on a football pitch and could back up the aggression by playing the game properly, too. The team was packed full of strong characters and had a backbone that refused to be shattered – committed players like our ox of a goalkeeper, big Jim Stannard, centre-half Paul Clark, who resembled a Viking warlord with his beard and long hair and was equally ferocious in the tackle, plus the industrious Glenn Pennyfather in midfield. We were very direct, but never played a Wimbledon-style route one, using the wings rather than just lumping it down the middle. I became the focal point of the attack, with every free-kick, throw and cross aimed at my chest, head and feet to flick the ball on for Richard Cadette to hit 30 goals in all competitions. And I relished that responsibility, throwing myself in where it hurt for the lads around me, better players than I had previously played with at the club who wanted to win at all costs.

Two of the new arrivals – Londoners Paul Roberts and Dave Martin – became friends for life. We ran that team on and off the pitch and were dubbed 'The Three Amigos'. Robbo was three years younger than me at 24, a fitness fanatic with long hair and not a bad-looking boy. A right-back who washed up on Southend's shores from Swindon, he had been Millwall captain at 18 and was the proverbial 'Mr Marmite' with his own fans, who either loved him or hated him. He was also the biggest wind-up merchant when it came to opposition supporters. Robbo had a super-long throw, and if he was getting stick, he could arch his arms and head back with the ball ready to launch it and send a gob missile flying backwards, hidden from the officials' eyes, into the crowd. But Robbo got his comeuppance on a return to the Den with Brentford, when a Millwall fan jumped the fence and chinned him. Robbo was also the club's Del Boy, who made sure we were the best-dressed team outside the top flight. He always had some sort of deal going on, lugging boxes of videos on to the team coach for an away trip or decorating the changing room in silk ties and suits that he was selling at knockdown prices.

Dave Martin was my permanent room-mate on away trips. The club's two biggest nutters were shacked up together, but Davey was different gravy to me in the mentalist stakes. Well over 6ft tall, 23, with a flat nose and shock of blond hair, he was another ex-Millwall player who had fittingly played his part in the Crazy Gang's rise to the First Division, before leaving Wimbledon for Roots Hall. Great warriors like Graeme Souness, Roy Keane and Mark Hughes have always held my utmost respect, but when it comes to true football hardmen I've never met anybody who holds a candle to Dave. Everything he did, whether it was playing football, shagging or eating, was aggressive. I've swayed into a bar pissed on foreign soil to retrieve my flip-flops to find Dave fighting off a group of angry locals, using the leather belt removed from his trousers. If King Kong had asked him to step outside, he wouldn't have even had time to beat his chest before Dave had smashed him to the floor. Equally at home in the centre of midfield or defence, he didn't know the meaning of pain and threw his body into the most dangerous areas to win a challenge with complete disregard for his own well-being. I've seen him take 12 stitches clashing heads with another player to dive in and nick a goal, before playing on with blood pouring down his cheek, grinning as if nothing had happened. The guy would have played on one leg if he'd had to, and they don't make them like that any more. Unfortunately, he is paying the price for all those years of bravery now, with the legacy of the injuries to his knees and ankles hampering his attempts to earn a living away from football.

We got well looked after at Southend and always stayed in a hotel ahead of an away fixture. But the pair of us completely abused the room service, drinking 14 pints the night before one game, with Davey ordering and hoovering down 18 plates of sandwiches. By 2am I couldn't move in my bed I was so pissed, and struggled to stagger to the toilet.

The drinking always started as soon as we arrived at our destination, thanks to a system of using the young pros as bar scouts. We'd get to the hotel late in the afternoon on a Friday, and I'd say to David Webb, 'Boss, is it OK for the lads to have half a pint before dinner?' He would agree, before heading to his room to get tarted up for the evening meal, while getting on the red wine himself with Kevin Lock. As soon as he'd gone, we'd place one of the kids at the end of the bar, watching the stairs, so they could sound the alert when Webby was on his way back. The rest of the players would sink four or five pints in that time, immediately returning their empty pint glasses to the barmaid, while keeping the half-pint glass on the bar for insurance. Some of the players were lightweights, though, and were only allowed half a beer, just in case they started getting silly at dinner and gave the game away. Webby would eventually stumble down the stairs in his designer gear thinking he looked a million dollars, and I'd pipe up, 'Any chance of another half before dinner, gaffer?' He would nod again, and we'd have another half with dinner, making it six pints each before we'd polished off the ice cream and peaches. After the meal, I'd push my luck one last time: 'Can we have a quick one before hitting the pillow, boss?' Webby would wave us on, and it all started again – a young pro watching the manager finish his meal in the restaurant, while we got down as many beers as we could before he stirred back into life.

The mood of optimistic change sweeping through the club was obviously reaching the terraces, as there was a real sense of 'we're in this together' at Roots Hall. That close-knit feeling between players and fans was born out of a pre-season friendly with Crystal Palace. I was preparing to come on at half-time when I noticed a few scuffles breaking out in one of the stands. I loved talking to the fans, always trying to have a bit of banter at a corner or throw-in, or saying hello to a little lad with his dad, as I knew it would set him up for the week that a footballer had spoken to him during a game. And one fan I always acknowledged was 'Big Ginge', who stood bulging through his vest in all weathers by the near post of the North Bank, where Southend's top boys made a racket behind the goal. Ginge had bright red hair and a matching beard and was the main man. He'd survived a nasty Stanley knife attack from Colchester fans which left him needing 50 stitches, but I'd always give him a nod and ask how the family were when I was waiting for the ball to come in. On this occasion, a few punches were being thrown at invading Palace fans, so I darted over to the wall and shouted out: 'If you need help, I'll come in.' They didn't need a hand, but these were my fans, who paid to watch me play, and I wanted them to know I was there for them. As it happens, it was only a minor punch-up, but if I'd seen one of our boys getting a pasting I'd have been off the pitch and on that terrace like lightning.

I did more damage on the pitch, though, when our towering central defender Shane Westley was screaming on the floor in our penalty area after Palace striker Ian Wright had stamped on his hand. I hollered, 'What's the matter Shane, you big soft cunt? Get up and head out the corner that's about to come in.' He'd dislocated a couple of knuckles, so I grabbed his hand, pulled the knuckles out with a click and straightened his fingers. Unfortunately Dr Roy's pitchside first aid had ruptured the tendons in Shane's hand and after the game he was sent to hospital for a five-hour operation.

David Webb only started me twice in the first 11 games of the 1986/87 season, which reaped five wins and had us hovering around the newly introduced promotion play-off places. I was recovering from my summer knee operation but felt fit, and his team selections caused me plenty of frustration. Paul Roberts was up to his old tricks again, goading the opposition fans at former club Brentford in a League Cup win. One of Brentford's punters hurdled the wall and grabbed Robbo as he took a throw-in, motivating some Southend supporters to run onto the pitch and defend their player. I was warming up on the touchline and yelled at our fans, 'Go on boys, smash the wanker.' Like most flashpoints in football, it was all over quickly and didn't get too messy, but my rallying call was acknowledged by a chorus of, 'Roy McDonough is a football hooligan', as our fans escaped the clutches of intervening stewards and reached the safety of the away stand.

There were more fireworks in our narrow 2–1 second-round exit at First Division Manchester City. Benched again, I trudged into the Maine Road changing room like a bear with a sore head to find Robbo tearing a strip off Shane Westley, who was a good four inches taller than him. Robbo had piled into Shane on the pitch for pulling out of a challenge and not covering a team-mate, and the defender had spat at him in retaliation. Shane was another one who thought he was tough, but only ever played for himself. I couldn't stand the bloke and as he stepped forward to strike Robbo he was instantly pinned back against the wall by me and Dave Martin. Webby walked into the changing room, looked at us and said, 'Fuck me, I've got a team full of gangsters', before walking back out again to let us sort it out.

Webby finally bit the bullet at the end of October and reinstated me to the firing line at the expense of the hapless Dean Neal. I rewarded him by sparking a run of five wins in six matches, with goals against Scunthorpe and Cardiff. Having me to bully defenders again also brought the best out of Richard Cadette, who netted seven times in that run. We were third in the table, in the last automatic promotion place, but miles behind Preston and Northampton, who both had one boot in the Third Division by Christmas.

We were handed a humdinger of an FA Cup second-round home tie with the leaders Northampton in December, after a brace from yours truly finished off non-leaguers Halesowen Town 4–1 in the first round. The Cobblers had some highly-talented players, such as Richard Hill who scored 29 times from midfield that season, and strikers Ian Benjamin and Trevor Morley, who also chipped in to a mammoth 103-goal championship-winning total. The game lived up to its billing and was a Friday night cracker of a 4–4 draw. Cadette got a hat-trick and I lashed in a right-foot volley on the angle after taking the ball on the chest. I was well pleased with myself after seeing it replayed on the *Saint and Greavsie* show the following Saturday morning before training.

I was full of beans (and booze) when I arrived at the training ground and Webby quickly gathered the lads, saying, 'Well done, you all did brilliantly last night, apart from the big fella, who was a fucking disgrace.' I couldn't believe my ears. Was this Webby's way of getting back at me, because he'd had to swallow his pride and play me? He needed to remember that I made that team tick, putting goals on a plate for that selfish little fucker Cadette. He had us all running round the pitch after that, but I made sure I was even slower than usual, finishing a lap behind everyone else in protest.

But I was no stranger to Webby's Saturday running sessions. Regular Friday night football at Roots Hall meant regular Friday night drinking, and Webby didn't need to be Columbo to suss out the drinkers at the club – which is why he put on the extra punishment running sessions the day after the game. One Saturday morning I turned up with Dave Martin and we were both still wearing our matchday suits, as we hadn't been home all night. Webby would run us hard for over an hour until our heads throbbed. If either of us had suffered from a heart defect, we would have been digging a hole for the other team-mate. But it did sweat out the beer and give me a clean slate again to resume bar duties in the afternoon.

We lost the cup replay at Northampton 3–2, and a frustrating battle against centre-half Keith McPherson laid the groundwork for another red card on a Boxing Day which certainly lived up to its name. Before that we had a tough league fixture in the Midlands at promotion rivals Wolves – another juggernaut of a club to spin off the rails and tumble down the divisions. It was virtually a home game for my family and friends, who were all at Molineux to see me tap in the winner for three priceless points after my old Exeter team-mate, Martin Ling, had got our first goal. The lads were toasting me at the bar after the match and I was milking the attention, when my pal Ian Atkins walked in, chaperoning this short fat girl with big knockers. My face went white as a sheet, as this delightful creature was my back-up shag if I was down on my luck and paralytic pissed on a weekend trip back to Solihull. I could see Ackers grinning as he called out, 'Roy, your girlfriend's here. Aren't you going to buy her a drink?' He'd done me like a kipper, and the Southend boys were pissing themselves at my expense. This stumpy bird waddled over and looked up at me with swirling eyes full of admiration. So I bought her a drink and gave her my full attention, praying for her sake that she didn't get wind of the other lads destroying me.

The top-of-the-table Boxing Day clash with Northampton burst our bubble as we collapsed 4–0 at Roots Hall. And I was well out of order, pole-axing their defender Keith McPherson – who I apologised to after the game. He was only 5ft 10in tall, but was getting the better of me every time. I couldn't back into him, or physically intimidate him, as I couldn't get close enough. His game was to come at you late and use an almighty spring to win the header, and he was snuffing me out. Finally being part of a side which was threatening to be successful had made me more cynical in the pursuit of glory and I had developed a Kama Sutra-like-manual of ways of inflicting pain on my opponents – with a razor-sharp elbow the device chosen to leave McPherson well and truly fucked. Just before the interval, I threw back my arm with full force, leaving him prostrate on the floor with a busted and bloody bugle. He didn't deserve that, as he had been doing his job fairly, and I was the one taking liberties now. Alf Buksh was the referee, a tiny Indian fella who must have booked me a billion times and had to stand on tiptoes to show me the colour of his card. There was no doubt it was a red one this time, and I just said, 'Listen, Alf. Don't ask my name, or how to spell the fucker, as you know it off by heart.'

After serving my suspension for red card No.7 in the pro ranks, David Webb put me straight back into the team for a January trip to Swansea, which would be the catalyst for major ructions. After just 20 minutes at the Vetch Field, I cushioned a pass and played it to Paul Roberts down the wing, when their midfielder, Phil Williams, whacked straight through me high and late. The fucker really hurt me, leaving stud marks down my ribs and left thigh. But I was one step ahead and could see Robbo running with the ball, which meant the game was still active and referee Paul Vanes was distracted. So I hammered the bottom of my boot straight into Williams's head. 'Want to do me you Welsh cunt? Then have some back.' But I didn't get away with it, as a linesman with bionic vision 90 yards away started waving his flag, earning me a four-game ban on my return.

Webby came down to the changing room as I soaked my wounds in the bath, telling me he couldn't trust me anymore, despite my protestations about the Swansea lad taking me out. I was being put on the transfer-list first thing Monday. We lost the game 1–0 and Webby's determination to ship me out didn't go down well with the chairman Vic Jobson, who said I was staying. Webby's response was to punch the chairman in the ribs as they sat in the stand, and a few weeks later he resigned as Southend manager.

Jobson had always been a big fan of mine, but he was off the wall at times. He was in his fifties and I'm sure I witnessed him go through a mid-life crisis, as he started turning up at the club with flicked-back blow-dried hair, wearing trendy young suits and ties with zig-zags on them. And I tested his patience too, as he had a bit on the side at the club – a brassy barmaid, who was all tits and arse. One of the directors clocked this blonde serving me grace after hours in my motor in the Roots Hall car park, and he must have grassed her up, as she got sacked the next day. But, thankfully, there were never any repercussions for me and, with our long-serving defender, Paul Clark, who was only 28, installed as the new player-manager in March, I returned from suspension to start the final 15 games of the season. I only managed one more goal against Cambridge, taking my final figure to eight, but gave everything I had to get us promoted, shoving my head between flying boots and goalkeeper's fists, or punching a defender in the eye to win the ball and set up a chance.

I could see the finishing line, but I didn't have it all my own way in another promotion fight at home to league runners-up Preston, which ended in a 2–1 defeat. Their centre-half, Sam Allardyce, had the biggest head I've ever seen, like one of those giant papier-mâché things you'd see on *It's A Knockout*. Like a Dave Cusack or Mick McCarthy, I'd already heard about how supposedly tough he was. But that always gave me added incentive, as I soon discovered that players like that usually weren't as hard as they believed they were. I was having a good, fair scrap with Big Sam, who caught me with an elbow, but I didn't think much of it until I went up for the ball again, which had a red splat in the middle of it. Next time the ball dropped out of the sky, it was covered in an even bigger patch of blood, so I rubbed my hand down my head and it was covered in claret. The physio ushered me off, and I was sent down the tunnel for my first set of head stitches – five of the fuckers without any injection – before going straight back on the pitch to resume a highly enjoyable battle with Allardyce.

We were still third in the table, and one game we could not afford to lose was the April Roots Hall promotion crunch against a Steve Bull-inspired Wolves, who were breathing right down our necks. More than 10,000 fans turned out, including 3,000 from the Midlands, and before the match there were rumblings filtering into the changing room of trouble around the town, which unfortunately left one supporter nursing a stab wound. But it all added to the buzz and the realisation that we were about to play in the game of our lives. I'll never forget the deafening sound the Wolves fans made as they smashed their feet on the terrace concrete and boomed and clapped out Queen's *We Will Rock You*. They were trying to lift their team, but as that great noise thundered across the turf it gave us an even bigger boost – it was like being back in the big time again. Martin Ling's goal gave us a 1–0 win amid chaotic scenes, which included the Wolves chairman pleading over the loudspeaker with his supporters to 'uphold the proud traditions of their club' following an ugly pitch invasion.

But we were soon brought crashing back down to earth after an horrific injury to right-winger Lingy on a Thursday night in our next game – a 4–0 whitewash at Wrexham, in front of just 935 people. I called Lingy 'Sponge', as he was only tiny but could soak up as much beer as anyone back in our Exeter days. He was my little mate and during the first half he told me that the Welsh side's left-back kept threatening to 'do' him. Keeping his word, he cracked Lingy so hard with an elbow that his nose bone fractured his skull in seven places. The defender didn't even get booked. But Lingy did, booked straight into an operating theatre, where the surgeon compared his horrendous injuries to a shattered car windscreen, almost writing off his career.

It was 0–0 at half-time, but the incident hit us hard and we went to pieces after the break, with my focus not on playing centre-forward, but drifting over to Wrexham's left-back berth to try and put one on Lingy's assailant. He knew I wanted revenge and made sure he was near the tunnel at the end, so he could escape me at the final whistle. But I sprinted after the full-back and, as he reached the home dressing room, I launched myself through the air, catching him with my studs and bouncing through the door. On the floor, surrounded by Wrexham players, I looked around for him, ready to ram my fist into his skull. But six of their lads grabbed me and chucked me back into the tunnel, blocking the door as I shouted out threats, trying to get back inside and finish him off.

We still had to win our final game at Stockport to clinch promotion and condemn nearest rivals Wolves to the play-offs. We flew up to Manchester on a white-knuckle ride in a rickety 70-seater plane with the fans, which was a first. Unlike now, teams didn't have to finish their seasons all on the same day, and our match at Edgeley Park was played on a Friday night. Over 1,000 fans travelled up to cheer us on to promotion, and there were 100 Wolves fans in gold and black colours there too, hoping to see us fail. But that was never going to happen and goals from Glenn Pennyfather and Richard Cadette sealed the 2–0 victory we needed, completely nullifying Wolves' 4–1 triumph over Hartlepool 24 hours later, and they suffered play-off heartbreak against Aldershot.

I was so relieved and burst into tears as I walked down the tunnel, finally releasing the season's tension as well as the resentment of so many past disappointments. This was the first thing I had achieved in football since winning promotion with Walsall seven years before and it was a great feeling – revitalising, even, as I realised that my biggest concern for the past 12 months hadn't been where to get my next drink, but when the next football match was.

It was weird winning promotion on opposition soil, though, as I watched our celebrating fans chucking scarves over a metal fence towards the players, or trying to strain an arm through the grills of the cage to touch one of their heroes as they saluted the supporters in front of the terracing. It is these kinds of displays of emotion and pride which are the lifeblood of the game, but I had forgotten that.

The beer was flowing on the plane home, as a couple of uniformed air hostesses in the party mood took turns sitting on my knee, buckling me in tight with the seatbelt, and shoving their hands down my pants. When we landed, the whole team rushed to TOTS, where the DJ announced the promotion winners' arrival and we were clapped in. The two air hostesses had winged it to the nightclub, thinking they were going to get sorted out by Big Roy. But not this time, girls. I'd finally done something that mattered, got a club promoted and played a good part in it – so much so, that Jimmy Greaves, whose son Danny was working at the club, demanded my No.10 shirt as a memento. There wasn't going to be any sex tonight. Free of my demons and the company of losers, I was going to happily drink myself stupid, knowing that just for once I had truly earned it.

16. THE BATE ESCAPE

All the Southend lads jetted out to Portugal to keep the promotion party flying. Turning our complimentary FA Cup Final tickets into beer, we stuck £500 behind the hotel bar and got leathered for a week. I was leading the way, of course, but this time for pleasure, and not to paper over the cracks of an imploding career.

We were staying in Albufeira, the former holiday destination of a committed young Birmingham City striker who had barely touched a drop and stood in awe watching his manager Jim Smith's hilarious drunken antics. Ten years on and I was the comedy drunk entertaining the club's kids, 'boat racing' cocktail pints against the young pros and taking £5 off them each time – as they couldn't get anywhere near my seven-second finish. While I was waiting for the struggling juniors to catch up, so we could refill the cocktails and race for their holiday money again, I was also having social beers with the senior lads.

I knocked back 10 cocktail pints in 20 minutes, as well as a good few lagers during the course of the night. But, not being able to handle the pace, everyone else disappeared, abandoning me to drink against myself. Trouble was, I didn't realise they had all gone until the early hours, and by that time I didn't know where I was, or where I was going. I still had money in my pocket, though, and stumbled through the humid darkness outside into a cab, rambling on to the driver about finding a hotel with a big, blue neon light. That's all I could remember – the hotel's name had long evaporated. I must have gone on eight different journeys, clocking up a £100 fare. The Portuguese cabbie wasn't even going the long way round to fleece me! Daylight had broken by the time we located the hotel, and I fell into reception to find a concerned bunch of the lads gathered around the main hotel phone. Finally remembering they had left me behind, they were about to ring the police to send out a search party.

Things had fizzled out with Wendy in Colchester, and adventurous football groupie Jackie had become more of a regular arrangement. Having moved out of Wendy's place, I spent most of the summer in Solihull, going out on the lash with my brothers and mates and ploughing through the easy meat. The weekend before reporting back for pre-season training, I was at the Scandals nightclub when all this whooping and cheering started going off. I revolved away from the beer pumps to gaze upon a vision on the empty dance floor. This older, attractive woman – stripped down to black stockings, suspenders and high heels – was doing a turn for the punters.

Maggie had a reputation around town, following a scrummage with the local rugby team. As the clapping and whistling continued, 50-pence pieces were thrown on to the dance floor, which knickerless Maggie skilfully picked up without using her hands, before depositing them in a pint glass. I was suitably impressed, although I'm not sure I'd want to handle her loose change. And once Maggie had finished her party piece, I bought the girl half a pint of lager and charmed my way back to her bedroom. She wasn't shy, ripping my kit off and dragging a big mirror over to the side of the bed so we could get an intimate view of the docking procedure. It was the time when wearing shoes with no socks was in fashion, so she got things going by sucking my manky, sweaty old toes.

After a rascal session, I got in the shower and as I dried off scanned her girly shampoos and conditioners on the bathroom shelf. I curiously eagled in on this white cream in a pickled onion-sized jar, with its label facing the wall. I slowly turned the container and the label read, 'Head and Body Lice Cream.' 'No fucking way,' I thought. 'The clap was bad enough, I can't catch crabs as well.'

Driving down the motorway to Southend, I felt something itchy on my skin. I had a scratch and found this little black thing moving about on the end of my finger, which had small legs or claws. I rested the tiny creature on the handbrake and put my foot down all the way to Roots Hall, where I fetched it in a hurry to give to the startled physio Buster Footman, who bolted for the pharmacy even faster. He got me a special body lotion and hair shampoo to get rid of the critters. I swore that was the last time I would be feeling the pinch, but I still rolled the dice again a few weeks later when I crawled back into Maggie's undergrowth for a second time.

It was all change at Roots Hall as we prepared for life in the Third Division. I got the breaking news in a phone call from the vice-chairman, John Adams. 'We've brought in a new manager, Dick Bate, and this fella's going to improve you by 20 per cent, Roy,' he promised. This was a real slap in the face for Paul Clark, who had completed the job of getting us promoted after David Webb had bailed out. But Clarky didn't throw his toys out of the pram and stayed at the club as a player, picking up his money and biding his time. He had obviously known what was around the corner. Adams had met Bate on an FA coaching course and the bloke had more badges than the Boy Scouts. He was a big northern bastard, 6ft 3in tall with a thick, dark moustache and he was the king of all Clipboard Charlies. Now, with my hair and tash I did quite a good impression of Basil Fawlty, but this guy was the real deal. Bate had the Three Lions FA insignia plastered on everything he owned – T-shirts, tracksuits, kitbags, diaries, and probably his underpants. He wore a slim-fitting tracksuit with huge white stripes down the side, gold rings and bracelets on each hand and wrist, plus a big chain dangling around his neck. When we turned up for his first pre-season training session, I'd never seen so many road cones, apart from the time they were flying over the roof of my car. It was like major roadworks on the M25. I'd finally got the bit back between my teeth, after too many seasons lost and drunk in the football wilderness, and the club had landed us with the god of all coaching-manual worshippers.

Bate set up four lines of cones for a dribbling relay with the ball, and took great pride in showing us how to carry out the task by dancing in and out of them like Torvill and Dean. All of the lads swapped knowing glances, and when it was our turn we just tripped and kicked our way through the lot of them, creating an exploded minefield of cones. Bate blew his whistle like a petulant kid. 'Can't you lot do better than that?'

'Sorry, gaffer', I smirked. 'We weren't sure how to do it, can you show us again?'

And he did as well, taking 20 minutes to set them all up immaculately, with the precision of an obsessive-compulsive disorder sufferer. So we smashed the fuck out of them for a second time.

The next day, I was fighting cat and dog in a practice match with one of our kids, Spencer Prior, when Bate's stopwatch started bleeping. He blew his whistle to stop the game and went to speak – but no words came out. Bate had completely forgotten what he was doing. He beckoned over one of the apprentices and whispered in his ear, sending the youngster scampering off to behind one of the goals to fetch his notes. Bate read through his notes, then dropped the clipboard, blew his whistle and started issuing instructions like a policeman guiding traffic. The players just pissed themselves, and Bate had lost the changing room before the season had even started.

It didn't take him long to lose Vic Jobson, either. The players were drinking non-league Basildon United's bar dry after a warm-up match, when Jobson came over to me and asked, 'What do you think of the new manager, Roy?'

I replied, 'Vic, I couldn't tell you. Ask me again in a couple of weeks.'

Bate appeared in the bar, saw Jobson talking to me and shouted at the chairman, 'You, a word', before stomping out.

Bate had just signed his death warrant, trying to lay the law down with Jobson, who didn't suffer fools. The players were stunned, and one of them asked, 'Seriously, Roy, how long do you think he'll last?'

'Eight to 10 weeks,' was my answer.

His new signings weren't up to much either. Eric Steele, who is now Manchester United's goalkeeping guru, arrived from Derby as our new No.1, but was soon suffering shell-shock at the hands of opposition strikers. The full-back with the shortest throw in football (all three yards of it), Chris Ramsey, came from Swindon. I genuinely loved Rams, who had been mangled by Manchester United's Norman Whiteside in the 1983 FA Cup Final when he was with Brighton. The poor bugger was on his last legs, but he was just happy to be at a football club and would always take the piss out of himself. 'Played another blinder today, eh lads!' he would often say after another shocker. But Bate's worst signing was Richard Young. Built like a brick shithouse but softer than butter, he cost money from Notts County and was earmarked as my younger replacement. But he couldn't cut the mustard on the battlefield and rarely got a sniff.

We started off the 1987/88 season with draws against Bury and Chester, but it was the lull before the mother of all storms as a short Saturday trip to bogey team Gillingham turned into the greatest embarrassment of my career. On the Friday, the manager called us into a team meeting where we found him standing next to a whiteboard with a black felt-tip pen. Bate had written down the whole Gillingham team and scrawled question marks over their goalkeeper and seven outfield players, identifying them as the Kent side's weak links during an hour-and-a-half-long yawnfest. We got annihilated 8–1 at the Priestfield Stadium, which was the biggest defeat of my career and that includes kids' football. We were so poor they even scored our goal for us, defender Gary West putting past his own goalkeeper. As we sat, heads bowed, in the changing room after one of the worst 90 minutes in Southend United's existence, Bate burst in and went to shout, but only a pathetic little squeak came out. He couldn't even give us a bollocking.

Let off the hook, the mentality of the players was to head straight to the bar and write Bate's obituary over a few pints. We joked that his eight question marks on the Friday must have been Gillingham's goalscorers, but we didn't remember the goalkeeper popping one in. Things didn't get any better under Bate's limp leadership, who rapidly went down as the worst manager in Southend's history. We lost the next five games, including a 6–2 tonking at Notts County and a 4–1 pulverising at Port Vale. I sifted through the wreckage of both disasters to get my first two goals of the season, which is of little consolation when you're bottom of the table and the butt of national jokes. Even Liverpool superstar John Barnes had a laugh at our expense, when he was a studio guest on *Wogan*. Our dreadful league record read: Played: 8; Won: 0; Drawn: 2; Lost: 6; Goals For: 11; Goals Against: 28; Points: 2. Thankfully, just as Mystic McDonough had predicted, Bate was on his bike by the end of September, with defender Paul Clark reinstalled as player-manager. The Coach of the Century had lasted just 10 weeks, but he has gone on to land other high-profile coaching jobs since. Bate is now the FA's Elite Coaching Manager, with the responsibility of overseeing an entire generation of England's greatest young talent. I really can't get my head around that one.

The only positive thing Bate achieved during his brief Roots Hall tenure was steering us past Brentford in the first round of the League Cup. That meant Clarky's first game back in charge would hand me an Essex reunion with England stars Peter Shilton and Mark Wright, who were both coming to town with First Division Derby. Five years earlier, Shilton's agile heroics for Southampton had denied me more than one goal at Colchester in the same competition, before I had taken great delight in giving Wright a torrid time as we bowed out in the second leg at the Dell. Our goals-against column was the highest in the country, so the Rams arrived at Roots Hall with the whiff of an easy kill in their nostrils.

But Bate's departure that same morning galvanised the players into an immediate response, making a mockery of our terrible start to the season. The startled Rams were butted into submission, with the form book turned upside down in the 28th minute. Derby defender Ross MacLaren handled in his own box and referee David Elleray had no hesitation in awarding a penalty. There was only one player ever taking it, and I grabbed the ball and placed it on the spot – 12 yards away from the bulky figure of England's No.1 filling the goal opposite me. The North Bank unleashed its fury on Shilton as the fans screamed 'Wife Beater', following allegations in a national newspaper, as well as throwing pink toilet rolls at him. None of that bothered me, or broke my concentration. I didn't do nerves on the pitch and knew exactly what I was going to do with the spot-kick. Shilton spat on his right glove. But the gob barely had time to rest on his other chubby paw before I'd powerfully laced the penalty inside the right post, not giving Shilton a split-second to move. A Southend fan ran onto the pitch and celebrated by dropping his trousers in front of Shilton, which must have been a new one for watching England boss Bobby Robson who was in the stand. We hung on comfortably for a 1–0 win with defender Wright, who hadn't got any tougher since our last meeting, handing me another 90-minute stroll.

It was the first time Southend had beaten a top-flight team on home turf in their history – some 81 years in the making – so the press were clamouring for an interview outside the changing room. When asked how I'd felt facing England's top goalkeeper, I boasted, 'I'd have been confident of putting the penalty away if there had been two Peter Shiltons in goal.'

All the lads threw boots and socks at me as I did the round of interviews. But it was a strange one for me, as I was never a glory hunter, always just as happy setting up chances for my team-mates, and it was only a penalty for fuck's sake.

I had a nice framed picture capturing the moment, though, taken through the net from behind the goal. A defeated Shilton is on his knees as I celebrate, arms raised in front of him. But the photo went in the dustbin after reading his comments about failing to save the Germans' penalties in the Italia '90 World Cup semi-final shoot-out. Beaten four times from the spot,

Shilton said he was more than happy that he had gone the right way every time. To me, though, it was cheating. He never took a gamble and just waited to see which way the ball went. So I questioned whether he'd even bothered trying to save my penalty on that foggy, freezing night at Roots Hall – a million miles away from a balmy evening in Turin against the Krauts. It didn't count in my eyes anymore.

I took far greater pride in our gritty away performance, which was probably an even bigger shock as we fought tooth and nail for a 0–0 draw at the Baseball Ground to get through on aggregate. Our reward was a short third-round trip to Second Division Ipswich. My old drinking pals, minus Ian Atkins, who was injured for the game, were lucky fuckers that night. The left-back, Graham Harbey, got the winner, when his free-kick deflected off the wall and ballooned into our net. They celebrated like they'd just won the World Cup which left a bitter taste in the mouth and I've detested Ipswich ever since.

Having Clarky back at the helm sparked a positive transformation in the Third Division, too, as we beat Brighton and drew with Northampton, before I was among the scorers in a 3–1 win at Grimsby. Our mini-revival came to an end as I found the net in a 3–2 loss at Bristol City, before the alarm bells started ringing loudly again. I was having a decent run in front of goal, hammering in another penalty in a 3–1 defeat at Chesterfield, but we greeted November without a win in eight games including a midweek massacre at Sunderland where I'd made my league debut as a fresh-faced 18-year-old striker with Birmingham City. However, my first return to Roker Park after 10 years was memorable for all the wrong reasons, as we got slaughtered 7–0.

I soon made things harder for Southend, earning a painful red card in a 1–1 draw at home to my old club Walsall. I'd been having a decent ding-dong with their long-haired centre-half, Graeme Forbes, who was your typical hostile Scot. When he caught me off balance, Forbes unleashed a few 'I'm going to fucking do you' digs, which were well disguised. But I let it pass, as he was getting it back with equal force and I was savouring the contest. The guy was a tough customer, and he had my respect. Even more so when he seized his opportunity to gain the upper hand. I slipped over heading the ball on and as I flung out a grounded arm, Forbes stamped six studs down hard onto the back of my hand. Fair play to him, though, as I would have done the same thing to get the advantage in such an evenly balanced duel. But there were no excuses for the referee's behaviour. As Forbes smugly jogged past while I clutched my hand in agony, he was closely followed by the official. The ref had been right on the spot, but he was playing on as if nothing had happened. What he should have been doing was showing Forbes a card for his hatchet job on my hand. I yelled after the referee, 'Are you going to do something about that, you cunt?' But you can't fling a C-word at a whistler, even if they are blatantly in the wrong, and I was soon running my swollen hand under a cold tap in the changing room following the ninth red card of my professional career.

Gradually we started making ground on the teams just above the relegation zone, which had a lot to do with some inspired signings from Clarky. He got Paul Sansome from Millwall, who was the most all-round solid goalkeeper I'd ever played with – a brilliant shot-stopper who had a strong kick and confident hands. Super fit Peter Butler signed from Cambridge, a midfield Yorkshire terrier who would purposefully surrender the ball to an opponent just so he could tackle them again and win it back. But the wisest investment of all was the £50,000 Clarky paid Cambridge for striker David Crown, who would fill the goals void left by Richard Cadette's summer departure. Crowny was an absolute gem who was always quick to acknowledge the role I played in his goals. He was the best finisher I ever had the privilege of playing alongside – and that includes Trevor Francis. Crowny was so deadly that if he went one-on-one with the goalkeeper I would just turn around and walk back to the centre circle for the kick-off. He scored 69 goals in 132 games for Southend, mainly in struggling sides, which some record.

The great recovery started with a five-game unbeaten run to

see out 1987, as I slammed home a brace in a 4–1 Roots Hall thrashing of Doncaster, before lashing a penalty past Nigel Martyn in a 4–2 home bashing of not-so-fat Gerry Francis's Bristol Rovers. The only time our manager let himself down was on the Christmas drink. Clarky turned up with his muscular legs threatening to burst through a pair of skin-tight Farah trousers, but blew us all out after a couple of pints, while the rest of us got wankered. He had refused to cancel training the next day and must have been up all night gripping a piece of chalk as we were greeted by a blackboard rundown of odds on who would throw up first during the running session. I was the hot favourite, surprise, surprise, and Clarky had called it right as he ran the bollocks off us. But I wasn't going to give him the satisfaction of knowing that, so I kept the foul-tasting vomit in my mouth before swallowing it straight back down again.

Dismissed as condemned men all season, we carried on nicking results here and there without ever threatening to put a run together and pull clear of the trapdoor. But that all changed on April Fool's Day at home to play-off-chasing Wigan as we embarked on a run of six victories in our last eight games. I had to settle for a place on the bench, having missed the last game through a yellow-card-induced suspension. Martin Robinson had hit a double in the previous match, a 3–0 win over Chesterfield, and rightly kept his place. But he was too similar to Crowny – small, pacey and an intelligent maker of runs, not the battering ram needed to break down the visiting defensive barrier. Leading 2–0 early in the second half, Wigan's back four were sitting in their deckchairs puffing on big fat cigars. But I got thrown into the fray and gave the northern fuckers the fright of their lives to turn that most vital of matches on its head. I also sparked the revival in the scoring department, stroking home from the spot, before Martin Ling pulled us level, setting the stage for the most worthy of all winners – a 35-yard rocket from Crowny.

We had a fighting chance of staying up now and the season went down to the wire, with Blackpool the visitors for a long-distance seaside derby. There was only ever going to be one winner on that final sweltering day, as we made the Tangerines look rotten. After the game, people whispered about survival bungs being chucked at the opposition, but the truth was that we wanted it more. Blackpool were comfortable mid-table finishers with nothing to play for, while our lads were competing for their futures – the chance to make sure their appearance money and bonuses didn't get halved by contractual relegation clauses. And who knows, staying up might also mean the opportunity to push your luck and ask for some extra dosh next season. Peter Butler, Martin Ling, twice, and Crowny – with his 17th strike in just 28 games – applied the finishing touches in a 4–0 great escape act. We finished 17th in the table, three points clear of the drop zone – which had not seemed possible after those respective 8–1 and 7–0 Third Division horror stories at Gillingham and Sunderland. Relieved fans swarmed across the pitch and ripped the players' shirts, shorts and socks from their bodies. Keeping our heads above water against all the odds was just as satisfying as winning promotion the previous year. I'd even managed to reach double figures for only the second time in my career, plundering 11 goals during our eternal struggle. These were all excellent excuses for a giant celebration drink – but there was an even bigger reason to get sloshed on 4 June, 1988, when I got married.

I'd been seeing Jackie on and off for seven years – ever since I bedded her to win a bet with Colchester boss Allan Hunter. Seven years younger than me, and no saint herself, she was only ever a phone call away during that period, and we'd started to see a lot more of each other during the last couple of seasons. It was a relationship with precarious foundations – built on lust, not love – and we'd somehow got to the stage of being engaged for the past 12 months. But there were no big romantic gestures in the marriage proposal. I was going through the motions again, just like when I put a token diamond on poor old Denise's finger. The whole thing was a sham.

There were two main reasons for walking up the aisle with Jackie: approaching 30, it seemed the right thing to do, and I needed future security. My brother Gaz and most of my drinking buddies had tied the knot over the previous couple of summers, so it felt like a natural progression. The other big attraction was that Jackie's dad, Gordon Parker, was absolutely loaded. Gordon was a developer, who had been on the board of directors at Colchester United. He lived in a massive house on the outskirts of town, in Lexden, which had an indoor swimming pool and a Rolls-Royce on the drive. I was having problems with my knees, which could threaten to call full-time on my playing days, so marrying into the Parker family would provide extra financial security. If it all went wrong, the millionaire father-in-law would bail us out, which must have made me a gold digger. Gordon even let us buy a knock-down detached house, which was on the market for £125,000, for £75,000 to set up our marital home.

We got married at Lexden Church – next door to Gordon's house – with Ian Atkins carrying out the best man duties, which had included a messy stag weekend back in Solihull. The reception was a flash affair for 250 guests, held in a giant marquee in Gordon's back garden. The champagne flowed and there was a free bar all day, which my pals rinsed. But the bubbles went straight to their heads as a couple of them tried to shin up the support poles of the marquee, while another group attempted to get a petrol go-kart fired-up in the garage. I was so relieved they didn't succeed, as they would have driven it straight into the party and started running people over for a laugh. It was a complete nightmare, which just about summed up our marriage from day one.

We had a week on honeymoon at Gordon's apartment in Tenerife, but the football season was just around the corner and I couldn't wait to get back to Roots Hall. It was a sad state of affairs, but at the time I'd convinced myself that I was in love with Jackie. I should have known seven days before the wedding that I wasn't. Like most footballers, I thought I was immune to the normal rules and regulations of the world, so I took a girl from the Colchester Hippodrome back to my flat. My betrothed was working nights as a nurse and didn't get home until 7.15am, so I knew I could pull it off. When my guest saw Jackie's pictures and make-up around the flat, I had to convince her that we'd just split up, before getting down to business. I pushed my pre-marital conquest out the door at 6.30am, so I had time to shower off her scent before a tired Jackie got home. But that was us, Roy and Jackie, the highly-sexed but insatiable couple, who were constantly craving attention but crap in our own company.

Mum gave our marriage a six-month shelf life at the wedding reception. God knows how, but we lasted seven years.

17. THE SECOND COMING

'Seventeen pints of Stella please,' I asked a startled Southend Airport barmaid at 8am. We were flying to Scotland for a pre-season tour and the boss, Paul Clark, had lost his marbles, putting me in charge of the travelling party. Clarky had to drive all the kit and balls 450 miles to Stirling, just north of Glasgow, in the club's white transit van. It would take him 10 hours as the old heap could only do about 50mph at top whack. But we'd be north of the border in a couple of hours by plane, and he wanted two of his senior players – me and Danny O'Shea – to keep the rest of the squad in line.

'Don't let the lads go out drinking all day,' he told us.

'Don't worry about that, Clarky, we'll make sure,' I said, trying hard to keep a straight face.

As soon as he'd gone, Danny laughed, 'Did he really just say that?'

So we got the girl working behind the pumps well before opening time. We were staying at Stirling University and by the time Clarky arrived we were all shit-faced, cheering and clapping him into the car park. It would be fair to say that he didn't see the funny side of our antics after such a long drive. The whole tour was a week-long piss-up, but with two major highlights. I played a round of golf at Gleneagles, making sure

I finished the beautiful course, despite turning my ankle, and I played at Hamilton where I was marked by some bald, fat bloke who was about 40, and we got stuffed 4–0. But I couldn't have been happier, as I was a big fan of Saturday morning's *Saint and Greavsie* show, on which they were always harping on about the 'Hamilton Accies', so I was just dead chuffed to play there.

There weren't any new faces around the club for the 1988/89 Third Division campaign, as Clarky had used up the budget in keeping us up the previous season. But one new arrival was chartered physio Ken Steggles. I was homing in on my 30th birthday and it was time to think about the end of my football days, so I spent a lot of time working with Ken towards a physio qualification which was one future option for me. It got me thinking more about my body and what I'd done to it over the years. I'd drastically reduced my drinking habits at Southend, but still felt it was quite normal to have a few beers on a Tuesday after a midweek game. It was also OK in my book to drink through a day off on a Wednesday, when I also played in Colchester's snooker league at night, plus Thursday – not Friday before a game – and Saturday and Sunday, relaxing after another weekend match. Eventually, I plucked up the courage to ask Ken if it was acceptable for a professional sportsman to drink 70 pints of beer a week. To this day, I'm still waiting for him to pick his jaw up off the floor and give me an answer. But it still didn't seem that much to me at the time, as I'd built up such a high tolerance to alcohol and genuinely believed I was a reformed character.

When I was at my worst, I could easily drink 24 pints during a steaming session, so it isn't hard to do the maths. The major difference now, though, was that I wasn't drinking to forget. It was purely social and there was a cut-off point. I had the strength to walk away and didn't have to be last at the bar, downing beers with company, or on my own, until kicking-out time. But I would never have classed myself as an alcoholic. I didn't pour lager on my Cornflakes, hold a cold can under my pillow at night or hide beers in the toilet so I could go off for a secret swig. I was always open about my boozing, and it makes me laugh when I hear about these so-called 'monster drinkers' like Arsenal's Tony Adams and Paul Merson. My Colchester pal Perry Groves was George Graham's first signing for the Gunners, so I got to meet a lot of the Highbury crowd at various functions. After the christening of one of Grovesy's kids, we went back to his house in Stanway and polished off two barrels of Kronenbourg, which his father had kindly donated from his Ipswich pub. That adds up to 160-odd beers, but Merson broke his neck after nine pints and fell asleep, just as the rest of us were getting warmed up. Like all the Arsenal lads of that era, Merson was a lovely guy and a top-class player. He loved a flutter more than a drink, and wouldn't bat an eyelid at betting £16,000 in one afternoon on crown green bowls.

We played against Arsenal at Roots Hall, with the Gunners bringing down a strong team for Paul Clark's testimonial. Tony Adams was a giant player in my eyes. He was a hard, uncompromising character, but was also a very talented footballer with excellent distribution skills. During the 'friendly' match, I elbowed Adams so hard on his rock of a nose that pins and needles shot all the way up my arm. I turned round expecting to see the England colossus kneeling on the floor, wiping blood from his face. He just smiled and said, 'Don't worry big fella, plenty of time.' I hadn't meant to catch him, but I knew what was coming. And sure enough, 20 minutes later, he smashed me to the deck with a crunching tackle. Adams picked me up, but there was no act of aggression – we were even now – and I just said, 'Fair play to you big 'un – on you go.'

You had to respect the guy, but the only thing I could never get my head around was his alleged alcoholism. The bloke would get locked away in an England training camp for weeks at a time – how did he get on the piss in there? By raiding the hotel mini-bar? All of these self-proclaimed alcoholics never washed with me. But we had a massive drinking session that night, and all the Arsenal boys followed us down to TOTS. Steve Bould and Niall Quinn particularly enjoyed themselves, as they were found suited and booted in the car park by the groundsman the next morning, resting their snoring heads against the outside door to the Roots Hall changing rooms.

The start of the season certainly packed punch as we beat Bolton Wanderers 2–0 at home. The Trotters had just come up from the Fourth Division and brought 1,000 fans with them. But they were another set of mugs living in the past of their knackered old club's glory days, and an army of them invaded the pitch at the final whistle in their Pierre Cardin designer jumpers. They soon got batted back by Big Ginge and his crew as Southend's top boy stood in the centre circle, repelling them with iron fists like Popeye.

The struggles soon set in again, though, as we managed just two wins in our next 15 Third Division outings – with my only goal coming in a 3–1 victory against Chesterfield.

We were occupying the relegation places again and the writing was on the wall for Clarky at the end of November after David Webb was spotted in the stands during our FA Cup exit at Bristol City. The jungle drums were beating loudly, and it wasn't long before Webby was announced as general manager, to work alongside Clarky. What a load of bollocks. Webby was never going to be second in command to anyone. He had to have full control and Clarky didn't deserve to be treated like that. He'd picked up the pieces twice, winning us promotion after Webby had quit, then saving us from relegation after the Dick Bate disaster. If Vic Jobson had wanted Webby back as manager, then he should have just thrashed it out with Clarky man to man. I thought Jobson and Webby's handling of the situation was poor, as it made life extremely difficult for Clarky and would have a massive bearing on the outcome of our season. For the following few weeks Clarky tried to organise the team in the dressing room with the silent spectre of Webby hovering in the doorway behind him, which completely undermined his authority in front of the players.

Unbelievably, despite having had two years away from the club, Webby still had it in for me. I'd been sidelined for a month with a ligament injury to my right knee and had only just finished my rehabilitation. The knee was feeling stronger but I was desperately short of match fitness. I played in a hastily arranged December practice match against a local Sunday League side – which was stand-on-one leg stuff – before being told I was playing centre-half on Saturday at Third Division leaders Sheffield United. I was already rusty and hadn't played in defence for two years. To make the job even easier, my central rearguard partner was going to be left-back Paul Brush, who had been my gym buddy for the last four weeks, recovering from an identical injury. It was a complete stitch up.

I told Brushy we might as well take a couple of shovels out and dig ourselves holes in the Bramall Lane pitch, as we were going to get murdered. But this was a route one Dave Bassett side, all rough and tumble, and we played a blinder against the Blades, snuffing out their muscular front two of Tony Agana and John Francis. I knew they would pump it long all day, which gave me the chance to drop off and head back everything that they launched in our direction. We pulled off a shock 2–1 win, and I was chuffed as nuts at the end. Webby winked at me when he bowled into the changing room afterwards.

'Fuck me big fella, you were like John Charles out there today,' he said.

Still red-faced, I replied, 'Really Dave. Well do you know what? My arsehole's as big as my head, as I've been breathing out of it for the last 90 minutes.'

He didn't know what to say to that, and I thought, 'Fuck you. I showed you, I'm not going anywhere.'

Players aren't daft, and we knew exactly what was going on. Webby was back in the managerial hot-seat at Christmas, with Clarky relegated to player status again. But there was no magic formula as our struggles carried on. I was automatically restored to the firing line and got the winner against Northampton at Roots Hall, but we only managed two victories in our next 14 matches under Webb. And I only got one more goal, a back-header from a corner that I knew very little about until I saw my team-mates running away celebrating, in a 3–2 January defeat at Huddersfield.

Stuck in the bottom four, the end of March and beginning of April handed us a Roots Hall double-header, offering six do-or-die points in our battle to beat the drop. Sheffield United were the first visitors, hunting another win on their charge to promotion. I'd always had a decent relationship with the Southend fans, but there was a small section who had started getting on my back about my three-goal total for the season so far. Well, I shut the fuckers up soon enough in a 2–1 success against the Blades, throwing myself full-length at the far post to meet Martin Ling's early cross and net a textbook diving header, before running over to their little huddle and flicking the V's. But the best was yet to come as I claimed Goal of the Season in the next match, a relegation dogfight with Blackpool. With time running out and a useless draw beckoning, the ball was chucked into the box and I somehow managed to defy gravity by hooking a leg above my shoulder in mid-air to bury an overhead kick and steal all three points. It was my fifth goal of the season and, unfortunately, my last, as we climbed to the giddy heights of 19th in the table.

We took another six points from the next two games against Bristol City and Reading, as David Crown carried on blasting himself to a 25-goal haul, and confidence was sky high. But the wheels came off another escape bid when we failed to win six matches on the trot going into the final game of the season – including a May Day bundle at Bristol Rovers. It was a sunny Bank Holiday Monday at Twerton Park, brightened up even more by goalkeeper Nigel Martyn spilling the ball under my aerial challenge for Martin Robinson to fire us ahead. But I didn't come off so well trying to flatten Devon White, their huge forward who was as big as a building. Running into that giant with everything you had was like throwing yourself at a stationary bus. We were pegged back for a draw by play-off chasing Rovers. But there had been a nasty verbal side to the game, mostly revolving around their little midfielder Ian Holloway. It carried on into the players' lounge after the match, as Holloway made it crystal clear that the row wasn't over, kicking-off a 16-man brawl in front of terrified families and friends. A few haymakers were thrown, but it was mostly all handbags – a lot of pushing and shoving – and it was all over very quickly.

When it's backs to the wall you have to stand your ground as a team, but I could understand Holloway's anger as one of the Southend lads had over-stepped the mark in the war of words. Holloway's wife had successfully battled cancer, and this player had twisted the knife in the midfielder's very personal pain by making derogatory remarks about her illness. That is the sort of gutter level some players will resort to in gaining the upper hand. As the red-hot needle flies around the pitch, a player will think, 'How can I go one better?', trying to come up with the final insult to destroy an opponent. But our player didn't need to resort to the lowest of the low blows, as he was a true hardnut who could have ripped Holloway to pieces with his bare hands. Holloway deserves credit for sticking up for himself and his family – all 5ft 3in of him.

I went to the Professional Footballers' Association awards dinner at the super-plush Grosvenor Hotel with Ian Atkins and my pal Kim Webber before the end of the season. All the PFA big-wigs were there, people like Gordon Taylor and Brendan Batson, plus all the top managers. But it's mostly a great excuse for 500 footballers from all levels of the pro ranks to have a good old Sunday piss-up together – many of whom get carried out horizontally during the course of the night. We had tickets earlier in the day for the Simod Cup Final between Nottingham Forest and Everton at Wembley – a 4–3 thriller – but as soon as those famous twin towers were in sight, we decided to fuck it off and hit the pubs instead. When we finally arrived at the Grosvenor sozzled in our penguin outfits, Kim bet me £20 that I wouldn't wrap my tie around my head Rambo style for the whole night. All that was missing was a machine gun, as giggling players pointed up at me from their lamp-lit tables as I stumbled down the spiral staircase into the main hall. As the drink carried on flowing, I went one better after getting lost on a trip to the toilet. On the way back, I poked my head (tie still on) through the stage curtains and looked out across the drunken throng from behind the top table. It all went quiet, so I ducked back out, then shoved my head through the curtains again to face the masses, Eric Morecambe-style, and got a standing ovation. I was out of contract that summer and already had a poor reputation for drinking and discipline on the football circuit. And with a host of managers – or potential new employers – watching my antics, it probably didn't do me any long-term favours.

Having not touched our food at the Grosvenor, we staggered on to a late-night burger bar with the munchies for some grease in a bun. Kim thought it would be hilarious to spray each other with the squeezey sauce bottles, and when I climbed out of a cab in front of my Colchester home at 4am, I was covered in gunk. I couldn't find my keys, so I tried to fish my hand through the letterbox to grab the handle and open the door. After about 10 minutes of rattling around, the door swung open and I was greeted by yelling goalkeeper Alec Chamberlain clutching a golf club. I was so pissed that I'd completely forgotten he was staying with me, and Alec thought I was a burglar trying to break in. But his anger soon turned to concern, as he started panicking and talking about calling an ambulance after clocking the red stains all over my suit. He thought I'd been involved in a car accident and needed medical assistance. I did find myself in the accident and emergency ward the next day, though, after my eye swelled up painfully. I'd got sauce in it playing silly buggers and had to miss training as my eye was swabbed clean by a hospital nurse.

The final day of the season at Roots Hall was a re-run of the previous year – we needed three points against visitors Chester to stay up. But this time we were also relying on our relegation rivals to get turned over to escape plummeting into the basement. We won the game, young centre-back Spencer Prior netting the crucial strike, and all the fans were jumping up and down, celebrating another Houdini act at the final whistle. Some of the players were joining in too, clapping and cheering, which was stupid as the other results hadn't been confirmed. Then, a blanket of silence smothered the crowd as the late Third Division results started crackling across the terraces on hand-held radios. And the players' smiles quickly disappeared as grim realisation set in. Blackpool had stolen a point at Cardiff to survive, while Reading had hit back from 2–0 down at half-time at Chesterfield to win 4–2. So we filled the final relegation slot, tied on 54 points with Northampton and Blackpool, but with a vastly inferior goal difference.

It was my fifth relegation, and at a club where the manager hated me and I was out of contract. What else could possibly go wrong? Well, I could always break my face playing cricket in the 20-overs Alehouse midweek league in Colchester. I opened the batting against a bowler I knew, Chris Tracey, smashing the new ball out of the ground and into the archery field next door at the third attempt. Two balls later, he delivered a wicked bouncer, which glanced me on the left cheek, sending me to my knees. Everyone gathered round to check I was OK, as Chris was a big lad who could chuck the ball at 70mph, but I dismissed the pain as nothing more than getting hit by an elbow on the football pitch. I scored a crap 24 runs before picking up the ball myself and trying to get my own back on Chris, sending in a few bouncers, although none of them hit the target. After the game, I had a few beers before driving back to the Midlands for a week on the piss. When I returned to Colchester I still had a dent in my cheek, which I put down to the seam of the ball hitting me. Despite my protests, Jackie urged me to go to hospital to get it checked out. The doctor told me I must have the constitution of an ox, as I'd unwittingly broken my jaw and busted my cheekbone, and I was operated on straight away.

With me unable to join in with pre-season training properly because of a serious injury sustained playing sport away from the club, David Webb hatched another recruitment masterplan to put an end to my stay at the seaside.

18. END OF THE PIER SHOW

David Webb lassoed Colchester's 'Italian Stallion' for £25,000 to lead us out of the Fourth Division at the first attempt. I saw it as another ploy by the Southend boss to finish me off – but just like all the other times, it backfired on him. At 23, Mario Walsh was seven years younger than me and a lovely lad. But that was the problem, he was too nice – a pretty boy with no balls. I was out of contract and Colchester wanted me to return in the opposite direction. But Shrimpers chairman Vic Jobson killed that one by asking their manager Jock Wallace for £100,000, which was outrageous. I didn't want to leave Roots Hall anyway and had signed a week-to-week deal, as I knew nobody at the club could do my job.

I drove Mario to training from Colchester every day, and my replacement would spend the journey seeking out advice on how to become a better player. 'Get tougher and win the ball in the air, for starters,' I told him, knowing full well he wasn't up to it.

I was confined to the bench for the first seven games of the season, as Super Mario scored a couple and we zoomed to the top of the table. The hardest fixture to swallow was a League Cup second round first-leg tie at top-flight Tottenham, which we lost 1–0 to Terry Fenwick's jammy header. I sat there seething with rage, not even getting on, forced to watch our pouting centre-forward, who couldn't punch his way out of a wet paper bag, strut around ineffectively at White Hart Lane.

Southend might have got off to a flier, but they still needed me, the aggressive fucker who imposed himself on any back four and caused damage physically, whatever the situation. And a 5–0 midweek thumping at our unhappy hunting ground of Gillingham soon made the penny drop with Webby. Mario was benched, I was back in the starting line-up, and I made my point, returning with a September goal in a 2–0 home win over Lincoln. Poor Mario hardly kicked a ball again that season.

I still hadn't signed a proper contract and by that stage was willing to walk if a decent offer came in. League new boys Maidstone wanted me and one of our youngsters, Justin Edinburgh, and set up a clandestine meeting at the Bull pub, in Hockley, just outside Southend, where £15,000 cash stuffed in a brown envelope was pushed across the table. It goes without saying that we turned it down, which was the best decision full-back Justin ever made, as he joined Spurs soon after, earning FA and League Cup winners' medals. Justin was a gifted lad, and not just on the pitch, as he was the king of the showers. Forget all the myths about the black boys, Justin was white as snow and had the biggest dangling weapon I've ever seen in football – a good seven inches on the flop. The boys would joke with him on a Friday: 'Don't be greedy Justin, let me borrow that for the weekend to put a smile on the missus's face.'

Starting the season in the stiffs, I'd got a buzz out of helping the youngsters find their feet. I also came up against Wimbledon's Vinnie Jones, who must have been coming back from an injury. We had a couple of challenges, nothing spectacular, and it's a shame we never played in a blood-and-thunder league game, as we could have had some fun. He wasn't hard in my book, or brave. He was just a bully who never had the bottle to do things face-to-face. He claimed to have intimidated Steve McMahon in the 1988 FA Cup Final. Do me a favour! He tried to do McMahon, but the Liverpool midfielder jumped his challenge and cut Jones's cheek open with his boot. That was the worst day in football history, as Wimbledon proved you can be successful just by being big and strong, pumping the ball long into the box and riding your luck. A few years later, Jones should have been banned for life when he more or less finished Gary Stevens's career, after scything through the Spurs defender's standing leg on the touchline. The kid was hanging out to dry, and if he'd been one of my team-mates I would have followed Jones home in my car and done time.

I liked the reserve-team boss Ronnie Hanley, who had gone to school with Spurs manager Terry Venables. Knowing I would be playing in the second leg of our League Cup tie, Ronnie marked El Tel's card, warning him that his defence was in for a rough ride. There was a full house of 10,400 fans at Roots Hall, and I was greeted by my old Birmingham team-mate Pat Van Den Hauwe, who was playing centre-half for Spurs.

'How you doing, "Donut"?' he asked.

'Not as good as you, I'm playing for fucking Southend,' I replied.

Then he pointed at my elbows, 'Keep them down tonight, big fella'.

And I warned him, 'Pat, I haven't signed a contract here, so I'll be going flat out tonight.'

Spurs showed us huge respect on that cold October night. They fielded a full-strength side, including stellar players Gary Lineker and Paul Gascoigne, who became national heroes at the end of the season, leading England to the Italia '90 World Cup semi-finals.

The game started at a frantic pace, which we capitalised on in the fifth minute, Dave Martin climbing above Terry Fenwick to meet Jason Cook's corner at the near post and beat Erik Thorstvedt with a bullet header which wiped out Spurs' slender first-leg lead. We were relying on goalkeeper Paul Sansome a few minutes later, who stood up strong to deny Lineker one-on-one, before Gazza drilled the rebound wide. I came agonisingly close to doubling our lead on 11 minutes when David Crown raced clear of the overworked Spurs defence and found me in the box, but my half-volley at full-stretch cannoned back off the crossbar.

Spurs were more at sea than Southend Pier at the back, and Pat Van Den Hauwe hadn't heeded my pre-match warning. Pat revelled in his tough-guy image and threw a punch in my direction after a skirmish on the 15-minute mark. With me, the first one was always for free, and I just said, 'Pat, behave yourself, pal.' And he nodded, 'Yeah, sorry big fella, sorry big fella.'

A few minutes later, we went up in the air for another big challenge and he chucked another fist at me, so I won the header and flattened him in the process. Venables then started chucking compliments my way, moving broken Pat to full-back and giving Mitchell Thomas a bite at the cherry. I bashed him about the park, too, leaving Spurs to make a second reshuffle, pulling Steve Sedgley out of midfield, but still they were failing to counter my aerial domination.

We had the upper hand, so I had time to admire the mercurial Gazza, who was still running the show in midfield. Peter Butler was given the impossible task of marking the Geordie genius, with the remit of following him everywhere – even if he went for a piss at half-time. Peter was the fittest specimen I'd ever come across in my life, but even he was left chasing shadows. Gazza might have been a bit tubby, but he had immense body strength and was like the Piped Piper, leaving behind a trail of pursuers he had skipped past for fun. Technically, the guy was out of this universe, but the thing I liked most was that he played with a smile on his face and chucked the humorous banter around: 'Fucking hell lads, how tight are ya shorts, like? Did you need a shoehorn to put them on? Surprised you Southend boys can even run, man.' He floored me with one meaty tackle, before jogging over, chuckling, to say, 'Sorry about that, mate.' I just said, 'Don't worry. You're Gazza, you can do what you fucking like.' He really was that good.

Just before half-time our mad Scouse winger Gary Bennett got the wrong side of defender Gary Mabbutt to prod home a cross from Crowny and put us 2–1 up on aggregate. Roots

Hall erupted, but Spurs midfielder Paul Allen soon doused the flames after the restart to level the tie. Southend's fans were soon up on their feet again when Paul Stewart got sent off for banging Paul Roberts with a flying elbow. Venables branded Robbo a cheat in *The Sun* the next day, and to be fair he had started doing the breaststroke on the track round the pitch after being floored. But he had an egg above his eye after the game, which must have been all the evidence his solicitor needed to get a retraction and a £20,000 out-of-court settlement.

One player who did con referee Paul Danson was Terry Fenwick. The defender jumped over my boot as I slid in to block him, but made a real meal out of it – holding his leg as if it was broken – then giggling after getting my name in the book. Spurs' Spanish midfielder Nayim skilfully dummied our back four on 55 minutes to grab an equaliser on the night and make it 2–2 – edging the north Londoners a goal ahead over the two legs – but we didn't know when to give up and rallied to score again 12 minutes later, squaring the tie once more. Benno raced on to my deft flick from Paul Brush's long free-kick to bamboozle the Spurs defence again and leave big Norwegian goalkeeper Thorstvedt flat-footed for a second time. A giant-killing was still on the cards, and there is always one gilt-edged chance in games like this to pull off the win. And with extra-time looming, it fell at the feet of the one man I would have put my mortgage on to swing the executioner's axe. In the dying seconds, Crowny found himself staring into the whites of Thorstvedt's eyes and pulled the trigger, but his clean strike brushed a post and Spurs survived.

Extra-time passed and we won 3–2 on the night, but an aggregate score of 3–3 meant we had bowed out on the away goals rule, which was very cruel. Equally harsh was the 10th red card of my professional career which I received in the additional period, after I had pushed my aching limbs to track back with David Howells. Trying to slide the ball out on the East Stand touchline, I caught the midfielder from behind, taking his legs away. The charitable Spurs fans screamed 'Off, off, off', and Mr Danson duly obliged. I was physically shattered, had no intention of fouling the bloke, and the referee could have shown a little more common sense after the Herculean effort we had put in. As I started to trudge off, the bitter feeling of injustice grew unbearable, so I angrily turned round to confront Danson. I wanted to call him a 'cunt', but luckily Robbo had seen the red mist take hold and intervened, pushing me towards the tunnel.

The next day, Terry Venables got on the phone to his old school chum Hanley and said, 'You know your mate, the big bloke up front. You were right – he is a fucking handful.'

I'd earned my spurs and Dave Webb slapped a two-year contract on the table, with a slight wage increase to £450 a week, and a £5,000 sweetener sprinkled on top. It made a mockery of the whole Mario Walsh fiasco. Webby had wasted £25,000 on somebody who could have never taken my place. I was a week short of blowing out 31 candles, but if Webby had given me £10,000 of the Mario fee I would have signed for five more years. And I wasn't the only one being rewarded, as the whole team was whisked off to Torremolinos for a five-day warm-weather training camp in recognition of our League Cup efforts. As soon as the plane skidded across the Spanish Tarmac, a raging monsoon half-drowned the Costa del Sol. It was so bad that people lost their lives, and the reception of our Billy Basic hotel – which Webby or Vic Jobson had obviously got as a cut-price deal from a pal – was already full of water when we checked in.

We couldn't do any training, as all the pitches were waterlogged, so the first day turned into an 18-hour drinkathon. Although, a hungry Dave Martin managed to tip the biggest bowl of king prawns you've ever seen down his neck. But he didn't realise you had to de-shell the things, and loudly crunched his way through everything, the heads and boots, the lot – which had the rest of us in stitches. Webby's No.2, Kevin Lock, was getting on the piss with the players, and I let it slip that Jackie had packed a big envelope in my suitcase. Locky couldn't get to my room quickly enough, finding the package and sharing the contents around the rest of the lads. Inside were eight photos of me and Jackie in a number of uncompromising positions, with a note reading, 'To Donkey-Boy Roy – just remember what you've got waiting at home.' The whooping players got a good eye-full of the McDonoughs in all their glory, before I collected the photos, counting how many there were to ensure nobody took home a holiday souvenir. I enjoyed the crack as much as them, but it wasn't normal behaviour to hand explicit pictures of your missus around a bar to hot-blooded footballers. That showed just how little I cared about Jackie – otherwise I would never have let it happen.

Webby was frustrated with us being on the piss in the hotel all day, and wasn't happy with Locky joining in. Happy Hour was 'double your drinks o'clock' and when Webby came down to the bar in the early evening, there were at least 100 empty beer bottles in front of us. His first attempt to put us in our place was outrageous. The relentless rain caused a power cut and, under the cover of darkness, he hurdled the bar and started pelting the over-65 brigade sitting across the room with packets of crisps and peanuts to try and get us in trouble. The unimpressed oldies gave us some very funny looks when the lights switched back on.

The pitches might have been unplayable, but the rain eased off after a few days, so Webby pulled out his ace to stop us drinking – fitness training on the beach with an 8am start. The bar was open all night, so we had to be inventive too. We made sure we had our training kits on so we could drink through until 6am, before crashing out on the reception sofas for two hours, already changed and ready to start running pissed.

I was never one to hydrate after a night on the sauce by drinking gallons of water, but as Webby put us through our paces I could feel my heart wanting to leap out of my mouth – I was convinced I was going to die on Spanish soil. As we stood there wilting in the heat of the early morning sun, Webby pointed at me and said, 'You drink with him, you laugh with him, now you can run with him. If anyone finishes behind Roy, then you can all go again.' Well there was no chance of that, and it wasn't long before I was lagging behind, nursing a queasy stomach and pounding head, as we ran three miles along the beach before stopping at a sea wall. There were 84 jagged concrete steps, which we had to spring up and down 10 times each, and I was struggling, asking Webby for a quick time out. Grinning with satisfaction, he thought I was going to be sick and sent Locky to keep an eye on me, which must have been a treat. I'd been running so hard with all the booze sloshing round that I had lost control of my bowels and panicked that I was going to shit myself on the steps. For the first time in my life, I had to take a dump outside, squatting between two sun loungers to release a chocolate Mr Whippy into the sand. It wasn't pleasant and I had nothing to wipe my backside with, so I pulled my shorts up and ran three miles back to the hotel again, squelching behind the others. When I got there, Webby was waiting outside, and he shook my hand, saying, 'I'm impressed you even got through it.' The players hit the showers, but I went to the bar to straighten out with four beers, before dealing with that dirty arse.

Back in England, I found the net in a 3–0 whitewash of Hereford at Edgar Street, before hitting the target again in a 3–2 Roots Hall triumph over Burnley, as Southend continued to lead the way. Promotion cruise control, however, would soon transform into FA Cup first-round meltdown, as the *Match of the Day* cameras handed Des Lynam a humiliating upset to show the nation that Saturday night. We got beat 1–0 at non-league Aylesbury, whose players rubbed it in with their stupid duck waddle celebration. And it was crossroads time in our season. We would either go on a great run in the league to get the cup defeat out of our systems or our confidence would take a major hit and it would all go wrong.

It was a time when cute man management was needed to lift the lads, even the hardened drinkers in our squad. We needed a slap across the face to wake us up, or a reassuring arm round the shoulder from the boss. But Dave Webb was never going to play the kindly father figure and we fell off our perch, yo-yoing between third and fourth spot following a wretched sequence of just six wins in 19 games. I only found the back of the onion bag twice more, signalling the end of the Eighties with a goal in a 2–1 home defeat to Exeter, before getting another in a 2–0 Roots Hall win over Doncaster in February 1990. As we struggled to find consistency, it was like my past was coming back to haunt me. My old drinking club, Exeter, were well on their way to being crowned champions while Grimsby, managed by former Walsall nemesis Alan Buckley, were in second place. As we tried to cling on to third spot, another of my ex-clubs, Cambridge, led by John Beck – the Dracula of football, who was on a one-man crusade to murder the game with his big-hoof brand of percentages football – were threatening to sink their fangs into our necks and dump us into the dreaded play-offs.

But there was little I could do to influence things from the dugout during a 1–1 draw at Scarborough in March. Times were changing. Dave Webb was planning for the future, bringing in younger and faster new faces like Andy Ansah, Dean Austin and Steve Tilson, to freshen up our promotion push. And it was one of these new pairs of legs, belonging to Ian Benjamin, which had taken my first-team place over the last few games. Webby was sitting in the directors' box with the chairman at Scarborough, but one of our boys got hurt in the first half and Kevin Lock told me to get warmed up. I was in a right strop about being benched and told him to 'fuck off' long before Carlos Tevez ever threw a hissy fit, so he put on one of the kids, Iain O'Connell, instead. Bored of watching us struggle after the break, I bit my lip and started to have a light run up and down the track, which always made me feel like a right cock for not being in the starting XI. And the opposition fans, who could almost grab me from the stands, always took great pleasure in reminding you that if you weren't playing, then you must be shit.

'Sit down you grey-haired old wanker', they started shouting, as I jogged between the dugout and corner flag. At least I had some form of contest now, so I threw in the old chestnut, 'How much did it cost you to get in today, lads?' The insults continued to be exchanged as I stretched out my hamstrings, until I finally stopped to take a good look at my new fan club. There were three fat northerners, all sitting next to each other in bright, fluorescent body warmers – yellow, green and red – with skin-tight jeans and cheap trainers. I couldn't believe it, I was getting hammered by the *Teletubbies* and called out, 'Blimey lads, that fashion will catch on . . . in about another 20 years.' They shut their gawping traps instantly, but when I stepped on to the pitch for a late run-out – subbing our sub, Iain – I had to burst out laughing, as someone in the crowd called out, 'Fuck me, they must be shit, they're bringing on the coach driver.' Credit where credit's due, it was a great line, which I told Webby after the game when he asked why I'd been chuckling. He smiled. 'I can top that, Roy. I was sitting next to the chairman's missus and when you came on, she tapped me on the shoulder and asked, "Who is that man? He looks like Omar Sharif. You never told me we had a Greek god on the team, David."'

My frosty relationship with Webby had thawed, and he put me back in the team to play centre-half for the promotion run in. He showed that he must have thought something of me after all by handing me the captain's armband for an April midweek trip to Burnley. I'd never been skipper before at a professional club, and I was bursting with pride when I led the team out at Turf Moor. It was just a shame that Burnley's Roger Eli decided to ruin my big night. I went to clear the ball up the line in the first half and Eli slid in to block, just like I had hundreds of times with defenders. But he tried to follow through and take me out. I knew the danger signs only too well, and read what was coming, steering my body out of his way and sending six studs to the floor, inches from his grounded head. I could have crushed his skull, but my only intention was to mark his card for the rest of the game. Eli rolled around on the floor like a wounded soldier, and despite pleading with referee Alan Wilkie to examine his face – which didn't have a scratch on it – my seventh red card in five years as a Shrimper was rubber-stamped. That's what a bad reputation does for you. I was so angry that he had fooled the referee into sending me off on such a proud occasion that I waited for him in the tunnel at half-time, and after the game, but a gang of security guards wouldn't let me anywhere near their changing room. He never turned up in the bar afterwards either, which was just as well for his sake as the fucking coward had cost me big time.

The rest of the players had battled on for a goalless draw at Turf Moor and they made sure Dave Webb knew I had been mugged off, but he still fined me a fortnight's wages. I kept my place at the back alongside Paul Clark – minus the armband – for a 2–0 win at Essex rivals Colchester, before waving goodbye to the season at the end of April in a 2–0 home defeat to promotion rivals Grimsby.

I was suspended for the last three games because of the Burnley fiasco and was forced to sit in the stands at London Road for another dose of final-day drama. Southend had to win at Mark Lawrenson's Peterborough to cement the last automatic promotion spot, a task made tougher by the fact that the Posh could still make the play-offs themselves by taking all three points. Fortunately for us, master poacher David Crown conjured up two goals to seal a 2–1 win and send us back to the Third Division, which was wildly greeted by 3,000 travelling crazies wearing Viking helmets, glittery wigs and rubber rings around their waists. But it was a horrible feeling for me. Despite doing my bit towards our promotion success – playing 33 times and scoring five goals – I felt completely empty as the players trooped over to the fans to thank them for their vocal efforts. I was delighted for the club – I'd headed, kicked and tackled every ball up in the stands – but I couldn't face walking on to the pitch and clapping the supporters as I hadn't played a single second of the biggest game of our season. I blotted out the cheering by disappearing into the bowels of London Road, waiting in silence for my celebrating team-mates to return to the changing room. After what had seemed an age, they eventually appeared, noisy and bare-chested after throwing their shirts into the crowd and wearing Southend scarves and hats which had been chucked back in the opposite direction.

They were all jumping up and down, spraying around the booze, and started throwing cans of beer at me – but I just sat there completely detached, which nobody noticed amid all the happy commotion.

Typically, the club had laid nothing on, no big promotion party. But despite being closer to my Colchester home than Southend, I still drove back to the seaside town and had a couple of beers with the other players, before slipping quietly out of a back door without saying goodbye. Now that wasn't me. But I just didn't feel part of it, at all.

19. OLD PALS' ATK

The Roots Hall culture was changing – signalling an end to the golden era of big characters and big drinkers. Manager Dave Webb made another couple of shrewd summer signings, picking up future England left-back Chris Powell on a free from Crystal Palace's reserves, before spending £100,000 on Stockport hitman Brett Angell. Both were squeaky-clean and in their early twenties – like an increasing number of the squad – and would earn Southend nearly £2 million in later moves to Derby and Everton, respectively.

Brett had replaced David Crown, who was the same age as me and had been shunted on to old foes Gillingham for £50,000. In Brett, Webby had a younger model, who could still guarantee 25-plus goals, and in the more experienced Ian Benjamin, who could play my targetman role and get a few goals, Brett had the perfect partner. In defence another local boy, Spencer Prior, was coming into his own, so there wasn't much chance of me getting a game there alongside Paul Clark. I was nearly 32 and had a year left on my contract, but the writing was finally on the wall for me at Southend after five years.

I had a much better relationship with Webby by now, and he saw my 1990/91 season role as focusing on bringing the kids through by turning out for the reserves, as well as sitting on the bench as an emergency utility player, who could do a job up top, or at the back. But I wasn't ready to pack in my career as long as I was fit and healthy. I still had the desire of a teenager to play the game and believed I had something to offer someone – and that person just happened to be my best pal from the Midlands, Ian Atkins, who was taking his first football management steps at my old club Colchester.

Living in the town, I still had a lot of connections with the club and in fact had helped Ackers get the job. Colchester wanted a young, hungry manager with all the coaching badges, and that was Ackers to a tee. I spoke to the club's physio, Charlie Simpson, whose advice was highly valued by the Layer Road directors, and he did the rest, landing my mate the gig. But it wasn't an easy first job, as Colchester had crashed out of the Football League. There was only one automatic promotion spot in the GM Vauxhall Conference, which meant you had to be better than the other 21 teams and win the championship to ensure promotion. Ackers's remit was to emulate Lincoln and Darlington who had bounced back to the Fourth Division at the first attempt in recent seasons.

He spent three months living at my house while he got his teeth into the job, but we never discussed the possibility of my Layer Road return. He needed me, though, the big centre-forward who could bulldoze Colchester back into the Football League. So he went out and gave grateful Southend back the £25,000 they'd spent on prancing peacock Mario Walsh.

Ackers's big problem was that the Colchester chairman, Jonathan Crisp, didn't want me and had even told him at his interview, 'Under no circumstances will you be bringing your big mate here – Roy McDonough, the drinker and shagger.' My reputation had put a dampener on things once again, and Ackers had to take it on the chin to get the job. But it was a bit harsh, as I had been trying to mend my reckless ways off the pitch. I'd already beaten Mum's six-month prediction. I was still married to Jackie and had played with a straight bat since walking down the aisle, palming girls on to other lads when I was out. I'd even curtailed the drinking, cosying up on the sofa to watch a film with 'her indoors' on a Thursday night instead of going to the pub.

Ackers cracked under the pressure and wanted to resign after his first game, a 2–0 defeat at Yeovil. I managed to talk him out of it, aided by my father-in-law, Gordon, who had a personal hotline to the club's directors. In the meantime, I was warming the bench for Southend, who had won eight of their first nine games to top the Third Division, and playing in the second string where I kept spotting Colchester scout Brian Owen in the empty stands. Colchester were still spluttering a little, clocking up a handful of wins, but drawing with those great football powers of Barrow, Fisher and Welling, as well as losing at Macclesfield. Ackers was increasingly desperate to get me involved and arranged a behind-closed-doors reserve-team friendly between Colchester and Southend at Essex University in the hope of convincing Layer Road's bigwigs that I was worth the gamble. I was struggling with a painful tooth abscess, my face was hanging off like the Elephant Man and I'd swallowed enough powerful painkillers to tranquilise a herd of his stampeding namesakes, but it was still child's play for me, even at about 70 per cent. I banged in a hat-trick in 35 minutes before walking off the pitch. I didn't have anything else to prove.

After the game I met Ackers and Jonathan Crisp – who warned his manager that his long-term friendship with me would be on the line by bringing me to the club – at the Red Lion, in Colchester, to discuss the deal. Ackers remained professional, sticking to the orange juices, even though I knew he could drink as much as me at a weekend. Despite the huge fears over my allegedly monstrous reputation, I matched the chairman, drinking four pints of Guinness over a two-hour period, while finalising a two-year deal. The money was a slight drop, £400 a week, but I pocketed £10,000 up front and, most importantly, I would be playing first-team football. And despite his initial reservations, the chairman grew to love me, branding me his 'Lionheart' for getting stuck in.

Another chairman who had always been great to me was Southend supremo Vic Jobson. He gave me a big hug and dragged me out to the centre circle to say goodbye before a League Cup match with First Division Crystal Palace at Roots Hall on a freezing October night. The fans gave me a standing ovation, including the fuckers on the far side who had always slagged me off and were probably clapping the fact I was leaving at last. It was a hard decision to leave Southend, as the club had rekindled my love for the game, but I was glad to be bowing out when they were in such great shape. As I scanned the stands one last time, it was amazing seeing all the supporters out of their chairs – people I had fought for over the years. It was a new, strange feeling, to actually be sad about leaving, but it also felt like I had finally left a mark somewhere.

At the turn of the century, Southend's fans voted me into their BBC Cult Heroes top three, behind Chris Powell and Brett Angell. It was a massive honour, but not to finish behind those two, or above the likes of Stan Collymore, it was because I came higher than such talented players from my era: Paul Clark, the Davids Crown and Martin, Glenn Pennyfather and Paul Sansome. Webby was also a different class with me in the end. He wanted me to stay, but knew I wanted to help out my pal, so he arranged an exchange deal with Colchester's young striker, Morrys Scott, who never played a game at Roots Hall. Southend were a top side that year, winning promotion to the second tier of English football for the first time in their history. At the end of the season, Jobson invited me back for the promotion dinner and handed me a commemorative decanter, which all the Southend lads received. Webby even piped up about me in his speech, telling people what a great influence I had been around the changing room over the years. It was the perfect ending to a fond batch of seaside memories that I will never forget.

To my eyes, the GM Vauxhall Conference was a Mickey Mouse league packed full of posties, washing machine repair men and all other manner of glorified pub players. Ninety-five per cent of the division was part-time, so as the professional outfit we were stronger both physically and mentally, and should have been bullying every team into submission with our superior fitness. We played good football, but Ian Atkins was over-cautious and kept playing a five-man defence, filling the sweeper role himself. Now, Ackers was a decent player in this position, but we didn't need to be so defensive against these non-league muppets. Every time we scored, he wanted to play deeper to protect our lead, when we should have been stepping up a gear and smashing them around town.

It was his first managerial job and he took it very seriously, even pulling me to one side to tell me to stop calling him 'Ackers' during games. He said, 'You must call me boss, or gaffer now.' I told him to go fuck himself. Ackers was also too deep when it came to thinking about the game, and would baffle the players with his complex pre-match instructions. When he left the room they would all look confused, so I would translate and put what we were supposed to be doing into basic language that the players could understand.

When I returned to Layer Road – which was still standing, just about – I weighed 14st, a stone overweight, so I spent my first two months coming off the bench against toilet teams like Sutton United and Kettering. But Ackers looked after me, joining me on extra runs after every training session to punish my body back into shape.

I finally got pencilled in for a Saturday start in December 1990 at Stafford Rangers. History repeated itself as, just as I had on my first full Colchester debut against Burnley nearly 10 years before, I marked the occasion with a goal – a beauty of an 18-yard header in a 2–0 win. Unfortunately, my 'friendly' reputation had followed me down the plughole into football's backwaters, too. Both the opposition players and referees were looking out for me, and I was given my latest set of marching orders. Stafford's Mick Tuohy landed me in hot water after taking a cheap shot, which was the first time I'd been attacked without a football anywhere in sight. He was obviously hoping to make a name for himself, just sprinting out of nowhere to dig his elbow into me and land a punch in my ribs. I might have been a terminally grey-haired striker, but I wasn't getting mugged on the pitch like a little old lady. So I booted the retreating Tuohy as hard as possible in the back of his calf and he hit the deck like a sniper had shot him. I had the raving hump after having the red card pushed under my nose, as I'd let Ackers down straight away, which I knew wouldn't go down well with the powers that be.

I met Dad and Gaz in the bar, ordering a pint, but not touching a drop, watching the door and waiting for Tuohy to make his entrance. He was playing with the big boys now and I let him know it when he came into the room, shouting and screaming at him and branding him an 'amateur cunt'. He didn't stick around for a beer, funnily enough. I'd only been back at Colchester two minutes, but I went to Layer Road on the Monday morning for a meeting with Ackers, convinced I was gone. When I entered his office, though, he was sitting giggling behind his manager's desk.

'You did him, didn't you?'

'Yep, but he asked for it', I replied.

'You know it can't happen again, Roy,' Ackers warned. And it never did . . . well, not that season anyway.

The goals kept flowing, another eight in total, but I don't know how much they count against the likes of Gateshead, Northwich Victoria and Slough. All I wanted was to haul Colchester back into the Fourth Division and start playing against proper teams again. Even visiting northern shitholes like Halifax, Hartlepool and Rochdale was a big step up from this utter crap. With a handful of games to go, Barry Fry's Barnet, with an 80-strong squad of players, and Altrincham, were our main rivals for the championship crown.

More than 7,000 fans squeezed into Layer Road for Altrincham's April visit, with the away side far happier with a 1–1 draw. I only lasted 12 minutes of the title six-pointer, but I was seeing a different shade of red this time. The ball bounced across me waist high and I managed to lash in a volley, despite their defender making a glancing block and clipping my ankle in the process, but the Altrincham goalkeeper saved. I thought nothing of it and carried on playing, but a few minutes later

I was waiting for a throw-in when I noticed a red tinge to the grass around my right boot. Blood was pumping out of my sock, so I hopped off the pitch and down the tunnel, spraying claret over the floor and walls. The physio, Charlie Simpson, must have had a strong stomach as he carefully removed my boot and sock in the treatment room. The ankle was cut so deep I could see the bone sticking out, so Charlie rang an ambulance to rush me to Colchester Hospital. I didn't want the indignity of being carried out on a stretcher, but Charlie made me, so I compromised by refusing to lie down, sitting up straight in the thing. I could almost hear the *Some Mothers Do 'Ave 'Em* theme tune in the back of the ambulance as it reversed too quickly, sending my prostrate body flying off the trolley to the floor, which was bloody painful. When I arrived at hospital, even more battered and bruised, a Chinese doctor said my ankle looked like a wartime 'shrapnel wound'. He gave me seven pain-killing injections before pulling the skin back together with tweezers, cleaning and closing it up with 12 stitches. I went back to the Layer Road bar on crutches and had a word with the Altrincham defender who explained that he'd christened a new pair of studs for the game. He didn't apologise, but didn't need to, and I had a few medicinal pints – before hobbling on to Valentino's nightclub to numb the pain further.

On the Sunday morning I woke up in a drunken daze completely forgetting about my injury and got out of bed by throwing my full body weight on to the ankle, which hurt so much it felt as if a double-decker bus had run over my foot. We had another game at Kidderminster the next day, and I was desperate to have more injections so that I could play, but Charlie ruled me out, believing any aggravation to the ankle could run the risk of me losing my right foot as there was a chance of gangrene setting in. With four games left my season was over.

Our final match was also against Kidderminster, which we won 2–0 at home. But we needed Barnet to lose at relegated Fisher to snatch the title by one point and win promotion. My old Southend team-mate, Paul Roberts, was playing for Fisher and rang me before the game to say he had turned down a bung to throw the match from Barnet's ticket tout chairman Stan Flashman. Robbo had been offered £10,000 for himself, plus another £10,000 to share around the other players. Fisher went a goal up, and Robbo celebrated in front of their dugout, labelling them 'corrupt fuckers', but Barnet went on to win 4–2 and we were condemned to another season in the Conference, which was a disaster. The fall-out was immediate. Ian Atkins refused to accept the runners-up trophy, which I respected as I also believed that second counted for nothing, and chairman Jonathan Crisp quit after wiping his nose for £1 million.

The new man at the helm was James Bowdidge, a City businessman who bought the club for £1 and wore even worse pinstriped suits than Sir Alf Ramsey had back in the Seventies. He wanted to 'give the club back to the fans' and would stand on the terraces alongside them. Ackers asked me to get more involved on the coaching side for our second attempt at getting Colchester back into the Football League, which seemed like common sense to me. We were a good team and had previously coached a Premier Division Sunday League side, Apex Asphalt, together in Solihull, with great success.

My brothers Gaz and Keith played in the team and I'd certainly demonstrated my passion for the management side of things during a cup quarter-final. Standing on the touchline during one game with a hangover, I was slaughtering the referee who wasn't giving striker Keith any protection from the opposition's heavy-handed centre-half. Keith lost his balance after one hefty challenge and the defender threw a fist then kicked him on the floor. I was straight on the pitch, running 80 yards to chuck a punch at the defender, but only half-hitting his chin and landing in the middle of a muddy mass of flying football boots as a 22-man brawl kicked off. It got quite tasty, with one lad needing stitches above his eye, and two noses got busted. The terrified referee ran to the safety of the changing room, blowing his whistle to abandon the game, with Ackers in hot pursuit, trying to smooth things over and save our club a huge fine. He said, 'Sorry, ref, he's a lad who comes from down south and watches us play sometimes.' The panting official replied: 'Bollocks, that's that fucking McDonough – he's a lunatic.'

I got more involved with the pre-season schedule, but only a few weeks in Ackers hit me with the bombshell that he was returning home to take up the first-team coaching role at Birmingham City. The club asked me to take charge for a pre-season game at Sudbury Town and I went to speak with influential physio Charlie Simpson, who had punted my name to the board for the manager's job. That put a whole new perspective on the meaningless warm-up match, which suddenly held massive consequences for my future. I rounded the boys up in the changing room before the game and said, 'Listen, I can do this job standing on my head. If you do things my way, I'll look after every one of you and we'll have the biggest beano of our lives.' I led by example, scoring a big header, as we beat Sudbury.

Two days later, I got summoned to the ground for an interview. Suited and booted, I sat next to Colchester coach Steve Foley, my only real competition for the post, waiting to be called into the boardroom. He asked me if I wanted the job, and when I said 'yes', he replied, 'Good, because I don't want it.'

I felt confident facing the chairman and directors – the club's most powerful men lined up in front of me like potential investors in *Dragons' Den*. They asked plenty of mundane questions about coaching and the youth team, as well as warning me about my drinking habits, as Colchester's manager couldn't be seen boozing around town. I agreed, of course, but bollocks to that, I went on the piss in Colchester every weekend once the season started. Before offering me the job, they wanted to know my masterplan for the new campaign. 'Simple,' I said. 'To win the league in style – by getting more goals than any other fucker.'

20. BRING ON THE CLOWN

The 'village idiot' or 'drunken clown' would be sacked by Christmas, they said. Half the town was having a massive laugh at my appointment, and that was all the motivation I needed to do the manager's job. We were a full-time professional outfit but didn't have a pot to piss in and I started the season with 14 senior pros and two snotty-nosed apprentices. But the biggest thing I had in my favour was that all the lads wanted to play for me, which they demonstrated by showering my car in champagne as I drove in after landing the job.

Our philosophy was to go for goals, and we played 4–3–3 most of the time, with two quicker, younger pairs of legs flanking the Big Roy battering ram and feeding off my tit-bits. My first action was to assure rock-solid defender Tony English that he was still the skipper. He'd led Colchester out of the Football League as captain and was desperate to make amends. With everybody fit, the team had a strong spine, starting with goalkeeper Scott Barrett, who was 'Mr Consistent' between the sticks. In midfield, there was my old Southend team-mate, Nicky Smith, a workhorse with an eye for goal, plus a couple of Irish rogues in Eamonn Collins and Mark Kinsella. Now 25, Eamonn had become the youngest player to appear in an English professional match when Alan Ball had handed him his Blackpool debut at just 14 years and 323 days. He was very comfortable on the ball, but I had to keep a close eye on him as he was a mischief magnet. Eamonn always had money troubles, and in one game I caught him trying to talk the linesman into having a bet on the outcome of the match. But that was Eamonn, who would gamble on two flies walking up a window. Kinsella, or 'Sheedy' as we christened him after the Irish Everton legend, was the proverbial old head on young shoulders. He was only 19, but was never intimidated by the rough stuff and played like a man, backing up the front three with bursting midfield runs. Mark won my full respect at that tender age, as he could match me pint for pint, and had also banged his landlady, 'Fishy Ann'. The nickname had nothing to do with her womanly cleanliness, it was because the old man was a fisherman, and as soon as he'd disappeared out the door with his rods it was Sheedy's tackle box that Ann wanted to open.

My strike partners were Gary Bennett and Steve McGavin, both in their early twenties, and too cute for the sluggish GM Vauxhall Conference defenders. I was particularly fond of Steve, who had everything in his locker that he needed to play at the top level. But he could be lazy and I branded him Michelin Man, as he slapped on an extra tyre very quickly if he didn't look after his engine. I did my best to keep him on track, betting him £50 that he couldn't score more goals than me that season, giving him an extra incentive to stay in shape. But four into three doesn't go and another of my first jobs was to ship out my old mate, Mario Walsh, to Redbridge for £10,000. The poor bloke must have been sick of the sight of me and I told him, 'I'll use you Mario, but we both know you can't do the job that I do up front.' 'I was top scorer last season with 17 goals,' he bleated. 'I'm not being sub for any fucker.'

Players claim to borrow a bit of something from each of their old managers when they land a first crack at the top job. Well, I'd played under my fair share, but most of them were useless. I wanted to be a driven, straight-talking winner, like Jim Smith – who was the best manager I served under – or have Dave Webb's keen eye for a bargain player. I also wanted the lads to love me, like I had Bobby Moore – so one out of the three was a start. When we reported back for pre-season, the most important thing was getting the training right. I had hated training as a player, mostly because it usually revolved around mundane exercises. But I believe football is a simple game with three basic principles: control the ball, look up and find a team-mate. Don't get me wrong, we did plenty of running for the first few weeks to get in tip-top shape, charging up and down the steep gradients of the Essex University ground's hills until our calf muscles were screaming. And there were plenty of cross-country outings, plus the infamous seven-mile Layer run, passing the ground and quite a few pubs, which was my favourite for wringing the booze out of the boys. But I wanted the everyday training to be enjoyable so that the players didn't switch off like I used to. I wanted us to play good football, so most of our exercises were based around building confidence with the ball; passing and keep-ball sessions, with the cones squeezed in tighter to narrow the pitch and intensify the skill level. I knew all the tricks in the book, so if I noticed players hiding, hovering on the fringes of training, I would change things in a flash to freshen it up. I wasn't going to plod on and bore everybody to death, but I would still crack the whip if I had to.

'We have to work together here, lads. If we don't, then we'll be running around the trees for the rest of the morning. You know I don't want to do that – because I fucking hate running.'

The idea that managers earned more than the players was a myth, but the board doubled my appearance and winning bonuses so I could bank an extra £200 on a good week. I didn't sleep for the first two months, surviving on cat naps, as my working hours changed drastically from just two hours a day as a player to as many as 50 hours a week as the boss. There was all the phone calls and the paperwork, most of which I fobbed off on the office girls, and the driving up and down the motorway to scout players in reserve games who I didn't have the money to sign. But the biggest difference is the mentality. As a player you are totally self-centred. But as the manager I had to consider everyone as I had a whole club to look after. Winning promotion wouldn't just safeguard the playing staff's future, but everybody else's at the club as well, right down to the tea lady. I'd thrived on pressure my whole career, though, and was up to the challenge – that's why I was the manager, centre-forward and penalty taker.

The new Conference campaign got off to a steady start with a 2–0 August win over Macclesfield at home, followed by a draw from the marathon trek to Barrow. Slough away was next and I provided a masterclass in three-yard finishes for a hat-trick before arrowing in a diving header for a fourth goal – equalling the club record for a player scoring the most goals in one match, completing the feat in just 37 first-half minutes. The centre-half volleyed me in the head as I scored the last goal in a 4–2 win, splitting the skin above my right eye. Blood started to pour out, but in the good old days you didn't have to get mopped up and change your shirt, you were allowed to carry on, and I came within a lick of post paint to notching a fifth goal. As I walked off with the match ball – which Slough charged me £40 to keep – Jackie was calling out from the crowd, 'Roy, Roy, are you alright?'

I couldn't believe it: 'Of course I am, luv. I've just scored four goals for fuck's sake.'

My head was still bleeding, so I shoved a big dollop of Vaseline on the cut to stop the claret leaking all over my suit. Then this stranger bowled into the changing room and asked, 'You ready, Roy?'

Miffed, I replied, 'Ready for what?'

'Sorry,' he said. 'I'm Slough's club doctor and I'm here to take you to hospital to get your head stitched.'

I burst out laughing: 'I don't think so, mate. The only place I'm going is to the bar for a drink.'

It was show time, and I bounced the match ball into the bar, so these part-time losers knew who was boss. I couldn't stand the non-league players – they were all cheats to me. Blokes who never had the bottle to play the game for a living, just turning out on a Saturday to buy their missus a new fridge or make the monthly credit payments on the car. How much did they really care about winning when it wasn't their livelihood at stake every time they went in for a tackle or header? They might as well have stayed in the Sunday park leagues. And we always demonstrated our contempt after an away win, camping ourselves at the bar and singing songs loudly to rub their noses in it. I'd tell the boys after the game, 'I've got £100 in my pocket and we're not getting back on the coach until we've drunk it.' It cost me a fortune that season in beers – at least £3,000 – but I'd promised to look after the players if they did right by me, which more often than not they did.

We sat proudly at the top of the table in September. I'd scored another couple of goals, but we'd also lost our first match, 3–2 at home to Farnborough. But one defeat in nine games – including 5–0 and 4–0 thrashings of Bath and Yeovil, respectively – wasn't too bad. As the month came to an end, we faced our toughest fixture of the entire season – Wycombe Wanderers away. They were the nearest thing to another professional outfit, with a similar-sized fan base to ours and a decent ground. But in financial terms they were vastly superior, splashing out £15,000 and £20,000 fees on players while we didn't have a dollar. I desperately needed another couple of bodies and was finally given the green light before the Wycombe match to get Southend's pint-sized midfield scrapper Jason Cook on loan. I also exhausted our entire transfer budget to sign my No.1 target, Paul Roberts, thanks to a little creative accountancy on my part. Robbo was still under contract at Fisher and had just been paid a £3,000 signing-on fee. I wanted him in my defence, as he was a great talker and would organise the back of the team, while I looked after the midfield and forwards. But Fisher wouldn't let him go for less than £2,000 – and we didn't have it. A few weeks after getting knocked back, I began nosing through the club's transfer records and discovered that Fisher still owed us £1,360 in wages from a loan spell that two of our boys, Steve Restarick and Mark Radford, had spent with them. I told them we'd wipe the debt if we could have Robbo for the difference – £640 – and he joined me for £200 a week, plus days off whenever he needed them to work towards learning 'the knowledge' as a black cabbie.

I didn't know much about Wycombe. I'd obviously heard of their manager, Martin O'Neill, a Northern Ireland international midfielder who'd won the European Cup at Nottingham Forest. It was pouring down with rain at Wycombe on the day of the big match, with a howling wind blasting around the rafters of the stands. They were a good side, but we were better footballers and played them off the park – if it had been a boxing match the game would have been stopped at half-time. Even then O'Neill was very direct, sticking to the only formation he knew, 4–4–2 and launch it – unable to adapt his team to find a solution when things were against them. Their talented wideman Steve Guppy equalised our midfielder Nicky Smith's opener and O'Neill never stopped jumping up and down for 90 minutes, like a cat on a hot tin roof, always moaning at the referee when decisions went against his side. He reminded me of the Kevin the Teenager character in *Harry Enfield and Chums*, the spoilt angry brat who was always so hard done by.

O'Neill had a dugout with about 85 backroom staff crammed into it. I looked at my bench and all I had was Ian Phillips, a part-time No.2 who still worked for the gas board but came and helped me out on match days. We may have been the professional club, but this was a battle of the haves and have-nots. As the clock ticked down, we were happy to settle for a 1–1 draw in the backyard of our biggest rivals. But our goalkeeper, Scott Barrett, had other ideas, as he finally forced O'Neill to sit down. We had the wind behind us for the second period and a couple of minutes into injury time Scotty launched a monster kick down the centre of the park. The ball bounced once, 30 yards from goal, then I went up with their centre-half and completely missed it, before it flew over the head of distraught Wycombe goalie Paul Hyde and into the top corner. The ground went deathly silent but my boys went ballistic, running over to our celebrating fans. I was too old to catch up, so I walked back to the centre circle knowing we were just a few seconds away from three of the most precious points won anywhere in the country on that blustery day.

Still ahead of the rest, we only lost once in the next 14 games, 2–1 at Redbridge, taking us up to the end of the year. Fulfilling my promise to the board, we were scoring goals for fun – breaking the 50 barrier in the league before 1992 began – and I was leading the way, netting eight more times in that run. The goals continued to rain down in the FA Cup as I was on target in a 5–0 win over Burton, setting up a home clash with my old club, Third Division Exeter. We'd flogged one of our boys, defender Scott Daniels, to the Devon club for £50,000, and I wanted to give him a warm welcome back. We won the toss and I told Paul Roberts to hit the ball on the angle as high as he could towards me and Scott straight away. Robbo carried out my instructions and I splattered Scott, cutting his head and lip, before trampling all over him on the floor. I picked him up and said: 'Scotty, how you doing, son?'

Exeter's player-coach midfielder Steve Williams didn't think much of our reunion and started spouting off. He was another flash fucker, born with a silver spoon in his mouth. Despite coming from money, he had been a top-class creative midfielder for Arsenal and played for England. But he was in my domain now and I left him in no doubts about that. He didn't last much longer anyway, getting dismissed for a reckless challenge, so I sent him on his way with a few fucks ringing in his ears, and he started ranting and raving at me once he had reached the safety of the touchline. We hit the bar and the post, but couldn't break the deadlock and ended up having to travel to Devon for a replay, which was the last thing we needed. I played at the back this time and it wasn't long before Williams started chipping away with the verbals to settle the score, before running past and spitting everywhere. But I held back – as much as I wanted to flatten him I was the manager now and had to take it. I had to be responsible and set an example to the rest of the lads. So I kept my cool and we battled through extra-time, with the match still goalless. Boos filled the air as I put the ball on the spot for the first kick in front of the

Exeter fans, before hitting the net and running over to blow them all kisses. But despite a brave effort, we lost 4–2 on penalties, going out of the FA Cup without conceding a goal. I'd held my nerve on the pitch, but it was a different set of rules in the bar afterwards, where I waited patiently for Williams. I held my pint in my left hand, as I always punched with my right, and was going to deck the fucker as soon as he stepped through the door. When he appeared, he had two burly minders either side of him and hid over the far side of the bar. There were a few 'unfinished business' stares exchanged, but I never got the chance to gain revenge.

December brought Wycombe to Layer Road for an eagerly anticipated rematch. Before the first game there had been no bad blood between the two sides. But things change quickly in football, and just two months after the first meeting the clubs hated each other – making it a big grudge match to this day, despite the teams being 100 miles apart. A reporter for Colchester's local paper, the *Evening Gazette*, was the main instigator of the feud. He was a Wycombe fan and faxed every story I did with the paper straight to Adams Park, where O'Neill would pour over every word of black ink. The Ulsterman initially got the hump after I told the newspaper that I believed Colchester was a more attractive destination for potential signings, as we were the 'professional club'. O'Neill took it the wrong way, thinking I was questioning his professionalism as a manager. But I couldn't care less about how upset he was, and as soon as I learned about the newspaper leak I fanned the flames as often as possible, questioning O'Neill's bottle, the quality of his players compared to ours and forecasting how we were going to batter them at Layer Road.

And the boys helped me keep my word, as we hammered them on home turf 3–0, with Gary Bennett and Steve McGavin, twice, smashing in the nails. The first goal was another stinker for their goalkeeper, Paul Hyde, who dived straight over Benno's 25-yard shot. I was following up and said to him, 'You haven't got any better, have you mate.' I've never seen a player melt so visibly. He was a bag of nerves and every time we pumped a free-kick or corner into their box, I was shouting, 'You ready Paul? I'm getting this one, I'm coming for you.'

O'Neill had brought his double-decker-bus-filling entourage, but he wasn't so animated this time. It was like someone had taken his batteries out. He was broken, just like his team, and I couldn't resist the temptation to rub salt into his gaping wounds. I was standing next to the Wycombe dugout when the ball went out for our throw with 15 minutes left. I fixed my stare straight into O'Neill's eyes and called out, 'Hey Robbo, tell the lads at the back no more goals. We'll play keep-ball for the rest of the game.' O'Neill's bottom lip hit the running track and a murderous look washed across his beady little eyes as he realised I was taking the piss. The fans didn't stop clapping as we finished the game playing 'olé' football, stringing together 30 passes at a time and increasing O'Neill's frustration with every cheer.

The humiliation increased a few weeks later on a foggy Monday night at Layer Road. We were drawn against Wycombe in the Bob Lord Trophy – which I called the Bacon Lettuce and Tomato Cup – a meaningless competition that I didn't give a shit about. With such a threadbare squad, the last thing we needed was to pick up unnecessary injuries or bookings against our main promotion rivals. But the Conference warned us that we faced a fine if I didn't field a first team. I obeyed the order, only bringing in two youngsters, including Andy Partner who played at the back with me. The team sheet was strong apart from those changes, but Wycombe soon discovered that I was taking the piss out of them again – turning the whole side, apart from the goalkeeper, back to front. It was just like an end of season Sunday League game, when all the players swap around positions for a bit of fun. I put the centre-halves behind a forward, and the full-backs and wingers traded positions as well. Before the game, I told the players, 'Don't make any tackles and don't say anything to the referee. Just go through the motions as best you can.' We got thumped 6–2, but I couldn't care less and underlined the fact by telling a reporter, 'It's a shame they didn't get 10.' I apologised to the Colchester fans through the newspaper, and our goalkeeper Scott Barrett took pity on eight freezing-cold Wycombe supporters, ordering them hot drinks from the coffee bar during the game and paying the bill. Despite having played a first team in my mind, we still got fined £500 by the Conference. But that was the best £500 we spent all season, as it got us out of that shit cup, saving our lightweight squad for the promotion race.

We were seven points clear at the top as 1992 zoomed into view but we hit a sticky patch, winning just three of our next seven games, including a 2–0 defeat at Merthyr and February's 4–1 walloping at Welling. Welling bruised and battered us, and it was their lads' turn to be singing all the songs in the changing room and bar after the game, giving us a taste of our own post-match medicine. But I was a bad loser and didn't like the bitter flavour. We didn't stick around long, and I left the bar to a chorus of ridicule from their players. But as I stepped into the car park, something clicked inside my head and I steamed back into the bar to confront the home team. 'See you fuckers. Enjoy your little sing-song, because next season we won't be in this piss-pot league, and you still will.' We had to win the Conference title now.

21. MAKE MINE A DOUBLE

The FA Trophy gave Colchester a chance to reach Wembley's famous twin towers. It was the non-league FA Cup and getting to that final would not only be a once-in-a-lifetime trip for most players, but the whole bloody town as well. Before we could even think about getting there a new category was pencilled in at the top of my football hit-list, right next to opposition defenders and referees – the board of directors.

I did manage to squeeze another two budget signings out of them, my old Southend room-mate Dave Martin and Northern Ireland striker Ian Stewart, who had played against Brazil and Spain at the 1986 World Cup in Mexico. Since I'd left Roots Hall, hardnut Dave had been banned from his local golf club after leaving three guys face down on the green around the 18th hole, when one of them had looked at him 'funny'. He was recovering from a serious knee injury and Southend boss Dave Webb did me a massive favour. He let my rock-hard centre-half buddy, who was a Second Division player all day long, do his rehab in the Conference for the rest of the season and helped with the wages. Ian was the other missing piece in the jigsaw, an ex-QPR forward who could put the ball on a sixpence with his left or right boot, which was tailor-made for my head. He had just left Aldershot and I met him at South Mimms services on the M25. I offered him £350 a week and said, 'Don't bother turning up for training, just keep fit and play the matches.' Job done.

Our Wembley dream almost died at the first hurdle. Kingstonian were our first FA Trophy opponents at Layer Road, in January, and we used up all of our cup luck in one hit. I was banned having collected too many yellow perils and was forced to sit on the bench in my previously unworn manager's jacket, watching us fall two goals behind. This competition was my only chance of treading the hallowed turf at Wembley, but the opportunity was slipping away and I was powerless to do anything about it. Their big bruisers were getting an easy ride against my replacement, Steve Restarick, who was a natural goalscorer but no demolition hammer capable of knocking the Kingstonian defence down, brick by bloody brick. Steve nipped in to pull one back and give us a lifeline, however, before Kingstonian continued to dominate, hitting the bar twice. With the game drifting away, we won a corner three minutes into second-half injury time – which our goalkeeper, Scott Barrett, fancied a bite at. Scott piled forward and steered a far-post header into the path of Tony English, who buried a last-gasp equaliser, despite being two yards offside. Just for once, I loved the referee and his linesmen for letting that one stand. Things are supposed to even themselves out in football – so this was my leveller for all the shit career decisions, crap clubs and bad luck I had endured – and I was eternally grateful.

We won the replay 3–2 at their place, before making a long trip to Wales for a 0–0 draw at Merthyr, who I dispatched from the penalty spot in the rematch. Morecambe were beaten 3–1 at home in February, with new boy Ian Stewart getting a couple, before Telford were torn apart 4–0 at Layer Road, setting up a two-legged semi-final against Macclesfield. Ian and Tony English steadied the nerves in front of 5,500 expectant fans, before I smashed a penalty into the top corner. We won 3–0 and six studs had sunk into the lush Wembley turf. The directors were already booking their seats in the Royal Box.

The night before the semi-final second leg at Macclesfield,

which could clinch the biggest date in the club's history, I had to sit through a brain-numbing Wembley merchandise meeting, to discuss tickets, programmes and T-shirts. The chairman and directors were all present, plus my father-in-law, Gordon, who was getting more involved in the club, and Peter Heard, a wealthy developer who had started putting a few quid in. It was like listening to the turn-off teacher warbling away in *Charlie Brown*, and I really didn't want to be there. By 11pm, I'd had enough, stood up and said, 'Excuse me gents, but I've got to get a team to Wembley tomorrow, so I need to go home and get some sleep.' The oblivious clowns all nodded their heads. 'But before I go,' I added. 'If we do get to Wembley, I don't want to see any of my lads buying their own drinks.' Looking after the players hadn't even occurred to them, but they shook the moths out of their wallets, handing over £250 in cash, which was better than nothing.

Macclesfield threw the kitchen sink at us, and it took a stunning 25-yard volley from Jason Cook to earn us a 1–1 draw on that Friday night to cement a Wembley place. The Macc Lads were putting it about, urged on by a hostile home crowd. I was only a couple more bookings away from a ban, so I took myself off with 20 minutes left, gifting the home fans a chance to spit their verbal venom in my face. Right in the middle of the angry mob, I spotted some familiar faces – Martin O'Neill and his Wycombe squad, who were playing at Altrincham the next day. They had been knocked out of the FA Trophy already, so it was nice that they got to see us reach Wembley.

A growing number of local louts were camping themselves around our dugout. The banter was swirling, then two haymakers came over the roof, just swinging past my head. I shouted to the copper next to me: 'Hey, pal, are you going to do something about this? I've got about 100 of your lot queuing up to slap me.' The bent fucker didn't say a word, so I pulled out the medical box and sat on it in the middle of the running track to avoid any more flying fists. As soon as the final whistle blew, I bolted for the tunnel like Billy Whizz, but my escape route was blocked by two policemen. They refused to budge, blatantly blocking me off in the hope that I'd get a clump from one of their fans. So I launched myself through the air shoulder-high, jumping past the idiots, which shocked the life out of them. It should have been the happiest few minutes of my life, but I went ballistic in our changing room after spotting just two lonely cans of Guinness on a table. I couldn't believe it – we'd just got to Wembley and there was no champagne on ice, not even a can of beer each. I told the lads, 'Go and drain the Macclesfield bar – I'll sort it.' Then I stormed off to dig out the chairman, James Bowdidge, who was all smiles when he saw the triumphant player-manager approaching. I soon wiped that look off his face: 'What the fuck is going on? My players have just got you to Wembley and they are buying their own drinks.'

'What about the £250, Roy?' he replied.

'That's for when we get back to the hotel, now sort it out!' I said. He hastily arranged a bar tab, but it wasn't good enough. He'd be lording it up at Wembley in a few weeks' time, but it was my boys who had lumps kicked out of them to give him that opportunity, and they deserved a reward.

We reached our hotel just outside Macclesfield before midnight. Dad and all my brothers met us there. Perry Groves had also come up on the supporters' coach, as he was out of the Arsenal side nursing busted ribs and had volunteered to be our mascot. I ordered 18 bottles of champagne – one for every member of the squad – and a pint of Stella for everyone there. When all the players, family and friends were gathered together, I made my address: 'We're at the bar together, we're going to Wembley together, and in the morning we're going to breakfast together. I fully expect everyone to have a pint in their hand still. And if you go to bed, don't bother coming down in the morning, or you'll get fined.' Speech over, I got two of the boys to hold my legs and I performed my party piece, downing a pint in seven seconds upside down. Just for once, my gobby old man was lost for words.

Nobody let me down that night and I was so proud of my boys – for getting us to Wembley and holding their booze. We drank right through the night, with everyone clutching a pint above their full English in the dining room at 9am. There were one or two green faces at the breakfast table, and a fully tanked up Grovesy had broken one of his ribs again jumping over the bar in the early hours. He was supposed to be at Arsenal for Saturday morning treatment, but had decided to stay on the celebration lash with us – which cost him a £2,000 club fine. There were more beers on the coach home and Dave Martin started a riot, tipping a pint of beer over my head, which led to a big bundle on the back seats as half the lads started play-fighting like school kids. I got dropped off at the Watford Gap services on the M1 for a rendezvous with Dad and my brothers. They weren't there when I arrived, so I collapsed in the car park flowerbed, which I blended in nicely with in the green Adidas shell-suit, with yellow stripes that I was wearing. I was woken by the ear-splitting car horn of Leicester striker Colin Gordon, who was en route to his Saturday match. 'What you doing, big fella?' he called out of the window.

Petals showered off my body as I rose slowly to say, 'We've just got to Wembley, mate. Been having a little party to celebrate.'

'Well done, pal,' he said, then drove off, leaving the dishevelled player-manager of a professional football team staring up at the clear blue sky from a flattened bed of daffodils. Oh, and the £250 donated by the directors? I stuck it in a pint glass behind the hotel bar – and it got nicked.

After the 4–1 Conference hammering at Welling, I knew I had to lift the players for the promotion run-in. We were 11 points clear of Wycombe at the summit. But despite our FA Trophy exploits our rivals had played four games fewer. I didn't want to run the players into the dirt, as I had hated that and knew it would push us apart, rather than pull us together. But there was no harm in letting them believe that was my plan. I was greeted by a chorus of groans when I told the players to pull on their running shoes and meet me at the Royal London sports ground in Colchester. When I turned up, they were stretching around the outside running track, fearing the worst. The looks on their faces were priceless when I bowled out of the sports hall, padded up, wearing gloves and holding a cricket bat. Maybe they thought I was going to bash them all. 'Right, pick two teams and get in the sports hall. We're playing two hours of indoor cricket,' I said. I'd already booked the hall, but they didn't know that, and it was a great session, ticking all the boxes for teamwork, fitness and, best of all, enjoyment. It gave the lads a new spring in their step by putting a big smile across their faces. It also allowed the resident master batsman – who had been courted by Warwickshire as a teenager – to blast them around the hall chasing the ball. They didn't have a prayer of getting me out, and in the end I had to retire with 200-plus runs under my belt.

We won three and drew one of our next four games, before entering a tight backlog of April fixtures to compensate for our FA Trophy run. We had four games in nine days and we played like champions, beating Slough 4–0, Telford 2–0 and Merthyr 2–0, all at Layer Road, with the cunning old silver fox of a boss sniffing out three goals, before bagging another couple in a 4–0 success at Boston. All that was left was another tough trip to Macclesfield, followed by home games against Kettering and Barrow – with Wycombe tugging hard at our shirt tails.

We stayed in the same hotel we'd used for the FA Trophy the night before we'd played Macclesfield. I always let the players have a pint when we checked in, and another one with dinner. My 33-year-old legs were dog-tired after playing so many games in such a short space of time and I needed to rest up, so I told Paul Roberts to get the boys another beer before packing them off to bed. The Macclesfield match was critical to our promotion hopes, and all the players needed to be in top gear. As I went up to my room at 9pm, Dave Martin passed me on the stairs, dressed in a black polo neck jumper like Basildon Bond. His club tracksuit had been discarded, but I was so knackered it failed to set off any alarm bells. I was out like a light as soon as my head hit the pillow, unaware of what was unfolding around the hotel. I didn't realise it was both

Eamonn Collins's and Robbo's birthdays that night, so they all stayed up on the sauce. And Davey had arranged to meet some horrible northern whale he had chatted up in the bar after the FA Trophy semi-final. His room-mate had to sleep on one of the other players' floors, while Davey harpooned Moby Dick's wife, whose mating wails were so loud she kept the rest of the lads up half the night.

I wasn't impressed when I heard about all the antics, as this game was pivotal to our season, which I had made crystal clear to the squad. We were 2–0 up after 15 minutes, but then I got a tap on the shoulder from one of Macclesfield's defenders. 'Oi! Put a £2,000 cheque in the post and I'll make sure you get the right result today,' he said.

I couldn't believe what I was hearing, and replied, 'Are you having a fucking laugh? Who the fuck do you think you're talking to?'

Now, I might have been a lot of things – aggressive, a drinker and a shagger – but I was never a cheat.

Just before half-time, Scott Barrett picked the worst day possible to have a stinker, flapping at a cross and letting them pull one back. We were 2–1 up at half-time but facing a strong wind after the break. It wasn't long before Scott threw one in, then blundered again to gift them a third goal and the lead. Then I got another dig in the ribs. 'Told you, pal. Get that cheque in the post and the result you need is yours.' I ignored the twat and buried a header from the edge of the box to equalise on the hour. Macclesfield scored a fourth time two minutes later but, thankfully, Tony English's second goal of the game stole us a 4–4 draw. Wycombe had pulled level with us on points, but we remained top thanks to our superior goal difference.

I was fuming about the players' behaviour the previous night and how we had made life so hard for ourselves. Dave Martin ran over to congratulate me at the end of the game, but I wasn't in a forgiving mood and said, 'Fuck off Dave, or I'm going to do you.' I was still seething about his hotel shagging antics. But the irony wasn't lost on me. It was the classic pre-match McDonough build-up, and in the past I would have taken my turn with Davey. But the boot was on the other foot now – I was the manager and there was too much at stake to fuck about. It really hit home just how self-ishly indulgent footballers can be. Not giving a fuck about the bigger picture on the pitch, if there was a whiff of pussy in the air. I destroyed the lads in the changing room, which wasn't my style, as ranting and raving at players had gone out with the Ark. But they had nearly thrown away nine months of hard graft for a hotel piss-up and I left them in no doubt about how upset I was.

There were two games to go, and maximum points would take us up. Part one, Kettering at home on a Tuesday night. Two goals for McDonough and Colchester won 3–1. Wycombe were playing at Redbridge two nights later, so we went down there mob-handed, knowing if they lost we were pretty much promoted. The whole Colchester team and chairman stood behind the goal alongside the Redbridge fans. It was a Thursday evening, with our last game of the season at home to Barrow on Saturday, but there was no harm in everybody having a couple of pints before the match in the clubhouse, and another one at half-time. The promotion race was going to the final day, as Wycombe ripped into a 3–0 interval lead. The chairman went home not long after, so I retired to the bar with Perry Groves and another pal of mine, Ipswich striker Steve Whitton. Three blondes had taken a keen interest outside and tagged along for a drink, and we were soon joined by the rest of my first team, as Wycombe went on to win 5–0. I got all the boys a couple of beers in, and when Martin O'Neill's team marched in wearing their immaculate blazers and club ties, buying soft drinks, they couldn't believe their eyes. Here was the Colchester manager, two days before the championship deciders, sitting with his team, two pals, three nice bits of skirt and a table with 40 empty pint glasses on it. I just nodded at O'Neill and thought, 'Fuck you. I've got strong lads here. They can handle a beer and still go out and win on Saturday.'

One of the Wycombe directors, Alan Parry, the TV football

commentator, was far too pleased with himself when he approached our table. 'Not all over yet is it, Roy?' he said.

I treated his smugness with the contempt it deserved: 'Alan, all our fans are coming to our game in fancy dress on Saturday. I tell you what I'll do for you. I'll make my lads play in fancy dress, just to give you a fucking chance.'

Everyone burst into laughter – people at the bar, the birds and the players. Alan had bowled over a confident 5ft 3in tall, but retreated defeated no more than 3ft 3in.

The players never let me down, and the fans got their promotion party as we trounced 10-man Barrow 5–0. I registered my 29th goal of the season – I'd finally found my level – far out-scoring any previous campaigns. But I missed out on the Conference's Golden Boot by one goal to Redbridge's Paul Cavell, which I might have claimed if I hadn't spent the last 30 minutes trying to chip the Barrow goalkeeper from long range at every opportunity. Our American striker, Mike Masters, blasted a hat-trick, and Nicky Smith got the other goal in front of an official 7,193 gate, although it was more like 10,000 as I couldn't see a square centimetre of standing room anywhere. Wycombe did their part, beating our FA Trophy Final opposition Witton Albion 4–0 to stay level on 94 points. But with a nine better goal difference than them, we were back in the Football League.

The fans flocked onto the pitch after the referee blew up, chairing the players high above their shoulders. I could already feel the taps of the waterworks turning and I evaded the grabbing arms of the supporters to clamber up the terrace steps to find Dad and my brothers. Then one of the most remarkable things in my life happened, right there in the middle of that shitty old ground. I threw my arms around Dad and gave him a big hug, which he returned, gripping me tightly. It was the first time in my life that I can ever remember us embracing properly – a real father and son moment, at last. I'd been playing to impress the old man my whole career. I had always been terrified of letting him down and equally afraid of showing him any affection. But we held each other at the back of the stand as if it was the most natural thing in the world, with pandemonium reigning everywhere around us. The big, tough centre-forward – who was all Dad's creation – holding his old man with tears in his eyes. I loved the old bugger so much, although I still didn't have the courage to tell him. But a hug would do for now.

After the game, we headed to The Lamb, my favourite Colchester drinking haunt. The fans always sang a song about me, 'You'll Always See Him in The Lamb on a Saturday Night', which the players had blurted out a few times on the coach, too, and I wasn't going to miss my cue. I must have beaten the drinking record that night – touching 30 pints – as an entire town wearing blue-and-white wanted to buy me a drink. I had been fairly disciplined with my drinking during the week, since I had a 'proper' job as the manager, but I still always rewarded myself by getting smashed around town on a Saturday – leaving one session so far into the early hours that a market stall had been built around my club-sponsored BMW. That night I took it to the extreme, surrendering any promotion party memories to a drunken blur.

Colchester's hierarchy wanted us to travel down to Wembley on the day of the FA Trophy Final in a convoy with the fans – but I wasn't having that. We were doing this the proper way, so I booked us into the Wembley Hilton the night before the big game. Our party was 26-strong – which I made sure included the groundsman and coach driver – and when we arrived I was knackered.

It had been a hectic week leading up to the Sunday showpiece, during which time I had arranged sponsored suits for the big day, and managed to get *The Sun* to cough up £10,000 for having its name plastered on the front of our shirts. You couldn't sneeze at Wembley if you didn't have the right pass, so I ensured all the players and their wives were sorted, as well as booking flights for our American striker Mike Masters's father to jet in from the States. I couldn't wait to crash out at the hotel, but when we turned up at 1.30pm our rooms weren't ready. It was

FA Cup Final day and a few familiar faces were milling around a packed bar, like pop star Rod Stewart and footballers John Hartson and Mick Harford. We were shepherded off to our own private 'lounge' while our rooms were prepared. But there was no furniture, only a TV set, so we had to sit on the floor like primary school kids and watch Liverpool beat Sunderland 2–0. Once the rooms were ready, we had a couple of beers and I went to bed early, sharing with my No.2 Ian Phillips.

All the boys were on their best behaviour and after breakfast we boarded the team bus – next stop Wembley Stadium. As those iconic twin towers zoomed into view we could see our fans' coaches parked up with flags filling the back windows, reading, 'Big Fella's Blue and White Army.' Another had a cartoon of me with a razor-sharp Freddy Krueger-style hand, with the message, 'Nightmare on Witton Street.' Our fans filled the road leading to Wembley – many of them wearing T-shirts displaying a patchy team photo, crudely printed from the programme, which Paul Roberts and his mates had knocked out to make a few grand. They cheered us into the ground before the coach was swallowed whole by the two big wooden doors that led straight into the famous old stadium. And then it all went quiet.

I took Dad, brother Jim and nephew Leigh on to the pitch, which was magnificent but not as big as I thought it would be from seeing it on TV. In fact, it had the same dimensions as Layer Road. As I watched our fans taking their seats, it occurred to me that it wasn't the Wembley pitch which saps the strength from your leg muscles, but the nervous energy and anticipation reverberating around the ground. My main concern was the players and making sure they weren't worried.

I inspected my troops, who were pulling on their kits and lacing up their boots, and who had rarely let me down in the muddy Conference trenches all season. I wanted them to enjoy the day, but we were here to beat Witton Albion – nobody goes to Wembley to lose.

'Player for player, we are better than them. Just get out there and do what you've done all season – pass them to death and we'll win the game,' I said. I also ordered them to jog off the pitch at half-time, to show Witton we weren't tired, that we were fitter than them. Dave Martin and Paul Roberts took out some insurance, pinning a couple of the Witton lads up against the wall and threatening to 'sort them out', as we lined up side-by-side ready to leave the tunnel.

I didn't usually get nervous, but the roar of the crowd and the flash of the cameras hit me like a ton of bricks as I strode onto the pitch. I waved at my family to the left of the Royal Box – 39 of the McDonough clan had made the pilgrimage, and I'd paid for half of the tickets myself. There were 32,254 fans inside the ground and most of them were ours, filling the rafters of the high stands with their favourite chant, 'Big Roy's Blue and White Army.'

I felt sick to the stomach during the warm-up, a mental and physical wreck as the pressure of the season caught up with me. And, like an idiot, I told Ian Phillips to keep an eye on me. We couldn't have made a better start. Mike Masters became the first Yank ever to score at Wembley after I stood on the full-back's toes so he couldn't jump and flicked on Robbo's throw. Nicky Smith put us two up inside 20 minutes.

But it was a non-stop battle as Witton's masterplan was to play on my reputation and get me sent off as soon as possible, which their boss, Peter O'Brien, even admitted after the game. I was spitting on their players' boots, giving them a dig and shouting in their ears, 'How are you going to wind me up, you useless part-time northern fuckers?' That played right into our hands, as they were too preoccupied with fighting me, which allowed Steve McGavin to run riot. Our biggest adversary was the referee, Kieran Barrett. The Witton captain, Stewart Anderson, had already taken his armband off, expecting to see red, after topping our defender Warren Donald so badly that he ripped through his sock. But Barrett didn't even book him. Then their centre-half, Steve McNellis, punched me right in the mush straight in front of him soon afterwards, so I asked, 'Ref are you going to liven up here? You need to get a grip, otherwise there's going to be a massive fight and we'll clear these cunts out, which isn't going to look snappy on TV.' No response. Then Witton's Jim Connor booted me in the ribs, so I lifted my shirt to show Barrett the red marks and at long last he took some action – he booked me for dissent.

The game should have been done and dusted straight after the break, but Mark Kinsella toe-poked wide when he should have rolled the ball to me for an easy finish, but I just patted him on the head and called him a 'greedy little fucker'. Witton pulled a goal back against the run of play when Mike Lutkevitch flicked in a header, and then we had Jason Cook sent off for swinging his handbag too hard. By this time, I was on the bench. Despite feeling strong, Ian Phillips had subbed me 20 minutes into the second half and I was gutted. But I had given him the power to make the big decisions, and I wasn't going to give him a hard time. We were still in control and Steve McGavin clinched a 3–1 victory with a final goal – his 28th of the season, which meant he owed me £50 – and I became only the second player-manager ever to win a league championship and Wembley final 'Double' after Liverpool's Kenny Dalglish.

As we climbed the Wembley steps for Tony English to lift the FA Trophy, I shook hands with Dad, Jim and Southend chairman Vic Jobson, who was my special guest. We did a lap of honour for the supporters, with two female fans passing me their phone numbers, before I chatted to Mum and Dad on the halfway line, looking like one of the Super Mario Brothers in a baseball cap thrown to me from the crowd. As I walked to the tunnel, 25,000 Colchester fans applauded me and I waved the cap, before breaking into a jog, when I should have crawled like a snail and soaked up the whole experience as long as possible.

A champagne bar had been wheeled into the dressing room, with a little bloke serving drinks, so I told the players to drain the fucking thing before we all stripped off naked and jumped in the big Wembley bath with the FA Trophy. Dad, my sister Lisa and brother-in-law Steve had somehow managed to blag their way into the dressing room, and the old man stood there with a glazed look in his eyes. I got dressed and gave a few words to the *Evening Gazette's* Francis Ponder. He told me that he'd been speaking to my old fella, who had already shown how much being at Wembley meant to him by wearing a tie I had won for taking nine wickets in a Midlands cricket competition as a youngster. He confided in the reporter that this had been the 'proudest day of his life'– which meant more to me than winning any Double. The trophies did have their uses, though, as I carted them round every pub in Colchester for three weeks that summer so the fans could have their pictures taken with them and buy me a pint.

My biggest regret about that day was not returning to Colchester for a party with the players' families and friends. We were forced to spend the evening at the London Hilton, in Park Lane for a stuffy £25,000 dinner paid for by the club's new sugar daddy, Peter Heard. It was strictly Colchester United club officials and players only and none of us wanted to be there. We had to endure a juggler who kept throwing his balls against the low ceiling before cancelling his fire act because of the same problem. Then we suffered a boring band, who were just like the Tremeloes. The club officials should have let us celebrate in our own way after earning them the best part of £500,000 that day. But they did reward us financially for winning the Double, with each player pocketing an £8,000 bonus, although it didn't stop the bean-counting tightwads deducting the Wembley bar bill from our wages.

Martin O'Neill had been Sky Sports's studio guest for the final and couldn't resist a jealous pot-shot, trying to make out that it was a close game by naming our goalkeeper, Scott Barrett, as Man of the Match. The next time I saw O'Neill was at the Conference awards ceremony, held at the Grand Hotel in Brighton. I'd tripped up drunk walking down the stairs with the FA Trophy and the lid had fallen off, rolling around the corner and landing at the feet of O'Neill and his wife. He thought I was taking the piss when I politely asked if he could pick it up for me.

Steve McGavin was crowned Player of the Year and I was

named Manager of the Year which, combined with the highest goalscoring club prize, landed me a £1,500 cheque which helped pay our Wembley hotel bill. There was a trophy table separating the Colchester and Wycombe parties, with O'Neill typically having three times as many guests as everyone else, and we made sure we smashed our gongs down nice and loudly to make a point. All poor old Wycombe had to show for their season was the Bob Lord Trophy, sitting between their salt and pepper pots, and Steve told them, 'You're welcome to that little fucker.'

The club arranged an open-top bus tour of honour around Colchester the week after our triumphant Wembley trip, and we were pissed out of our heads as we waved both trophies around to 15,000 fans who were filling the streets, hanging off lamp-posts and poking their heads through flat windows above shops. The bus slowly made its way to a civic reception at the town hall and I swayed on to the balloon-covered balcony with all the players to address the fans. I thanked them for their support as they really had been magnificent, following us up and down the country and taking over most grounds.

As I looked across that sea of blue and white, I thought, 'The drunken clown didn't do too badly, did he?' The 1991/92 season had seen me lead the club to promotion and a first Wembley appearance as well as smashing several records, including the highest points total in the Conference (94). Colchester's 19 home wins was a club record, as were the 29 league and cup clean sheets and the 123-goal total in all competitions. And we had done it the right way, by playing football, not just lumping it forwards for 90 minutes. I'd even managed to go a whole season without getting sent off. But I was soon putting my foot in it again, announcing to the fans, 'We haven't just won the Double – it's a Treble.' Jackie was pregnant.

22. CRUSHED BY A HEARD

Playing at a tip like Layer Road might have been acceptable in the GM Vauxhall Conference, but it didn't meet the strict safety standards of the Football League so our 1992/93 arrival in the newly named Third Division – thanks to the inaugural season of the Premier League – had the fans rallying around to fund £100,000 worth of ground improvements. The supporters were brilliant, getting sore blisters on sponsored walks and shivering naked in baths of cold baked beans to help pay for the cement mixers and brickies to carry out basic upgrades.

Eight weeks into the summer break, just before a fundraising golf day, I got a phone call from the hospital. I answered it to hear Jackie sobbing away on the other end – she'd had a miscarriage. I burst into tears too. I was distraught, as I had wanted to become a father so much, and told my wife that I would be straight by her side. But Jackie told me to go to the golf day as the team needed me. She was with her mother and said she was OK, which I found very odd and I didn't know how to react. But as the months passed, my attitude changed. It sounds very harsh, but losing the baby might have been a blessing in disguise, as the way we both conducted our lives wasn't the proper environment to bring up a child in.

It was all change at Colchester that summer. I decided to make a fresh-faced start to life back in the Football League, shaving off the moustache which had been the trademark of my so-called hardman image for nearly 20 years. I also booked into the hospital for some repairs, and had 13 pieces of floating bone removed from my right ankle. It was all change at the top too, as James Bowdidge quit while he was ahead and was replaced as chairman by my father-in-law, Gordon Parker. He wasn't the true face of power at the club, just a caretaker for the publicity-shy millionaire Peter Heard, who was signing the cheques and pulling the strings.

Unfortunately, however, he wasn't prepared to pull his pen out to keep our promotion-winning squad together – which had a great chance of at least making the play-offs. Meagre pay rises were refused for goalkeeper Scott Barrett, defender Shaun Elliott and midfield maverick Eamonn Collins, so they left for pastures new, with no sign of replacements on the horizon. A fit-again Dave Martin returned to Southend, weakening us even further.

Then Pinky and Perky rolled back into town – sunburnt and overweight strikers Gary Bennett and Steve McGavin. Both lads were too good for this level, and I'd told them to come back for pre-season fit as fleas and in return I would get them big-money moves to better clubs before Christmas. But Gary had piled on a stone enjoying his holiday, while Steve had fallen off a wall in Corfu pissed and hobbled back into the ground on crutches with torn ankle ligaments. So my main job that summer was getting them back in shape, especially Steve, who I ran with around the fields and hills after we had finished morning training. But he pissed me off, as I was nearly 34 by then – 11 years his senior – and he couldn't keep up, constantly moaning about the pain. But with that type of injury you have to run through the agony, to break down the scar tissue and get the blood flowing again. One afternoon, Steve was a lap behind me, so I abandoned him and drove off, forcing him to walk six miles back to the ground on his own. We fell out about it for a while, but I wasn't punishing him. All I was trying to do was make his mind and body stronger, to get him a decent move to a bigger and better club.

Against all the odds, we got the new season off to a winning start at Layer Road, beating Lincoln's long-ball giants 2–1, and I chipped a goal from 18 yards. But things soon turned sour as we lost four on the spin, including a 2–0 home defeat to Shrewsbury, which proved old habits – and reputations – die hard. Visiting centre-half Mark Williams was torturing my ears, giving it the old big-man routine. So I gave him the benefit of my vast experience by telling him to go and find a new hairdresser. He had bright yellow highlighted streaks running through his hair and looked like a tart. How was anybody supposed to take this big woman seriously? But I swear that I clumped him by accident to get back on the red-card trail. I was backing in to Williams, waiting for a goal-kick from our new goalkeeper, Paul Newell, to arrive, and thought he was behind my left shoulder. Williams wasn't there, so I pushed my right arm back to feel for him just as he came charging in behind me and headbutted my elbow, making a right mess of his gob. I protested my innocence to both referee and bloody-faced player, but they weren't buying it. I was off after 15 minutes, which didn't go down well with the father-in-law and his controller.

God knows how many stitches they put in Williams's mouth, but I couldn't hold back a chuckle in the bar after the game. He was trying to get his swollen mouth around a pint glass and slobbering half the beer down the front of his shirt.

I scored again in a defeat at Bury, before signing off for a three-game ban by blasting a penalty past Walsall goalkeeper, Mark Gayle, in a 3–1 win, putting some daylight between us and an instant return to the Conference. But this sentence started early, thanks to my popular standing with Walsall's fans – some 15 years after fingering them at Fellows Park. I was standing by the near post when one of their fat ginger fans started calling me a 'wanker', so I turned round and said, 'Yeah mate, fucking murder playing at Wembley last season', knowing full well they'd never graced the stadium. In the changing room after the game there was a knock at the door and a policeman came in. 'Mr McDonough, we've had complaints from the away fans that you have been swearing at them, and I need you to come to the station with me.'

All the players, with their towels hanging round their waists, were gobsmacked, and I replied, 'Give me some credit, mate, I've been playing this game 20 years and you'd expect me to come up with something better than that.'

But the copper was adamant: 'If you don't come of your own free will, we will have to arrest you.'

I could see he was itching to pull the handcuffs out and I replied, 'Are you serious? You must be some sort of jobsworth, pal.'

So I ended up having a mugshot picture taken with a criminal serial number running under my chin at Colchester police station, before my fingerprints were inked and recorded. Then I was shut in a cell for the first time in my life, still wearing my muddy football kit for over an hour while they 'processed' me. A lot of the defenders I played against probably think they should have locked me up and thrown away the key years before. The whole episode was scandalous, and the Crown Prosecution Service kicked it out straight away.

The relegation fears eased off, as we were 12th by Christmas and I'd managed another four goals in wins over Halifax, Crewe and Torquay, plus a draw with Rochdale. My lightweight team was punching above its weight and the club's directors had taken over from brutish centre-halves as my biggest opponents. Every few weeks I was ordered to attend a four-hour brain-drain board meeting. It was the last place I wanted to be as my office was on the training ground, trying to improve the few players we still had.

These meetings were like chimpanzees' tea parties, where the faceless power behind the throne, Peter Heard, would tell a joke and all the spineless directors would turn on the canned laughter. It was embarrassing – not my cup of tea at all. Heard decided that he wanted me to write things down for the meetings, a weekly report on what I was doing at the club. So I obliged, jotting down '£25,000' in black felt tip and handing it to every director on a white sheet of A4 paper. They looked confused, so I explained, 'That is how much it has cost me to bring in five different goalkeepers this season – which is more than we needed to spend to keep Scott Barrett here.'

We never had a concrete No.1 all season and I had to borrow Paul Newell from Leyton Orient, as well as loaning Carl Emberson and Fred Barber, from Millwall and Peterborough, respectively. I also used one of the kids, Nathan Munson, who couldn't kick the ball further than the penalty spot, and looked up my old Walsall drinking pal Ron Green, who we paid a £150-a-week pittance.

Ron was 36 by then and got destroyed by the fans after throwing in a couple at home to Rochdale. I'd missed a penalty and was also getting the rough stick off my own fans, in particular five blokes at the back of the stand who were obviously getting bashed up at home by her indoors and came down to Layer Road to take it out on me and the players. We were 4–3 down with 10 minutes to go, when I turned in a tight spot and dinked an equaliser over the goalkeeper, jumping up on the concrete wall of the stand like a crazy man and digging out the hecklers. I was balancing on my studs and could have broken my neck, but was in such a rage as I pointed at the fans, shouting, 'See you, you no-good fuckers, I'll see you all at the back of the stand in 10 minutes.'

The only way they could leave the ground was via the back of the dressing rooms, so I ran off the pitch at the end, throwing off my boots, so I didn't slip over fighting. But the shithouses had scarpered early, not men enough to square up to my face. In the bar afterwards, Peter Heard asked me what had happened. 'Oh that, it was nothing. I was just celebrating the goal with a few of my mates in the crowd,' I lied. But poor old Ron was finished. He was staying at my house and I had to get us both pissed before I could muster the courage to sack him after just four games.

Directors don't understand the mechanics of football. They couldn't see how vital it was to have a capable goalkeeper on the books, training every day of the week and building an understanding with his back four. We rarely got to work on defending set-pieces as a group, as we couldn't afford to pay our loan goalie's travel expenses to drive up from his parent club. They were just thrown in on match days, which was an utter shambles. The board wouldn't sanction any money to sign players, when my aim was to make the play-offs and bring some more cash into the empty coffers, like I had the previous year. I was praying that I would turn up at one of these tedious meetings to find our wealthy benefactors donating £5,000 each into the transfer pot to bring in fresh blood. But I was living in dreamland and had to beg, borrow and live off favours to get cut-price bodies into the club. Centre-half Peter Cawley was playing non-league down the road for Heybridge Swifts for £80 a game, so I poached him. I also hailed a part-time cab driver from Southend, Adam Locke, who was a bit of a space cadet but had a great first touch and could play anywhere, giving me more options. But the old detractors soon started crawling out of the woodwork again. Everyone from the directors' parasitic hangers-on to the burger bar woman had an opinion – 'the drunk was building a mates club'. But they didn't have a clue what was going on behind the scenes. What was I supposed to do without a penny in my pocket for new players?

We retained the team spirit that had won us the Conference Double, remaining in mid-table, within spitting distance of the play-offs. I also made sure we still had plenty of the other spirit, too, which helped long coach trips home from the darkest pits of Darlington and Doncaster pass easier. Playing a few porn videos on the coach TV also helped to gobble up the motorway miles quicker. Although, the X-rated action glowing through our bus window would get a few stunned glances from passing truck drivers and other coaches packed full of grannies on their way back from a day out in York. All the nutters got bollocksed at the back of the team bus with me, while the sensible ones, 'the Trainspotters', sat quietly up the front. On one trip home, our boisterous behaviour was pierced by a loud pop, and one of the lads shouted out, 'What the bloody hell is that, gaffer?' I tottered down to the front and four of the boys – Warren Donald, Tony English, Mark Kinsella and Nicky

Smith – were sitting there with a bottle of red wine and a cheese and biscuits selection box.

Straight or crazy, I could never knock any of those lads who stood by me all season. To prove that point – and a team being the mirror image of its manager – we clocked up three red cards and 70 bookings that year. We got fined £10,000 by the FA for our pandemic disciplinary problems and I was hauled over the coals by the directors who wanted to introduce a spot £100 fine for any player picking up a yellow card, which I refused to back. What they didn't understand was that the mountain of bookings was a reflection of just how much the players cared for a club running on empty. We may have been a bunch of reprobates but we fought for our lives in every game, which is a lot harder than sitting behind a desk glued to a calculator. Tony Sorrell got one of our three red cards that season and I added a second of the campaign – my 13th in professional football – at Rochdale in March, complementing eight yellow cards.

I'd got two more goals in the three previous matches against Cardiff and Hereford, and we still had a chance of stealing into the play-offs. Scrawny kid Paul Abrahams was playing up front with me. A product of the youth team, he was 5ft 8in tall and nowhere near strong enough to handle the crude punishment dished out by Rochdale's defenders.

I was trying to protect him as best I could, taking whacks to the face and body in the process. But we were well in the game and I'd sent two far-post headers back across the face of goal for Nicky Smith and Paul to grab goals and keep us at 2–2 going into the break.

When we reached the changing room our goalkeeper, Fred Barber, revealed that he knew one of their boys, who had been ordered to target me by Rochdale No.2 Mick Docherty, as I was good value for an early bath. That old chestnut again. I'd literally taken all their first-half assaults on the chin but they started pressing the 'taking liberties' button too hard after the break. Alex Jones was the biggest culprit and I could never resist a window of opportunity. I really should have learnt from past mistakes by then but, believing the officials were distracted by another lad crashing to the floor further down the pitch, I gave him a short, sharp jab with my elbow. Jones hit the Spotland canvas like he'd been KO'd by Mike Tyson and we had another linesman miles away with binoculars who started waving that annoying flag above his head. As I left the field contemplating yet another dismissal, their coach Docherty was giving it large, pleased that his plan had paid off and feeling safe behind the white line. I stopped a few yards from him, sniffed hard and fired a snotty green lump of flob at his feet, sending the message: 'I'd fight you for tuppence, you arsehole – but you aint worth it.'

We lost 5–2, and I listened to the home fans cheering each goal hitting the net, as I sat dejected, all alone on a cold wooden bench in the dressing room. I still hadn't calmed down in the bar, and chairman Gordon tried to approach me but I just shook my head – I really wasn't in the talking mood.

On Monday morning I got a letter with all the directors' names on it, signed by Peter Heard, warning me that I would be sacked as manager if I got sent off again. What was I supposed to do now? I couldn't afford to lose my job, as I didn't have thousands squirreled away in the bank, but I couldn't have the board controlling me either. Heard even suggested that I should retire from playing but he didn't realise that, even at 34, there was still nobody else who could go out there and fight for the team like I did – attacking and defending set-pieces. I even finished the season as our joint-top league goalscorer with Steve McGavin on nine goals. But the board wanted me to sign a younger replacement. Someone who could do the same job in the air, but was quick and could score with both feet. They wanted me to bring in that mythical player for shirt buttons and I told them they had missed their chance, as Stan Collymore had just left Southend for Nottingham Forest – for £4 million.

When my ban had ended, Gordon would ring me before every game, asking if I had named myself in the squad. I replied, 'Why? If I do, is Heard going to sack me?' All he would say is that 'he wouldn't advise it'. The lads still had an outside chance of nicking a play-off spot, even if I had to be quarantined to the bench. My brave shoestring warriors were still in contention in April, but a desperate gung-ho attempt to make the promotion shake-up ended in a 7–1 thumping at Crewe. I was gutted, but you can only paper over the cracks for so long before a gaping chasm appears. I couldn't accept sending us into games weaker by completely excluding myself anymore, but I worked my way back into the team gently from the bench and we bounced back with a 1–0 home win over Scunthorpe. I dusted myself down for battle again, clambering off my seat to try and make an impact in our penultimate game at Darlington, but we got beaten by John Reed's first-half goal and any faint hopes of promotion were finally extinguished.

Realising our season was over, young striker Paul Abrahams cried his eyes out in the changing room and his shattered teammates were all wearing glum expressions. I did my best to lift them. 'I've been fighting the directors for months, but we've still come so close to achieving what we could have done without their help. Thank you so much for all your efforts – you've been magnificent this season.'

Gordon heard every word and had the front to come and sit down next to me, saying, 'Never mind, Roy. It wasn't meant to be.' That was the worst thing he could have said, and I called him every name under the sun in front of the whole squad. He was gone in 60 seconds and I'd made my mind up. If they didn't fire me over the summer, it would be a new season, with a new stance. I'd had zilch support from the board all year, when we were just two players short of making the play-offs. It was criminal, as it would have been another good payday for the club, with another chance of getting to Wembley. The fact that we finished in 10th place, just four points short of Bury, who took the last play-off spot, was a tremendous achievement, but still left a bitter taste. But things were going to change. I wasn't dealing with the puppet Gordon the Gopher any more, I was going straight to the hand that controlled it – Mr Money, Peter Heard.

23. BY GORD! IT'S OVER

We had a new jailbird kit for the 1993/94 Third Division season – blue with white arrows – which most people thought was a great fit for me. But I didn't get sent off all season, and disciplinary problems were the least of my worries.

I was still struggling to shop in football's answer to Oxfam, and was also told to ship out a few players to balance the books. I had to start playing myself again – I had no other choice, as we didn't have enough bodies. I made sure I was ready for another bruising nine-month slog as a targetman, undergoing surgery on my left ankle during the summer to remove a painful piece of rogue bone growing from my shin, which was as big as a thumbnail.

We made a solid start, winning two of the first three games, and our 3–2 home win over Northampton brought about a first for me – I let somebody else take a penalty. I put the ball on the spot and Paul Roberts shouted out, 'Let Martin Grainger have it.' It turned out that most of the boys had backed him at 19–1 to score our first goal, so I begrudgingly handed it over, threatening to kick him out of the club if he missed. But thankfully he didn't and the players were quids in at the bookies.

Left-back Martin was another product of the youth system, who also had a great chance of playing higher but could lose concentration, pile on a few extra pounds and thought he was a gangster. He was one of those players who was always knocking on the manager's door, demanding to know why he wasn't playing, and we had a big half-time changing room bust-up after I had slaughtered him for a poor 45 minutes. He got up and started walking towards me as if he was going to thump me. I warned him, 'Think very carefully about what you do next, son, because if you come another step forward I'm going to throw you out the window – now sit down you fat fucker.' And he did. But remember, I'm a nice guy.

My first goal of the season was against Fulham, in a League Cup exit. But my next strike, in September, came in a 5–2 home defeat against Rochdale and I was booed off the pitch for the first time. Eighteen months before I had been a god at Layer Road, but now the fans didn't deem me good enough to clean the toilets. The goalkeeping situation still hadn't been resolved, and I'd brought in another old Southend mucker, John Keeley, who was in his early thirties, to fill the gap. He'd gone to top-flight Oldham for £250,000 and earned the ironic nickname 'Lucky' for a catalogue of injuries and for reversing over a team-mate's cat in his motor. He was a London boy who wanted to come back south and Joe Royle said I could have him for nothing. John wanted a £5,000 signing-on fee, but the Colchester directors weren't willing to cough up.

One Sunday morning I went into my local paper shop to buy the *News of the World* to check the football scores and I bumped into a Colchester fan, Terry Kershaw. He was a local businessman and we got talking about the Keeley situation and my latest battle against a stubborn board. A sympathetic Terry told me to call round his house in the week, where he handed me £5,000 in cash. Not a loan, but a donation, so I could go over my masters' heads and get John into the club. Thanks Terry. But our new goalkeeper didn't like taking shit off the supporters and, after copping flak against Rochdale, John smashed the ball straight towards his agitator in the crowd, which just missed its intended target but rebounded around

Peter Heard and his ducking cronies in the directors' box – almost killing two birds with one stone.

The football pressure cooker was simmering at Layer Road and I'd adopted a siege mentality – it was me against the world now: opposition players, referees, home and away fans, plus the directors. Just to turn the screw a little bit more, our old chums Wycombe were up next at Adams Park. They had finally made it into the Football League and had got off to a good start, remaining unbeaten at home. I'd been tipped off that Martin O'Neill was still festering over our past encounters and had told his players he was going to blank me. As luck would have it, though, when we arrived at the ground he bowled out of the home dressing room into the corridor. So I seized my chance in full view of his players. I grabbed his hand for a forced shake and put my arm round his squirming shoulders, half-dragging him to the side of the pitch, saying, 'Hello Martin, how are you? Lovely to see you again,' which made him look even tinier.

And we gave Wycombe a proper welcome into the league. I hit a volley with the outside of my left boot into the top corner to put us 3–2 up in front of the home end, before Martin Grainger and new boy Steve Brown added a couple more. At the end of the game, I paraded in front of their fans, blowing them all big kisses, before walking back across the pitch slowly with my hands raised high in the air to milk the 5–2 win. When I got to the tunnel, Alan Parry was waiting with a couple of members of the local constabulary who were trying to arrest me for inciting a riot, which was never going to happen. There were a few scuffles between the fans in the car park, though, and when a reporter asked for my view, I candidly replied, 'It takes two to fight. One to punch, the other to stand there and be punched.'

The Adams Park bar had an open hatch into the directors' lounge, so I put £150 behind the ramp and ordered the players to drink themselves silly and make as much racket as possible. I was dismissed as some sort of thug, while O'Neill has been credited as being a deep-thinking managerial intellect, but he could never win mind games or football matches against me

– and I wanted to emphasise the point. We were eventually told to leave by the club security as we were the only ones still there.

Colchester plodded along in mid-table, still a couple of players short of promotion, winning a few, losing a few. But the goalkeeper situation was killing us and we used six different pairs of hands between the sticks that season, including mine at Hereford when we got stuffed 5–0 in October. John Keeley got red carded for conceding a penalty, so I went in goal until half-time, as I had been the designated emergency goalie since my Birmingham days when there was no spare goalkeeper on the bench. The penalty flew past me and we were 2–0 down at the break, so I had a reshuffle and put Nathan Munson in goal but he got dismissed as well after letting in two more, leaving me to pick up the gloves and get beaten again.

Back at Layer Road, chairman Gordon was on the phone all excited, telling me Peter Heard had liked the look of one of their goalscorers and asked if I'd like to sign him. The player in question was a 24-year-old striker, Chris Fry, who looked like a paperboy and I really didn't want him – I certainly didn't want him forced on me. But they brought him down and I offered him a shit contract, which he agreed to, so I swallowed the £5,000 signing to get another pair of legs into the club. I had an eye for a player, but wasn't allowed to use it, pushing the names of forwards Neil Shipperley, Paul Moody and John Hartson in front of the board, all of whom went on to have good careers and moved for big money, but they wouldn't rubber-stamp the signings.

I helped us recover from the Hereford collapse with a double in a 3–1 home success against Wigan a few days after my 35th birthday, but had to wait until the end of December to score again in a 2–0 win at Scarborough. In between those goals, we were humiliated 4–3 at home by non-league Sutton United in the FA Cup and got destroyed 7–3 at Darlington. I could feel the noose tightening around my neck, but any attempts to confront Peter Heard were buffered by my father-in-law, so I had to play cute to try and strengthen the side, laying a board meeting trap.

They still wanted me out of the team, even though I'd been

behaving myself and was still doing a sound job. So I offered to go on the bench if they brought in the younger replacement they were so keen on recruiting. I told them there was a young forward at Cambridge United called Michael Danzey, who was a big lump but about as brave as Mario Walsh. I said I could get him for £15,000 – £7,500 straight away and the same amount the following year, with a £5,000 signing-on fee. It was a cheap deal, so the lightbulbs started flashing above their heads. They took the bait and sanctioned the move. Then I pulled the rug away: 'Forget that, what I'm really going to do is sign Steve Whitton on a free transfer from Ipswich. He's a pal of mine, 32-years-old, and an experienced Premier League striker, who can be wearing a Colchester shirt by Saturday. He'll also be my first-team coach. We can give him £10,000 now, and £10,000 next season. Deal done.'

My juggling masterplan was to put Whitt in my place up front, so I could drop back into the centre of defence and free up another body to slot into midfield. One of the directors was a big Ipswich fan and was all for it while Gordon, concerned that money man Heard was being made to look stupid, worriedly asked wearing a frown. 'What have you done now, Roy?' And what did Heard do? He turned his chair away from me and faced the wall. 'Not going to happen, then,' I said, and left the room.

Heard was willing to bring in players, but it had to be on his terms. I was told to go and watch a player at Brighton, who Heard's City business buddy, Millwall chairman Reg Burr, had suggested would improve our club – which just about said it all. So off I toddled to Brighton to watch this left-back, sitting in the stand next to David Pleat. Unsurprisingly, he was a shocker, nowhere near as good as what we already had. When I got back home, Gordon was on the phone, all feverish. 'So Roy, what did you think of the player?' I told him he wasn't up to scratch and that that was the end of it. An hour later, Gordon rang again, asking, 'Peter Heard wants to know if you really went to the game – did you get a programme so you can prove you were actually there?'

He was questioning my integrity now, and I went absolutely nuts. 'Why don't you ring up David Pleat and ask if I was there? Otherwise, the programme's in the back of my car if you fucking want it.'

The pressure must have been getting to me, as I'd started to up the midweek drinking, taking more risks in the process. One night, I was driving home blind drunk from Valentino's in my club-sponsored BMW, cradling a hot kebab in my lap, when I shot across some red lights at a junction and spotted a police car in the opposite road. Expecting to see blue lights in my mirror next, I booted it down Hythe Hill in Colchester as fast as possible, thinking I could out-run them. It had been raining heavily and I completely lost control, skidding straight across a roundabout and smacking to a halt in a wall on the other side. This was another drink-related dice with death, and as I sat tightly gripping the steering wheel, with the front of the car mangled and smoke billowing out everywhere, I was just waiting for a tap on the window. But there were no police, I wasn't even being chased. I was just being paranoid. Luckily, the car started and I wasn't far from home, so I reversed out slowly and drove the wrecked motor back to my house. I'd got away with it again.

By Christmas I'd lost another two players. Defender Martin Grainger went to Brentford for £60,000, with a 30 per cent sell-on clause, which gave the club another pay day when he later joined Birmingham for £400,000, and Steve McGavin linked up with Barry Fry at St Andrew's for a club record £100,000.

I had two chances to move on at the end of 1993 but, like an idiot, stayed loyal to Colchester. Barry Fry had quit the Southend manager's job to take up the reins at Birmingham, and Roots Hall's vice-chairman John Adams had tapped me up for the role. Southend were flying high in third spot in the First Division, but I was under contract at Layer Road and not comfortable at all with breaking my word to Colchester. The future England Under-21 boss Peter Taylor, who was working for an insurance company at the time, got the gig. And not pursuing that job was one of the biggest regrets of my life, as I would have walked the 40 miles back to Roots Hall.

Then, on New Year's Eve, I got the most bizarre call from Martin O'Neill. He was dropping big hints about moving on from Wycombe and me joining his coaching staff. Now, I didn't like the bloke very much, but I knew he wasn't too hands-on with the training side of things and I could have lifted the players for him and put them through their paces. It was quite a compliment – perhaps there was a mutual respect between us after all of our battles – and maybe we could have made a successful partnership.

With Colchester still in the middle of the Third Division pack, Wycombe came to town in March for the grudge match, but for the first time I couldn't face our old adversaries. Gordon was up to his old games again, ringing before the match and advising me not to play. It probably hadn't helped my cause by being stitched up in the *Evening Gazette*, who I had confided in about all the off-the-field problems I was having to contend with, 'off the record'. But they had quoted me directly, and Wycombe went on to beat us for the first time in a 'proper' game, 2–0, and the fans invaded the pitch, singing 'sack the board' in front of the directors' box. I found Gordon and Heard cowering inside the ground, and I had to escort them into the car park so they could drive home.

Then I got the big summons for a face-to-face with Heard in the City, at the Hilton Hotel in Park Lane. We talked for a couple of hours over a five-star meal, but there was no hint of danger – he praised me for doing so much for the club, taking us to Wembley and winning back Colchester's league status. I couldn't get out of there quickly enough, as it was a total waste of time – nothing had been resolved or offered to improve the strength of my squad. I was coming to the end of my tether with the complete lack of boardroom support and unwarranted abuse from the crowd and reinstated myself in the team, powering a far-post flying header into the net at Bury in March to seal a 1–0 victory.

Squeaky-bum time kicked in as we went six games without

a win and started nervously sliding towards the trapdoor. But I still had Steve Whitton on ice and a group of local businessmen – not the directors, though – donated the money to bring him in from Portman Road before transfer deadline day. But the directors were still obsessed with dominating the club's non-existent transfer policy. I started getting phone calls from some guy who clearly wasn't the full ticket, masquerading as a football agent, who told me Barcelona and Borussia Dortmund wanted to sign Mark Kinsella for £500,000. I still had to inform the board and they started clucking like chickens, so close to warming the golden egg, before we found out the phone jacker was a local con man. And then I heard that Millwall chairman Reg Burr was trying to convince Peter Heard it would be good business to sign Lions rejects Carl Emberson and Tony Dolby for £55,000 a piece, which I politely refused.

We beat Walsall and Ian Atkins's Doncaster, with Whitton bagging a couple, to stake a claim on safety in 17th spot, before making the long trip to play-off chasing Carlisle, a few miles short of the Scottish border, for our final game. Ahead of the kick-off at Brunton Park, Gordon and Peter Heard presented me with a commemorative silver plate on the pitch in recognition of my 500th league appearance. Heard couldn't look me in the eye, and I knew I was 90 minutes from facing the firing squad so I threw the stupid dish across the changing-room floor. We lost the game 2–0 and Carlisle squeezed into the play-offs, while some of our officials were serenading another manager, Mel Machin, in the stands.

In the bar after the game, Heard put £100 in my top pocket to buy the lads an end-of-season drink for the seven-hour coach journey home. Before he disappeared, he asked, 'What about the two Millwall boys, Roy? Emberson and Dolby?' I explained to him in no uncertain terms that both players would be free transfers when the PFA list came out in a few weeks' time – which they were – but my bluntness didn't go down too well.

The following Thursday I got summoned to Gordon's house for a meeting with Heard, so I told Steve Whitton to tag along as I was about to get the bullet. But when we arrived they wanted to talk about playing budgets for the new season and I was stunned. What they put on the table wasn't enough to run a youth team, so I managed to up them by another £75,000. Relieved we were back in business, I got straight on the blower and primed striker Ian Juryeff and defender Chris Day, who had both been at Leyton Orient and would come to us on free transfers.

But the next morning, the phone rang again and I was ordered back to Gordon's house – this time I knew I was finished. When I turned up, my father-in-law was bawling his eyes out in the living room. After Thursday's meeting, Gordon and Heard had returned to the Layer Road boardroom to vote on my future, with the ballot ending tied. Heard was going on holiday that night and left Gordon to make the final decision. So who did he side with, the man who was ploughing £250,000 a year into the club to keep it afloat or the 'troublesome' manager whose face didn't fit anymore?

I just said, 'I'm not fucking stupid, Gordon. I know that I'm gone.' He tried to soften the blow by saying I was going to get a £30,000 pay-off for the rest of my contract, as well as keeping the club-sponsored BMW, but I didn't care about any of that – I just needed football. It was a sunny day, so I went home and drunk 14 cans of beer in my back garden with Steve Whitton. We both went back to Layer Road to play in a friendly that night against local side Stanway Rovers, winning 7–0, which allowed me to say a proper goodbye to a disappointed set of lads in the bar.

My wife Jackie was employed as the club's lottery manager and she officially broke the news of my sacking to the fans. I was gutted about the whole thing, but she didn't even shed a tear, by all accounts, even making a joke on Anglia TV about her being the 'bread-winner in the McDonough house now'. Her pal, on the other hand, Liz Blacknall, the wife of the Layer Road groundsman who worked behind the club's bar and in the ticket office, cried her eyes out. But that's because she truly loved me.

24. DAGGERS IN THE BACK

very summer cash-strapped managers take a fine tooth-comb to the PFA's list of players available on free transfers, hoping to pick up a bargain. For the first time in nearly 20 years there was a new name marching with the legions of unwanted – Roy McDonough; striker or centre-half; approaching 36 years of age; nearly 600 professional games and over 100 goals, including seven league goals in 36 starts last season. They were the positives at the top of my CV, with 18 red cards hidden away somewhere at the bottom.

But the disciplinary record wasn't my biggest barrier in finding fresh employment, it was the other section which read: Player-manager; won Conference and FA Trophy Double after spending £640 on team, before keeping Colchester in Third Division play-off hunt on peanuts. I could still do a playing job at league level, but what manager was going to take me, knowing full well that as soon as he lost three games on the spin the fans would be calling for me to take over? Maybe that's why Ian Atkins didn't take me to his new club, Northampton Town, despite making positive noises about it, which left me feeling betrayed. Rejection from my best mate, the harsh treatment Colchester's board had dished out and the prospect of a bleak future hit me hard, propelling me into the welcoming arms of some old friends – lucky landlords and a swarm of grateful barflies.

I drank nearly a third of my £30,000 Colchester settlement in pubs and clubs in just two months, getting wrecked seven days a week with anyone who wanted to join me to keep reality at bay. And I did most of the buying. I didn't bother searching for a different job, as football was my profession and I didn't want to do anything else. But for the first time in my life I had no stringent routine, which meant no training and my body flopping out of shape.

My pal at Chelmsford City, Joe O'Sullivan, tossed me a life jacket so I didn't drown in beer, swapping a bar stool for running up and down steeps hills with his boys twice a week.

While I forced myself back into acceptable shape, my former Southend strike partner, David Crown, rang, telling me to get my CV into GM Vauxhall Conference side Dagenham & Redbridge as their manager John Still was off to Peterborough. A few days later I drove down to east London for an interview with the chairman, Dave Andrews. It was a part-time club, but they were operating on the same playing budget as Colchester, which was far better than I had expected. I tried to convince him that I could improve their youth and reserve sides – as I'd been forced to drag the kids at Layer Road into the first team – and that he was getting a player who could piss the Conference, as well as a manager who could take Dagenham into the Football League. But he just kept repeating, 'How much is it going to cost us?' The annual salary was £30,000, plus a car and phone. I told the chairman I wasn't motivated by money, as I still had a nest egg tucked away from Colchester, and asked him to give me the job on a three-month trial. But I never got the chance, as it went to my old Millwall foe, Dave Cusack, as Dagenham believed I was double-dealing them, holding out for a Football League club, when my offer was totally genuine.

Something else beyond doubt was my true feelings for Layer Road barmaid Liz Blacknall. Originally from Nottingham, Liz was Colchester groundsman Dave's wife. Six years younger than me, she was tall and blonde – the complete opposite to diminutive Jackie – and a beautiful person, as well as being a stunner to look at. We'd started seeing each other while I was still manager at Colchester, which proved awkward, especially as there were times when Liz, Jackie, Dave and I could all be in the office at the same time.

Liz was Jackie's pal through work and the talk of the changing room, as most of the players had taken a shine to her. But she always made it perfectly clear that she was unavailable, politely rebuffing any attempts to chat her up across the football ground bar. And I loved that. Women rarely said 'no' to me, and for the first time ever I was doing the chasing – I couldn't believe how exciting it was. But Liz was different to what I was used to, timid, a little insecure even, and I acted like the perfect gentleman, never showering her with the gutter-mouth act.

It took me six months – as Liz put it – to 'wear her down'. Believing I was happily married, she fought hard to stop anything happening between us. But, in the end, fending off my advances exhausted her and Liz agreed to meet me at a safe house I had arranged, hoping to get me off her back. But this wasn't just about sex, a one-night stand and me disappearing having snatched my prize. I felt a connection as I had grown to know Liz properly during those six months of unsuccessfully hunting out her affections. By actually talking to her, I learned that not everything was rosy with her marriage either and we became good mates. There were no secrets, as I could be open with Liz about anything. I didn't have to worry about the consequences of exposing my innermost thoughts and feelings. It was natural, not a weakness, and Liz wanted to share these things with me, which knocked my socks off. After kidding myself so many times in the past, I had finally found my soulmate. This was true love.

Braintree Town manager Frank Bishop saved me from the pub – and tempted me into his snooker club instead. The club's ground, Cressing Road, was a dump and a homing beacon for middle-aged men clutching carrier bags on a Saturday afternoon. But it had a cracking bar and Frank's snooker club was next door. The savings were disappearing, so I didn't have much choice when he offered me £250-a-week cash to slum it in the Beazer Homes League Southern Division at such illustrious venues as Ashford Town, Bashley and Erith & Belvedere. Most of the players had real jobs, so training was held on Wednesday and Thursday evenings under floodlights, which was a novelty as those nights had always been for drinking.

I was handed a quick reunion with Colchester in a pre-season match, which we won 1–0. George Burley had been given my job. George was an ex-Ipswich player who turned up for work suited and booted with his sandwiches and apple in a briefcase, which must have got a big tick from Peter Heard. Ever-sensitive father-in-law Gordon had called to gauge my opinion on the 'new acquisition', and I asked him if he was 'having a fucking laugh' before slamming the phone down. After the friendly, Burley came up to me in the Braintree bar. He said Colchester had given him some money for players, which was more than I ever got, but he was struggling to get people into the club. He'd heard on the grapevine that I had some lads lined up before I got fired and would I mind telling him who they were. Burley got told to fuck off faster than the speed of light. I couldn't believe the Scotsman's cheek.

I hated every minute of playing for Braintree because I was still far too good for that level. I scored eight goals in 14 games at the start of the 1994/95 season, but it was so frustrating as nobody was good enough to get the ball to me – 90 minutes had never seemed so long. The games were always close and we only lost four times but Peter Collins, a coach who had won a few pots at Spurs, was elevated to Frank's job in the middle of October before a home game with Weston-super-Mare. None of us liked Collins, another training ground turn-off, and we certainly didn't want to play for him. The players' loyalties belonged to Frank so we held a 'union' meeting before the match and, as the most senior player, I was sent to the changing room as spokesman to deliver our ultimatum. Collins had taken out insurance, calling up the reserve and youth-team boys to play if we bailed out. He was standing next to the chairman, so I told him that none of us wanted to play for Collins and if Frank wasn't reinstated immediately we would all walk, adding, 'You pay me £250 a week, which I'm very grateful for, but if you pay me £1 today to play for that bloke [Collins], then it will be £1 too much.' The chairman refused, so eight of us headed to the club bar for the rest of the afternoon, leaving the stiffs and kids to get on with it.

Word flies round the non-league circuit quickly and two days later I got a call from Dave Cusack offering me £300 a week, plus a £50 win bonus, to drive through the smog of the Ford car plant again to join Dagenham in the Conference. I made my debut in a 2–0 October defeat at Merthyr Tydfil, a few days after my 36th birthday. The Daggers were struggling, so I found myself shoring up the defence more often than leading the attack. I was only on the winning side once in the first six games, at Altrincham, but managed to write myself into the history books at home to Stafford Rangers in December.

One thing I loved about playing for Dagenham was that the team caught the train together to away matches, which was much better than being stuck on a coach for hours. There were half-decent toilets, you could get up and stretch your legs, and the buffet carriage meant beers galore and card games all the way home. I even managed to pull off my old party trick on an Inter City speeding at 90mph into Euston, draining a pint of Stella standing on my head in 10 seconds – it was harder on a moving train, so took a few seconds longer.

There was no kitman with us, so I had to look after my own gear now, and I'd left my boots at Runcorn. Perry Groves had a boot sponsorship deal with Lotto, which meant he had loads of old pairs hanging around his house. He gave me a pair of his top-of-the-range footwear, which was designed to mould itself around the shape of your foot, but Grovesy had twisted and gnarled feet, so they were curly boots – it was like wearing winklepickers. Those smelly old cast-offs came up trumps against Stafford, though, as we were 3–0 down at half-time, but I banged in a four-minute hat-trick after the break – a perfect left foot, right foot and headed treble. It was the quickest in the club's history and earned us a 3–3 draw, with just 554 witnesses of this stellar moment.

My scoring off the pitch was almost detected before Christmas in an FBI-style interrogation from the wife. Jackie was doing the rounds in Colchester with the King Coel's Kittens charity, singing *Good King Wenceslas* and all the other festive carols around the streets to raise money in buckets. Thinking I had a couple of hours to sneak off, I arranged to meet Liz. When I got home, I went straight to the bathroom for a good scrub up, making sure there was no trace of giveaway smells for Jackie to get a whiff of. The golden rule was to only use warm water. If I'd covered myself in soap, Jackie would have been suspicious of my super cleanliness – it was better to keep things plain and simple.

When Jackie got home she had the right hump, demanding to know where I had been. The generator had packed up on the charity float, so she'd come home early, singing carols at the front door with a couple of kids to surprise me, but I hadn't been there. The brain kicked into gear instantly and I spun her a line about having to go down the squash club to rescue a mate who was trying to drive pissed out of the car park. But she wasn't buying the story, and insisted on carrying out a thorough inspection for evidence by sniffing my groin and placing her hand on my heart while asking me questions. She was trying to gauge whether my heart rate increased to see if I was telling lies. But I stayed calm and passed the test. It was like an audition for the Secret Service.

Even Perry Groves's signing for Dagenham couldn't halt the downward spiral. He'd retired from the pro ranks at Southampton, as his Achilles tendon had gone, and he was struggling. He was getting picked out for rough treatment because of his Arsenal past and the hatchet men at this level could get to him now as he didn't have the legs to accelerate away from them anymore.

It all kicked off during a 4–0 home defeat to Altrincham in February 1995. I'd had a run-in with their pathetic Scouse striker Andy Green up there, following through the back of him with knees, elbows and studs, which was punishment he couldn't handle. Even then, having played so many years in professional football, my body was much stronger than the part-time Conference players, and 13st hitting him at full pelt was painful. Green had come into the bar after the game threatening to shoot me, pointing a pretend gun in my direction with his arm. I told him to 'fuck off back to playschool' – so the return was always going to have a bit of extra spice to it. We had three players sent off, Grovesy for a late tackle and sub midfielder Robbie Gammons, with me proving that things run in threes.

We were 1–0 down when I cleared the ball out of play, at exactly the same time as the referee blew his whistle. He booked me for time-wasting and I protested, 'Ref, why would I do that, we're losing the game?' His shoulders went back and he grunted, 'Fucking McDonough', before jogging off. 'Lovely,' I thought. 'We've got one here, and it's going to get personal if I don't watch out.'

After the break I bent a pass down the wing, which I'm sure stayed in play, but the linesman started waving his flag, indicating the ball had gone out. Without any hint of aggression, I commented sarcastically, 'You're just as bad as the ref.' That earned me a second yellow card, followed by a red, and the crowd went mad. The little fucker on the touchline was sneering away after claiming my scalp but not for long, as two grannies in the stand chucked their steaming-hot cups of Bovril at him.

I was just plodding round the pitch in an angry daze, unable to comprehend how these two wankers had kippered me. Grovesy was already showered and up in the directors' box, shouting to the Dagenham bench, 'Get Roy off! Get him off, or he's going to wreck the place.' An irate crowd was ready to lynch the officials, who needed smuggling out of the ground at the end of the game, and Dagenham tried to get them charged with inciting a riot.

The linesman wrote in his report, 'that he had feared for his life' as I approached him. So I had to accompany boss Dave Cusack to the FA's headquarters at Lancaster Gate for a disciplinary hearing which, despite my long list of football crimes, was only the third time I had been there. I was under strict instructions not to speak and every time Cusack saw my mouth about to open he kicked me in the shin under the table. My judges and jury consisted of eight people: the referee and linesman, plus six of the FA's cobweb-covered *Spitting Image* puppets, who I felt like poking to see if they were still alive. One of the FA ancients read out my previous misdemeanours, which took a while, and they wanted to slap me with a 10-game ban. The linesman gave his evidence, recalling how he'd got showered in Bovril by two 70-year-old biddies, before spouting bollocks about how I was going to strangle the life out of him. I couldn't listen to any more and interrupted, 'Sorry gentleman, I know I'm not supposed to speak, but this is unfair. The linesman was safe as houses as he ran away. Even at the height of my career, I was never quick enough to catch him up.'

I played them at their own game. Putting an emotional choke on my voice, I apologised to everyone and explained things had been bad at home with the wife, I told them we had just lost a baby (despite it being over two years ago) and it was still affecting me. It was a low tactic, but I wasn't going to let these cheats stitch me up – a 10-match ban would have sent me into extinction. They adjourned the meeting, and I stood outside like a lemon as they discussed the case. But they bought my sob story, delivering a reduced verdict of a five-match suspension.

I was out for a month and during that time I worked hard at my new occupation, taking a leaf out of Dad's book as a travelling salesman. I was driving across the country flogging mineral water, vitamin pills, carrot cake, flapjacks and muffins to shops, petrol stations and newsagents. Sales must have been in the genes, as it turned out I was good at it, using the old charm to rake in £800 most weeks. It was a new buzz as I enjoyed the challenge of convincing complete strangers to part with their cash – a new game I wanted to be the best at.

I arranged my business calls around our away matches, and my second game back from the ban was a 2–2 draw at

Bromsgrove in March, where I'd agreed to do an interview with the *Sunday Times* about me, referees and red cards. I was playing centre-half but still stuck a goal past my old mucker Ron Green, before getting my head split open by their forward's flying elbow. I had blood trickling down my neck but I was relishing the battle, so I got the physio to whack a lump of Vaseline on the cut so I could continue playing. In the second half, the ball dropped on the edge of the box and I half-volleyed clear with a short, sharp follow through, but their lad ran across me and my sock exploded.

There was blood everywhere, so I sat on the floor. The referee ran over. 'McDonough, get up!' I pointed at my ankle, saying, 'I need a physio mate, and stitches.' But he wasn't having it: 'Fucking get up, McDonough. It's a corner.' Once he started swearing, the temper kicked in and I replied, 'Are you taking the piss? I need stitches.'

I got another straight red and I had to hobble off the pitch in agony, covered in blood. In the dressing room, I asked the bloke who made the teas to get the doctor, so he could start sewing me up. As he left the room, I called out jokingly, 'And do me another favour: get me a baseball bat for the fucking referee.' I didn't realise, but the *Sunday Times* reporter was scribbling everything down outside the door – and that quote took star billing in his story.

Before the next game, Dave Cusack phoned and told me to head to the Essex coast and turn out for the reserves at Concord Rangers, who played next to the methane terminal on Canvey Island. He also said to meet him at a pub after the game but he didn't show, so I knew I would be looking for a new club. I was unimpressed that he didn't have the balls to front up and tell me, so I went round to his house, got the money he owed me and that was that – there was no big sacking drama.

I felt poorly treated, as the referee had spoken to me like I was a piece of shit and I had ended up with six stitches in my ankle and five more in my head. Stories started to appear in newspapers about how I had been fired by Dagenham for picking up too many red cards. Cusack told journalists, 'Roy

McDonough would eat Vinnie Jones for breakfast', and while admitting I was 'a genuinely nice guy off the pitch', he added that I was 'the most ill-disciplined and occasionally terrifying player he had ever known'.

25. JACK-ING IT ALL IN

'**S**occer Boss Runs Off With His Wife's Lookalike Best Pal' ran *The Sun* headline. I finally made it as a Page Seven Fella when it was rumbled that I was playing extra-time with Liz.

I was hardly a football love rat, as there was only one real woman in my life, and I wasn't a boss either. I'd been sacked by Colchester 12 months before the secret got out in August 1995. I was still married to Jackie, but had booted her out of the house and she was back living with her parents. As far as I was concerned, my marriage had been over for years. I'd been messing around with other girls again long before Liz came on the scene and Jackie, who was no shrinking violet herself, must have realised it, as I was getting in at 5am on a Sunday stinking of booze and perfume. She confronted me once about my dalliances, and I reeled off a list of 39 girls – Susie, Louise, Nicola, Anna, Jane etc . . . – I had slept with over an 18-month period. I didn't care if Jackie didn't like it, as we were a nightmare combination and it wasn't healthy for our marriage to continue. I'd also suspected Jackie of playing away with a team-mate and when I heard the whispers I rang the alleged culprit, saying, 'When I see you I'm going to give you a dig. And then I'm going to buy you a beer.'

By the time Liz and I were going strong, Jackie had become a big fan of male strippers, the Chippendales, and I would give her £400 to go and follow their oiled torsos around Europe for the weekend, just to get her out of the way. But Liz and I had been lucky to go undetected for so long. Jackie found an itemised phone bill with Liz's home number printed on it at least 50 times, which I played down as calls to groundsman Dave about the state of the Layer Road pitch. And one week I had to wait anxiously each morning for the postman after being flashed by a road speed camera. In the picture there was a tall blonde in the passenger seat next to me, while brunette Jackie wouldn't have reached the dashboard. It wasn't much of a 'lookalike'. I also arranged a weekend away in Bournemouth to tie in with a business trip. Liz had met me at a pub when I got a surprise phone call from Jackie saying she was waiting for me at the hotel. Fortunately, Liz hadn't dropped off her suitcase and we got away with it.

I went to see Liz working at the Prince of Wales pub in Colchester one Friday night and recognised a few U's fans in the bar. We were taking more risks and her husband finding out was the main concern, as well as the obvious pain it would cause Liz's young son. But the plan was to leave in separate cars and she would follow me home. Just before I left, one of the Colchester fans offered to buy me a drink and I politely refused his offer. He said, 'Blimey, I never thought I would see the day that Big Roy turned down a beer.' Typically, the one time I did got me into a lot of trouble.

Jackie must have been suspicious that something was going on and must have been following me around town in her car. I took a quiet country lane back route to my house, so we wouldn't be seen. I was driving a BMW, with Liz following in her Vauxhall Astra, and when we got to a single-lane humpback bridge, where I had to give way, there was Jackie on the other side in her Mitsubishi Colt. She let us pass and turned round, while I sped home. Liz wasn't so lucky, though, as Jackie over-took her car and stopped in front of her, forcing Liz to pull over. Jackie ran out and confronted her about our affair through the car window, before heading back to the house to find me. I admitted everything to her, telling her I was in love with Liz, and she flew at me all hair and nails, demanding a divorce. I had to restrain Jackie and ask her to leave, relieved that everything was finally out in the open.

I was still playing the odd game after I received a couple of SOS's, guesting for Heybridge Swifts and Bishop's Stortford in one-off matches. Then I joined Canvey Island, who I believed wanted to have a go just as much as me. They were only in the ICIS League Division Two but were an ambitious outfit. There were giant container ships floating slowly down the Thames behind their wide-open Park Lane home, which had no defence from the strong salty winds that blew in from the sea. My old Southend team-mate, Glenn Pennyfather, was there, and Canvey had a cracking bar, which was always the deal-breaker. The club was fuelled by the cash of manager/owner Jeff King, whose old man owned half the island. Jeff was a big character with an unsavoury reputation, like I had. In his own playing days, he was rumoured to have threatened opposition teams and referees with baseball bats, and was also alleged to have tried to bite someone's nose off. But he was a big softie off the pitch just like me and pulled me after one game, asking, 'I thought I'd signed a raving lunatic?' But I didn't want any trouble, I just wanted to play football.

Perry Groves followed me to Canvey and we signed deals in the kitchen of Jeff's nightclub, King's – a rough-house in the middle of a caravan park, with wall-to-wall white stilettos and handbags. The money was decent, £250 a week in the hand, but I stuck out like a sore thumb at these empty little grounds with my white hair, as fans called out 'pack up old man' and 'you're well past it, McDonough' when I walked on to the pitch.

I was 37 by then and played centre-half in my first game, a 2–2 draw at home to Bedford Town in October 1995, and their ugly, toothless twat of a forward had been doing his homework.

He tried to goad me, saying, 'I've read about you in the newspapers, with the girls and getting divorced, you fucking mug.'

I never said anything when I played at the back, shutting out the verbal and getting on with it. But he pushed his luck, giving me a slap, so I warned him, 'Leave the girls out of it, son. And behave yourself with your hands or you'll be going home in a fucking ambulance with broken legs.'

We got on alright after that, but that was the stage I was at then. I'd become a big trophy for young pups on the non-league circuit who wanted to test themselves against 'McDonough the hardman', so they had a story to tell their mates.

Déjà vu kicked in during the return at Bedford two days before Christmas – when our goalkeeper, John Keeley, got sent off. Just like I had done at Hereford for Colchester a couple of years before, when we got beat 5–0, I went in goal to face the penalty. I took an age to change shirts, playing on their striker's nerves by asking, 'How's your bottle?' The poor bloke stubbed his toe in the run-up and shinned the ball goalwards, which I almost dived over but saved to my left, and we went on to win 7–1.

But I was out of there in the new year after 11 games and three goals. I'd had a falling out with Jeff King over wages. I was still working away as a travelling salesman and he told me that if I wasn't at the twice-weekly evening training sessions then I would only get paid half my money – which wasn't part of the original deal. It gave me the hump, as there was nothing he could teach me about the game at my age. Training was a joke. I would put everything into it, preparing for the next game, while most of the other clowns were running the clock down, desperate to go home. I wasn't driving back hundreds of miles for them, and the first time Jeff deducted my wages for not showing on the training pitch I shook hands and we parted amicably.

Before leaving Canvey's shores, a writer from the *Telegraph Magazine* interviewed me at the King's Club. It was a big glossy piece across four pages, getting under the skin of my hot-headed status and describing me as 'football's Vlad the Impaler'. The article also claimed that opposition players would ring in sick to their clubs the day before a game if they had to face me, which was just hilarious. It wasn't until many years later, when Liz was working for holiday firm Thomas Cook, that I even found out who the reporter was. Her boss had been lapping up the sun, reading a compilation of a famous writer's favourite interviews. 'You're not going to believe this Liz, but I'm reading interviews with Elton John, Mick Jagger and The Clash. Then I turn a page, and your old man's got his own section, too,' he told her. The journalist who interviewed me that day was none other than best-selling author Tony Parsons. It was nice to see I had made a good enough impression to rub pages with such renowned celebrities. I had finally found fame on Canvey Island.

A month later I was cruising beside the River Blackwater at Essex village team Heybridge Swifts in the division above Canvey. Their manager, Garry Hill, got me down to Scraley Road, which had one of the best pitches outside of the Football League, and I revelled in a centre-half role. Garry had put his own money into the club to attract better players but, like Jeff King, he wasn't the greatest on the training ground, and his pre-match tactics revolved around reading out the team and giving everyone a big 'C'mon' in the changing room. I made my debut in a 3–0 win against Staines in February 1996 and played with my slippers on as we won promotion to the Isthmian League Premier.

I got 20 games under my belt, scored once and only managed five bookings. But I was tempted a few miles away from Heybridge in the summer, installed as manager to try and revive sleeping non-league giants Chelmsford City. Unfortunately, my wake-up call was too loud, as the club wanted to stay in a coma. Chelmsford always had huge potential, able to attract a couple of thousand fans if they were doing well, in leagues where most teams were only watched by a couple of hundred.

They gave the trumpets a blast when they announced 'former Colchester manager Roy McDonough' as their new player-manager. It was still a part-time job, but £26,000 spread over two years wasn't a bad little contract. Chelmsford were paying top-three money in the Southern League Premier Division, but their players – some on £300 a week – were going through the motions, and City had only beaten off relegation on the last day of the previous campaign. That wasn't a good enough return on the club's investment and I labelled them 'Comfort City' in the local rag, which didn't go down well with the players.

I brought in some of my old team-mates, Jason Cook, Paul Roberts and Ian Benjamin, who were better than what we had and cheaper too. But the omens weren't good from the very start. The ex-Wolves defender Gary Bellamy was the commercial manager at New Writtle Street, but when I got the job it put his nose out of joint, as he wanted it. The day before our first game at Newport County he was pencilled in to play centre-half, but he cried off with a calf strain the night before. I didn't believe he was injured and told him, 'Don't treat me like a cunt. Play the games and I'll look after you, or I'll make life fucking difficult for you here.' But it made little difference, as he stuck to his own agenda.

Taking his place in the team for the 2–2 draw at Newport, I continued my love affair with the Welsh in football's backwaters. Welsh international Steve Lowndes was playing for them and he tried to make his mark, launching a flying headbutt straight into my cheekbone. But the stupid prick knocked himself out and ended up getting carried off on a stretcher, though not before I'd had a chance to lean over and curse him. 'I hope you get brain damage.'

Local firm Britvic wanted to cash in on my disciplinary record – which didn't bother me as long as it earned the club some money – by bringing out a new sports energy drink called Red Card. As the club's main sponsors, they were given permission to change Chelmsford's traditional claret shirts to blood red, and we went to Wembley for the brand launch, where I was photographed in the *Daily Star* with top fashion guru Wayne Hemingway who had designed the kit. The Red Card branding was launched with a nationwide advertising campaign, but when they held a photo shoot for the posters I was working away so my picture wasn't on them – which defeated the whole object of the exercise.

Chelmsford only tasted victory once in our first 10 games – 2–1 at Crawley – and I had a player rebellion on my hands. I'd tried to ship out the players on big wages, the cheats who didn't want to work hard for the club, but they refused to budge, content to sit in the club bar on a Saturday afternoon and pick up their money. My hands were tied and the fans' cheers soon turned to jeers as the New Writtle Street atmosphere became hostile. I found respite in the FA Cup qualifying rounds, beating March Town 5–0 and picking myself for a derby replay with Heybridge. I scored the winner only to be greeted by a banner unfurled by Chelmsford fans behind the goal – 'Go Home McDonough And Take Your Mates With You'.

I could take flak all day long, but one thing I wouldn't tolerate was the supporters venting their frustrations at Liz. She hated coming to Chelmsford, as she could feel the bad vibes as soon as she sat down in the main stand behind my dugout. She came to one game with her sister and my two nieces and had to sit through 90 uncomfortable minutes as people shouted at her, 'Why doesn't your old man fuck off?'

I went to meet the girls in the bar following another disastrous display and all the usual suspects were in their positions. Trevor Wright, the chairman, was twitching with a couple of directors, and the sneering players I'd binned from the first team for not trying hard enough were knocking back pints, hanging in there to get me out. Then there was the 20-strong group of fans who thought they were the club's firm of hardmen. Now it takes a lot to get to my Liz, but I could see she was really upset and I soon found out what had happened. I was certain it was the gang of idiots who'd given her such a hard time, and as I went to the bar one of the 'thugs' started bogging at me as if he meant business. Trying to stay calm, I turned away, looked back again and the knob end was still staring. I flipped out and fronted him up.

'Are you the hardest fucker here, pal? Are you the tough bastard who has been swearing at my missus? Let's me and you go out the back now and, once I've sorted the fuck out of you, send in the next hardest one and he'll get the same. And do yourself a favour, before you come out, find the biggest lump of wood you can, as you're going to need it.'

The Chelmsford 'firm' shrank back like weak little girls, so I turned on the quarantined players. 'That's the trouble with this club. You're all spineless, like those fuckers over there who raped this club of top money last year. Now you can all go and fuck yourselves.' Then I got my drink, stood my ground with the girls and had a few more pints before going home.

I got the inevitable message 12 weeks into my turbulent reign after a 2–1 Southern League Cup defeat at Baldock Town. I was relieved of my duties as 'things weren't working out' according to the chairman, and Gary Bellamy took over the job. Usually, I wouldn't be bothered about compensation, but Chelmsford had tarnished my reputation by dragging my name through the dirt. I wanted my pound of flesh – all £20,000 of it. They weren't playing ball, making random allegations about my conduct as manager, so I got myself a lawyer and was going to march into the club on a match day with a winding-up order. I was prepared to close them down, but the lawyer had built a case against the wrong club, as Chelmsford City had technically ceased to exist a few years before, following financial problems, and had been reformed as The Supporters of Chelmsford City Football Club. The winding-up order was powerless.

In the end, the compensation claim went to the FA at Lancaster Gate. Paul Roberts got £6,000, more than the ex-manager, who waited a year to pocket £5,000. The hearing was a joke, as two of Chelmsford's directors reeled out a cata-logue of lies – claiming that I'd been trying to cook the books and syphon money out of the club. During a recess, I found the Chelmsford officials in the toilet in their three-piece suits holding their pricks, in front of the urinals. I couldn't believe my luck, pushing them both up against the wall, sending piss flying everywhere, and persuading them to do the right thing.

I tried to get back into football management, applying for jobs at Blackpool, Kettering, Kidderminster and Woking, but my reputation was coming back to haunt me. None of the club bosses could see past my 'troublesome' history and stack of red cards, when all I had done throughout my career was try and be a winner by wearing my heart on my sleeve. I got one interview, for the job at Dover Athletic, but that went to Gary Bellamy, which was one knockback too many.

I was finished with football now. And it wasn't tough to walk away from a game which had kicked me in the bollocks for the best part of 20 years, as in Liz I had something far more important now. For the first time ever, football wasn't the dominant factor in my life – Liz had taken its place. But she had one last battle to win before the transformation was complete – divorcing me from Perry Groves and Steve Whitton, who were determined to keep hold of their third Musketeer.

26. HEYBRIDGE TOO FAR

The happiest day of my life was 20 June, 1998 – because I married the woman who saved me. It wasn't anything like first time round, all pomp and splendour, surrounded by 250 people I mostly didn't know or care about. Just 64 guests, handpicked by me and Liz, with my twin brother Gaz as best man.

We tied the knot in the Midlands, in Sheldon, at a Methodist church which resembled Colditz but was lovely inside. When my Lizzie glided down the aisle she was a vision of beauty and I welled up. I loved this woman so much and wanted to spend the rest of my days with her. When I repeated my marriage vows in front of the priest, I wasn't just going through the motions – I heard and meant every single word. It was a moody day weather-wise, but they say the sun shines on the righteous, and when Liz stepped out of the church the currant bun put in a smiling appearance.

The whole weekend was memorable for a multitude of reasons, especially spending the day before the wedding with all my brothers, drinking on the boundary with Dad while he played cricket for Old Silhillians. And the wedding reception got emotional, as I almost broke down in front of everyone while making my speech about how beautiful Liz was on the outside, but 'turn her inside out and she is even better'.

Gaz sobered up proceedings with his best man's speech, though, providing a tumbleweed moment with gags about Jackie and the Chippendales. I'd been an idiot for as long as I could remember and felt so fortunate to have found that special person who some people don't find in a lifetime of searching. It had always been football, football, football, in the past. That's all I had cared about. But all the big regrets, especially not making it at Birmingham and Chelsea, had gone now, as finding a good woman like Liz was much better than being a top-flight footballer.

We went to the Greek island of Skiathos for our honeymoon. It was a wonderful place with friendly people, great food and amazing scenery, boosted by a rainbow of brightly coloured flowers. These were all things I had never noticed before, as my sightseeing abroad had never ventured much further than the bottom of a pint glass. One of the best things about our relationship was our similar senses of humour and the ability to giggle at most of the things life chucked at us. And there was plenty of laugher ammunition on Skiathos's aptly-named Little Banana nudist beach, which was packed with needle-dicked Germans who couldn't stop farting on their beach towels. Wedded bliss? Without a doubt. But it had taken a lot of hard work to reach that stage – with Liz doing most of the graft.

The biggest obstacle to our happiness was my inseparable drinking bond with Perry Groves and Steve Whitton. As our football careers were winding down we got back on the booze in a big way. And as my first marriage went down the same route, miles ahead of meeting Liz, the random sex games had also upped a gear. Grovesy would follow me around town like a Jack Russell, hoping to sniff out some action. We'd play tennis on Sunday mornings to sweat out Saturday's alcohol before starting again at Colchester's Cellar Bar, a gathering place for girls in their mid-twenties to late thirties, most of whom were familiar faces from the nightclub circuit. I was the fixer, with other footballers, especially the Ipswich boys, taking Grovesy's lead and clinging by my side, knowing full well that the sure-thing girls wouldn't be far behind. One adventurous blonde became a regular fixture, with Grovesy taking on the Marco Tardelli man-to-man marking role and following us back home to score in a threesome. And three soon became four, as this fine young woman got her girlfriend involved. She was up for anything and one night I started flicking fivers on the floor of a packed Cellar Bar in front of her. By the time the third one had hit the deck, she had my cock in her mouth. Thinking I was taking the piss, her mate flew across the wine bar in a rage to give me a slap, but missed, hitting an unhappy Grovesy and ending any chance he had of getting it on with his assailant.

We were acting like pubescent schoolboys again and, although I was never unfaithful to Liz, she had to wedge a crowbar between me, Grovesy and Steve Whitton to pull us apart – or end our relationship. When we first got together it was a riot and I would be out with Liz every night. She'd always look stunning, dressed up in a sexy catsuit and boots, with the figure to match, standing next to the white-haired old man, who most people must have thought was her father. But the lads didn't want to let me go – Roy McDonough, the party animal who was good with the girls – as I held the golden ticket to their social lives. Some nights I'd have 25 missed calls from Grovesy as he tried to lure me down the pub or to a nightclub. And most of the time I couldn't resist, sneaking off late at night to go on the piss. I found it difficult to abandon the pack, which was threatening to ruin something so special.

It sounds clichéd, but Liz did save my life. If it wasn't for her determination to change my mindset and make me appreciate what we had together, I would have tumbled to the bottom of the slippery slope, drinking and fucking myself into lonely oblivion. Liz was the first person ever to support me fully, who I could confide in without fear and who nudged me in the right direction, pointing out what was wrong and what was right. And she fought hard for me, hiding my phone so I couldn't be distracted and ripping the buttons off brand new shirts as I walked out the door to join Grovesy and Whitt. Eventually, the penny started to drop and I began drinking left handed, which I'd never done before. My right hand had always been for holding a beer, as I could sling it down quicker. But now I had something else in that hand, Liz's hand, and I would stand at the bar gripping it tightly all night when we were out. I'd never have done that in the past – held a bloody bird's hand. But I didn't care about any of the macho bullshit any more, or what Grovesy or Whitt felt about it, as your mates are two bob when you've got a strong woman like Liz on your arm. One night, Whitt came over to me at the bar, looked at me holding hands with Liz, and said, 'Big fella, I want that.' To this day, I don't know if he has ever managed it.

God knows how I managed to keep a vice-like grip on that hand. When Jackie discovered our affair, Liz went on holiday to Ibiza with her husband Dave and came clean straight to his face, which took real guts. The situation wasn't great, as I knew Dave the groundsman well. I'd spoken to him regularly about how I wanted the Layer Road pitch cut, and I took him to Wembley and let him sit on the bench. I even knew their little boy, David, who held a grudge against me for years, blaming me for splitting up his parents. When Liz returned from Ibiza, I made my intentions clear, that I loved her completely and I wanted us to live together. Liz had gone to stay with Grovesy's missus, but was in pieces, as she'd just split up with her husband and left her six-year-old child behind – the hardest thing for a mother to do – all painful sacrifices she had made for me. So what did I do? Went out on the piss with Grovesy and Whitt at Lexden Squash Club, when I should have been comforting the woman I loved on one of the most terrible days of her life – which was disgusting behaviour. Despite all her doubts, she stuck by me and we got through it.

The big turning point came months later when my old goalkeeper, Scott Barrett, came to live with us for a while, with his other half, Jill. Things started to get more sedate as we began doing normal couple things – going out for a quiet drink and having a meal. And I soon realised that I didn't need to get battered with Grovesy and Whitt – as this was all I wanted now. I was fully content.

There was one final stupid moment before we got married, though – my genuine attempt at a romantic proposal on Christmas Day 1997. It was our first Christmas together in our new house, in Peartree Road, Stanway, near Colchester. I bought a solitaire engagement ring and Sellotaped it to the inside of Liz's Christmas card, next to my written words, 'To my guardian angel – will you marry me?', which I left under the tree in the living room. Liz's sister, Jo, and her husband, Warren, were staying with us, and in the morning their excited daughter Katie got up early to start opening her presents. We'd had a decent Christmas Eve drink and I was struggling in bed with a thumping hangover while everyone else was downstairs. A shocked Liz opened her card, discovering the ring and message, while Casanova was still under the duvet. It wasn't quite how I had planned the proposal unfolding, so I lumbered downstairs in a pair of football shorts, with my hair sticking up everywhere and breath stinking like the bottom of a budgie's cage, praying that she would still say 'yes'. Well, who could have resisted that perfect picture of male morning beauty? And she gave me the best Christmas present ever, making me the happiest, if not the most sober, man alive.

A few weeks after our wedding in the summer of 1998, a bolt from the blue opened a door back into a world I thought had long washed its hands of me. My involvement with football for the past two years had been restricted to watching the TV from my living room armchair. But a phone call from Heybridge Swifts chairman Andy Barber proved the old desire was still buried away deep down, reignited by the opportunity to return to the leafy surroundings of Scraley Road as manager. I'd had a great time in my previous spell at the club, winning promotion as a player, but I couldn't deal with amateurs anymore – not after the way I had been treated by Chelmsford and I only agreed to take the job if Andy promised that all club decisions would be made by us alone. He shook on that stipulation, and I agreed to take over.

The money was crap and we were low on numbers, as Garry Hill had taken the best players to St Albans with him, but I sent out an SOS and soon got a few pals in to help me out, like Jason Cook, Tony English and, of course, Paul Roberts. Using my contacts, I got West Ham and Norwich down to play pre-season, with the promise that I could use the boosted crowd proceeds to strengthen the squad. But I never saw a penny, which should have been the first danger sign.

I tried to get the players passing the ball, to make the most of a smooth carpet of a home pitch, but we got off to a nightmare start in the Ryman Premier at bumpy Bromley in August. Their playing surface was better suited to growing vegetables than playing football and after we gave the ball away twice to concede early goals, the players' heads disappeared up their arses and we got drubbed 6–1. Next up was Purfleet at home, which was a major improvement as we picked up a goalless draw, but a familiar friend was waved in my face as I shouted the odds from the dugout. The referee was full of energy and anger, desperate to make a name for himself, when he charged over to pay me a visit. I questioned his 'crap decisions' and told him to 'do his job properly' and he sent me to the main stand. But another red card made little difference, as I stood in the middle of 25 seated Heybridge fans shouting at my players. It didn't matter if there were 10,000, or 300 fans in the ground – nothing was going to stop me getting instructions across to my lads. My third match in charge was at home to Basingstoke, and we'd finally turned the corner, going in 3–1 up at half-time. But we had a player sent-off just after the break and folded like a house of cards, losing 9–3, which must have been some sort of record.

Five games in and we still hadn't won, which included a 1–1 September draw at Sutton United – ringing the last bell on my football management career. The referee was the classic homer and had given them something ridiculous like 43 free-kicks to our two. A month away from my 40th birthday, I believed I had mellowed and really didn't want to get into bother anymore.

But I still wanted to win, even if it meant being polite when it came to conversing with my dear old friends the match officials. At half-time, I followed the referee down the tunnel, and asked, 'Excuse me ref, could I please have a word?' But he was downright rude, replying, 'McDonough, don't you talk to me – get out of my face.'

As soon as he spoke to me like I was something horrible on the bottom of his shoe, the Mr Nice Guy act was finished. 'Do you think 43–2 to Sutton in free-kicks was a fair reflection of the first half then, ref? Now, I'm telling you, you fucking muppet, do your job properly.'

Rant over, I paced straight past him and could hear his studs breaking into a jog behind me, and soon enough he was knocking on our changing room door. I was already inside with the players, but I held the door handle while he tried to open it on the other side. When I could feel the ref putting his all into cranking that handle and pushing his shoulder into the door I opened it quickly, and he flew across the changing room, landing in a heap by the physio's table. He had eyes like saucepan lids as all the players broke into a crescendo of laughter and he started swearing madly at me. I clicked back into gentleman mode. 'Do yourself a favour, ref. I've done nothing wrong here. Just calm down and we'll go and talk about it.' He marched off to the referee's room, where he regained some composure and gave me a light dressing down, taking my grievances on board.

But we still didn't get the rub of the green after the interval, as the fucker got even worse. Foul, foul, fucking foul – he must have been doing it on purpose, so I started spitting lava from my technical area. Fifteen minutes into the second half he blew his whistle and stopped the game, calling over a linesman and policeman for back-up, before ordering me into the stand. The crowd were booing as he looked down at me in the sunken dugout, stubbornly refusing to get the game started again until I disappeared.

Well, the copper got it first, as he stank of lager. 'Cheeky little lunchtime, pal? Best you piss off, as you wouldn't want anyone to know you've been drinking on duty.' He vanished straight away and after a five-minute stand-off I agreed to take a seat in the stand. As soon as his linesman witness was out of earshot, I got up close to the ref and said, 'Listen to me you no good part-time cunt. See this shit league you referee in? Well you know those dark little December and January car parks? Watch your back in them, as I'm coming for you with a baseball bat.'

He remembered every word, as it was all in the report which eventually got sent to the club by the FA, along with my nine-month touchline ban and £500 fine.

Ahead of sentencing, I was in charge for another five games and we finally got a win, 1–0 at Walton & Hersham, and I made a defensive playing return in my final game at the end of September, which ended in a 2–0 defeat at home to Carshalton. The chairman – the man who had promised to do everything face to face – called a 16-strong committee meeting, which included the burger bar lady, the window cleaner and the jobsworth who ran the car park, to discuss my future at the club. They voted unanimously to give me the flick, but what did I expect from a bunch of non-league amateurs? Red card No.22 looked to have consigned me to the retirement home once and for all.

During the next four years, I briefly flirted with local football clubs near my Colchester home. I trained with Cornard United to keep fit and held a soccer school there, as well as turning out a handful of times for ex-Layer Road team-mate Steve Ball at Stanway Rovers, chipping the goalkeeper from 45 yards in one game. I'd changed jobs by then, working for the Mitsubishi dealership in Colchester, which got me off the road and stopped me being away from Liz during the week. I'd always had an interest in cars and used to follow Formula One, especially British driver James Hunt who, like George Best and Barry Sheene, was a sportsman at the top of his game, but also a maverick who lived life to the full.

I was good at selling cars, flogging £85,000 worth of Shogun jeeps in my first week, as I fast-tracked to the No.1 salesman position. I'd moved on to BMW by the time I got one of those 'can you help me out' phone calls in 2002, asking me to pull my boots back on at the age of 44. I bombed up the Essex coast in the company X5 to Harwich and Parkeston, not to catch a ferry to the Netherlands for a booze cruise, but to pick up £50 boot money turning out for my former Colchester student Steve McGavin. He wanted me to liven up the boys in the dressing room and do a bit of organising, and I breezed through 90 minutes at centre-half, as we beat Jewson Premier Division top-dogs Gorleston 3–1, who were run by ex-Norwich duo Robert Fleck and Dale Gordon. I didn't bother warming up, as playing football was like jumping back on a bike, and all the old joints felt fine. I didn't get any stick from the fans and there were no punch-ups with the opposition striker – the biggest problem I had was getting Gary Bennett to buy me a drink in the bar afterwards. I told the local reporter to make sure he included my age in the report, which was accompanied by the headline: 'McDonough Masterclass'.

What a fitting end to my playing days . . . that should have been. But I couldn't resist one final curtain call and we got stuffed 8–1 at Sudbury, with me getting the hook at half-time. We were 6–0 down at the break, but the man I was picking up never scored a goal and I felt fine. I was too long in the tooth to start questioning Steve's decisions by then, though, and went for a pint instead.

27. DRIVEN TO SPAIN

With my football career well behind me, I was living a second life with Liz. Thanks to her employer, travel firm Thomas Cook, we managed to nab plenty of cheap holidays to destinations I'd never dreamed of seeing. We visited Antigua, Bali, Mexico and Thailand, opening my eyes to cultures which were completely foreign to the football team piss-ups on the Algarve that I was accustomed to, brought to life by a multitude of strange but wonderful smells, tastes and sights.

A huge disappointment for me was never having kids, a curse which also hit my twin brother Gaz. And with Liz by my side offering a loving home, I think I would have made a great father. We did try for two years after getting married, with no success. We took all the tests and the doctors discovered that Liz's body was reacting against mine at the pivotal moment. But we didn't give up, trying to bypass the problem by getting medical staff at Colchester Hospital to inject my sperm straight into Liz when she was ovulating. I would announce to everyone in the office at work, 'Right, I'm off for a wank.' Then I'd sit in the toilet and fill a jar, which I had to hold close to my chest to keep it warm as I drove to Liz at the hospital in 15 minutes flat. I'd been through all of this before with my first wife, Jackie. She couldn't get pregnant, so we had IVF treatment three times at Harley Street, in London, at £5,000 an attempt. The specialists tested my manic sperm, which were swimming in all directions under the microscope, and I joked it was because my white tadpoles were all pissed. That prompted serious questions about my alcohol intake, as it could have been affecting our chances. So I lied, halving my weekly amount of beer to 50 pints. The doctors put me on a course of iron tablets, ordered me to cut down the drinking and my sperm count climbed up to 93 per cent. I was still surprised that Jackie got pregnant, before the miscarriage, and she has given birth since we split up. I genuinely hope Jackie is happy with her life now, as everybody deserves to be.

I had nothing to show, financially, for all my years playing football. I still had a mortgage and hardly any savings, as any cash I earned during my career went behind the bar. The little money I had put by was what I had collected since meeting Liz and becoming more responsible. I had grown up at last and was good at my £30,000-a-year job as a car salesman at BMW, in Colchester. The drinking was minimal by then, a few lagers at home or a bottle of wine with dinner and pubs and nightclubs had long fallen by the wayside as I loved nothing more than a night in with my wife.

But a corporate golf day for BMW customers at a course in nearby Frinton gave my old drinking demons an encore in June 2003. We were told to park our company BMWs around the 18th hole, so they could catch the eyes of potential buyers. There was a party of 75 people – which included Jason Cook and Paul Roberts – and after having an egg buttie and pint of lager for breakfast, we played a morning 10-hole Texas scramble. I was useless, but I refuelled with a couple of lunch-time Stellas before hitting the fairway again, playing like Nick Faldo in the afternoon and winning the competition. Because I finished so far ahead of everyone else, my boss wanted me to become the entertainments officer, meeting and greeting the clients as they returned to the clubhouse. I was in my element but got carried away and drank another 12 pints before the evening dinner at 7pm – then got on the wine, red and white.

I left the club at midnight, refusing Robbo's offer of sharing a cab. I felt fine and I had to work the next day, so I wanted to get the car home. But as soon as I stepped outside and the fresh air hit me, I felt slaughtered.

I was pulled over by blue flashing lights, which turned out to be an ambulance, on the A133 Frating slip road, 10 miles from home. I could have been anywhere, though, and can't even remember the police turning up and taking me back to the station at Clacton. It turned out that somebody at the golf club had grassed me up and the police had been searching for my car on the roads heading back to Colchester. When they tested my breath I registered 104mcg of alcohol – just short of three times the legal 35mcg limit. But after two and a half hours in a cell, they gave me my car keys back and phoned a taxi. I was still battered and ran up a £50 fare while the cab driver searched for my car, which was sitting in the same place with all the doors unlocked and the hazard lights still blinking. I got back in the car, despite the cabbie's protests, and drove home to Stanway, where Liz caught me trying to climb over the back garden fence, despite having keys in my hand.

The police had finally caught up with me after a lifetime of drinking and driving – ironically, when I was selling cars as a job and couldn't afford not to be behind the wheel. Knowing I had some good commissions coming in over the next few weeks, I didn't tell work and rang the police to say I was going on holiday, stalling my court appearance for three weeks.

When the big day arrived in July I was worried about going down, as a teacher had been handed a six-month prison sentence a few weeks before, after crashing her car with a smaller amount of alcohol in her system. I prayed the judges might be Colchester United fans and show me some leniency, as technically it was my first offence. As I stood in the glass box, that hope was crushed as two women wearing glasses, who looked like they had been carved out of rock, took their seats in front of me, and I got handed my longest suspension yet – a 30-month driving ban, plus 80 hours' community service and £55 costs.

The judge asked me if I had anything to add, and I replied, 'Don't you think it's a bit harsh?'

I had to cut the grass at a cemetery to work off my community debt and turned up for the first day in flip-flops, shorts and a T-shirt. The church warden told me I had to change into jeans and trainers for health and safety reasons, then brought out the lawnmowers – a biggie for the grass, and a smaller one for getting up the sides of the hundreds of grave stones. The cemetery was huge, but my competitive streak was kicking in and I asked him if anybody had completed the task in a day, to which he shook his head. As soon as he disappeared I got stuck in, pushing those mowers hard, and I was halfway there after two hours when the smoking big mower blew up. I was gutted as I wanted to put the church warden in his place, who at first thought I had destroyed the mower in an attempt to skive off. But there was plenty of time for that during the remainder of my sentence, as I'd lie behind a shed and work on bronzing my tan as soon as the lawnmower monitor had vanished. I was also ordered by the court to attend a drink-drive rehabilitation scheme. But fuck that, I was off to Spain – and I could still drive over there, despite my English ban.

Liz and I had talked about Spain for a long time, in pursuit of a better quality of life – a fresh start with the sun shining on our faces. Despite losing my driving licence, BMW kept me on, but one of my old Heybridge players, Dave Greene, offered me the chance to help him run a Charlton Athletic soccer school in Torrevieja, on the Costa Blanca. So we sold the house, took the gamble, and it paid off.

Charlton manager Alan Curbishley came over to officially open the training camp, and we had 200 kids, aged eight to 15, mostly ex-pats' children, plus a few Spanish and German youngsters. We had a link-up with Valencia and played tournaments against Barcelona and Real Madrid, who wiped the floor with us. But I was surprised by their kids, as they were all big, powerful boys, not full of flicks and tricks as you might expect.

I also started a men's seven-a-side league under the Charlton banner on Friday nights at the posh La Manga club, which England boss Glenn Hoddle used as a pre-World Cup training base in 1998. This gave me my first taste of standing on the other side of the fence – taking on the role of my arch nemesis, the referee. I refused to wear all that black shit, just putting on different colours to the other teams, and I thought I did a good job. I didn't have any problem keeping up with play and, having been a professional footballer, I was alert to what was going on around me, never missing a thing. But I couldn't handle the verbal – which I had been so keen to hand out as a player. I'd go to the bar after the games were finished and couldn't talk for half an hour, as the abuse would tire me out, rather than the running around. It started to hit home how harsh I had been to officials during my playing days and consequently just why I'd totted up so many red cards. The players' unwelcome opinions wound me up so much on a couple of occasions that I offered to have it out with them in the car park.

The role reversal was complete when I red-carded a player during the league's enforced final match. The top team were all ex-pats with chips on their shoulders who believed they should have been professionals. The whipping boys had been the Q Bar, but they had started importing Spanish ringers, who were all decent players, and rapidly climbed the table. The English boys were 3–0 down at half-time and didn't like it. I had to send off one of the Spanish lads, who had gone straight through the goalkeeper's leg with a firm ankle, which was the catalyst for a massive punch-up. I was trying to drag people shouting, swearing and fighting apart, and bricks were being thrown across the car park. Two old boys paying £4,000-a-month club fees for the privilege of walking their dogs didn't like it, reported the uncouth behaviour and the league got kicked out.

So it was back to the soccer school, but I got bored after three years and frustrated by the lethargy of some of the parents. Their kids would turn up in expensive multi-coloured boots, listening to their iPods and playing around on Gameboys – not fully focused on their football training. I wasn't having that and told them to chuck all their electronic gizmos in the bin, which didn't make me flavour of the month after the parents had forked out a £400 package fee for the soccer school. I needed a challenge, something to test the old grey matter and get me at it again. Liz was making a few quid selling clothes on a market stall before taking an office job at a property company. And that was my next move, back into sales, flogging apartments, townhouses and villas, ranging from £150,000 to £250,000, around the beach and five-star golf resort. I went to work for MacAnthony Realty International, the company owned by Peterborough United's Irish chairman Darragh MacAnthony, who branded me his 'money-making machine'. All I had to do was drive five minutes from my home to Murcia Airport to pick up the clients and then show them around the properties, and I pulled off 10 big deals in the first couple of months.

Things were great, but then I was sent to southern Italy, right in the toe of the football boot, selling properties around a big marina. It meant I would only see Liz once every six weeks and it broke our hearts as we sat crying down the phone to each other most nights. But I stuck it out for 15 months before pulling the plug over a row when I didn't receive a big commission that I believed I was due – which would have paid off the mortgage in Spain.

I did a brief stint in Bulgaria selling property near a ski resort, before going back to Spain to work full-time, promising never to leave Liz's side again. Family has always been important to me. So much so, that I helped Liz's ex-husband Dave get a job as Torrevieja football club's groundsman, so that when their son David – who I have a great relationship with now – was in Spain with us they could all still be close together. I was even more than happy to let Dave live in our house for 10 weeks, while he settled into his new Spanish life.

The hardest thing about living abroad was leaving Mum and Dad behind in Solihull, who never made it over to see us. Neither of them was getting any younger and Dad was beginning to lose the plot. He only packed up playing cricket when he was 82 and was still physically strong, which probably saved his life one December. The silly old sod walked down the side of the back garden, tried to climb over a fence, fell off and knocked himself out. He slept outside all night and woke up covered in a blanket of snow. After that, he was moved into a care home in nearby Yardley for his own protection and was reunited with Mum in the same place for the last 18 months of her life. They were still fighting cat and dog, even then, bless them.

Mum passed away first in September 2009, at the age of 84. She'd had a bad fall, breaking her hip and leg, and never recovered properly. Liz knew about my childhood, brought up in a house of warmly-felt, but never expressed, affection. Mum and Dad had never actually said they loved me, but I knew they did. Liz encouraged me to let out my true feelings, pushing me to tell Mum I loved her with a big hug every time I visited during those final months.

When Mum died we thought Dad had completely lost his marbles. But after the funeral, he got into the hearse and started to sing the words to *Beautiful Love* which he always sang just for Mum. He knew exactly what was going on, and it was breaking his heart. The wake was held at Moseley Cricket club, where both Dad and I had played and he had also been an umpire. I had to take him to the toilet, taking his cock out and holding it while he had a slash and he said to me, 'It's alright, Roy. It's only a little one.' So I looked down, as the piss was flying over my arm and down my shirt, replying, 'It ain't too bad, Dad.' I'll always cherish sharing that moment in the cricket club toilet.

It was difficult watching Dad deteriorate. The intimidating nutter and loudmouth, who had lived life to its very fullest was growing weaker in front of my eyes. Dad had been a great sportsman himself, without hitting the same heights as me, but it was his single-minded determination that made sure I didn't fail. He pushed me relentlessly as a young lad in Solihull, fanning the flames of desire he knew I possessed deep inside.

He may have been unapproachable when I was desperate for a shoulder to cry on at the start of my football journey, but when I was crushed by Aston Villa's rejection as a kid he was there to pick up the pieces, getting me through the door at Birmingham City for a second chance, when I could easily have joined my brothers on the factory floor. It was tough love, and everything he did was to strengthen my shell so it wouldn't be shattered by the numerous knockbacks and disappointments which would plague my efforts to make the grade. We would often chat for 10 minutes in the care home, about football, or cricket, but then he would drift off, which was gut-wrenching to see.

Mum had only been dead three months when Dad followed her just after Christmas 2009, at the age of 90. I still had one last thing to do before he went and I knew when the time was right. He looked up at me from his bed and I could read what he wanted to say through his tired eyes. I leant over and said it at last, 'I love you, Dad', and a tear of confirmation appeared in his eyes, so I know he heard me. I'd been waiting to say those four words my whole life.

I called on the inner steel that Dad had forged in me by taking my place in front of the church lectern to read funeral eulogies I had written myself, paying tribute to both him and Mum, which was much harder than facing a rampaging Tommy Smith or growling Graeme Souness. I may not have been a top-flight star name, with a big bank balance and cabinet full of medals, but I had had a longer career than most, surviving 20 years on football's bloody battlefields. And it was Dad who had made that happen, giving me the drive to succeed and make my mark. I owed him.

EPILOGUE

Lying in a queue of trolley beds resembling a motorway traffic jam gives you a lot of time to think. It was the spring of 2011 and I was stuck in a corridor staring up at the ceiling of Faro Hospital for 24 hours, waiting for a shared room. Liz and I had upped sticks to Portugal to work for another property company. We'd left our house in Spain for a bright yellow Moroccan-style apartment community with a swimming pool, behind electric gates. We'd moved to the Algarve, chasing an even better quality of life, just a goal-kick from Vilamoura's huge marina cradling billions of euros worth of private yachts, tied up beside Luis Figo's bar and Cristiano Ronaldo's shop.

But after working my nuts off for the first two months, whisking clients from the airport around the lush golfing paradises, white beaches and wonderful apartments, as far up as Lisbon's Silver Coast, I got sick as a dog. I woke up one morning with eyes as yellow as cheese, which I dismissed as dehydration, but a concerned Liz made me visit a medical clinic. The doctor asked me for a urine sample, which was so dark in colour it looked like a pint of Guinness. I tried to laugh it off, but I'd felt like shit for weeks, and the doctor left me in no doubt as to how serious my condition was. Tests revealed acute Hepatitis B, which kept me in hospital attached to a drip for a week. A few months earlier I'd stubbed my toe on a discarded needle, walking my dogs in flip-flops across the dusty orange groves next to our Spanish house, which is all the doctors could pinpoint the infection to, as everything else came back clear. The liver-attacking disease wasn't going to kill me, but serious lifestyle changes needed to be implemented straight away – which meant completely giving up alcohol for six months, allowing the organ's regenerative powers to kick in.

It was the first time in more than 30 years that I couldn't have a drink, and represented the toughest challenge of my life. Some people snort cocaine and others pop mind-altering pills, but drinking was always my vice when it came to escaping my football disappointments, pulling on the careless playboy footballer mask in the process. My happy life with Liz was another world away from those dark times, but the fondness for a beer remained, and having that option taken away was extremely difficult to cope with. For the first five months I felt permanently worn out, like a pensioner with a bad bout of flu. My wrists and ankles painfully ached non-stop and for the first time in my life I was sleeping during the day. It made me realise just how much alcohol had polluted the workings of my body.

But I gradually got stronger as I fought off the temptation of having a swift pint on the quiet, and when I play tennis now I feel fitter than when I was at my peak as a professional footballer. I had my first drink after 26 weeks of abstinence just before Christmas 2011, at Gogarty's Irish bar in La Zenia. It was a cold pint of Estrella and it tasted bloody good. I had one more and just left it at that. I still have a social drink, a few pints a week and a bottle of wine with dinner some evenings, but the messy 20-pint-a-night sessions are long gone, as is my almost superhuman tolerance to alcohol. Liz had to drive to the pub and rescue me after I watched the Premier League clash between Manchester United and Liverpool in February 2012 as I was falling off my chair after just four pints.

When I was in Faro Hospital with all that time on my hands, not knowing how serious my condition was, I did a fair old bit of rewinding inside my head. It was a Saturday and the first thing I wanted to know was how my old clubs Colchester and Southend had got on, plus Manchester United, who I have always followed through a respect of the way they play the game with such attacking flair. Then I started thinking about my football career. I was a good targetman and played with my heart on my sleeve. I'd taken liberties with my family, team-mates and the fans of the clubs I played for, hitting the booze and abusing my body, but I don't think anybody that watched me play could honestly say that they never got their money's worth out of me. If I needed to apologise for anything to the fans of clubs I played for, it would be that if I had remained sober, and prepared properly, then they might have had an even better player in their team, who could have exerted more influence on games. But football broke my heart at such an early age, when I was completely dedicated to reaching the top level, and like a faithful husband getting dumped by the love of his life I hit the bottle to numb the pain.

The game bit me on the backside, but I should never have walked out on long-term contracts at big clubs like Birmingham and Chelsea. With most players in the modern game attached to their agents, that would never be allowed to happen now, although I'm sure there are ulterior motives behind certain transfers, filling somebody's pockets, and I could have been a victim of that.

Plenty of other things flashed through my mind, like winning at Wembley with Colchester, whose fans also voted me into their BBC Cult Heroes top three alongside Mark Kinsella and Lomana LuaLua, who both went on to grace the Premier League. Then there was winning promotions with Walsall and Southend, plus scoring in my much-missed mate John Lyons's shirt at Tranmere. And there were plenty of what-ifs. Millwall stuck in the mind most, wondering just how my career might have turned out if I had broken my promise to Gerry Francis at Exeter, to enter the Lions' Den with George Graham.

One thing I don't regret is the number of red cards I collected. I was too honest as a player and wouldn't get through the warm-up now, especially not with all the cheating that the foreign players have brought into our game. A lot of my dismissals were for verbal, but referees used to wind me up. I could feel my fist clenching when a bank manager or headmaster who had never played the game professionally tried to lecture me on the pitch. And I used to have this fantasy about finishing my career by knocking one of the fuckers out in the centre circle when my legs were shot to bits. I'm glad I didn't, because refereeing a football match is one of the hardest jobs in the world, as I found out at La Manga Club.

Some of them were OK. I always had a laugh with Neil Midgley and Graham Poll, who both had a sense of humour. But that was the biggest problem, the mentality. A football match is conducted at factory-floor level, the language and banter, which some posh twat who works at a private school in the week is never going to understand in a million years. And these so-called professional referees are even worse. Liz finds it hilarious when I sit at home, still berating them and shaking my head from an armchair in front of the TV. But there is a solution – get more ex-professional footballers picking up a whistle. I would have done it to stay in the game, if it hadn't meant going through eight years of qualification to make the Football League list. My old Walsall team-mate Steve Baines slogged it out and proved it can work. If the top retired referees fast-tracked their knowledge of the laws of the game into ex-footballers at an intensive summer training course, you'd be surprised how many old pros would take it up. It would make for a much better spectacle as these guys know the game inside out, especially all the dirty little tricks. But from my own perspective, a player would have much more difficulty questioning the rulings of a referee who has actually made those split-second-decision tackles for a living to pay his bills. We live in hope.

When we moved to Portugal we were promised the world, but the financial goalposts moved so we headed back to our house, in a small Spanish village well away from Murcia's Little England community. I am a partner in a property management company now, selling apartments and houses on the Costa

Calida. Paramount Pictures have planning permission to build a theme park in the area, so we're waiting for the property boom to land us a comfortable retirement. But I'd be a liar if I said the football flame doesn't still flicker – and a route back into the game is the only thing which could tempt me back to England. I still believe I've got a lot to offer football and I find it frustrating when I see people landing decent club jobs who have never achieved anything near what I did at Colchester with my hands firmly tied.

My biggest downfall was that I never stuck around in the directors' bar after games, as I wanted to drink with my players. I should have been 'networking', or brown-nosing as I call it, with the home and away directors, feathering my nest for a future job. My pal Ian Atkins was a great networker, landing eight management jobs, and made a decent living out of the game, which I don't begrudge him at all. He's got a cushy number now as a European scout for Sunderland – but I couldn't have gone through all that bollocks just to get a job.

I loved Stuart Pearce as a player, for his take-no-prisoners approach to games. But when I watched him on the England bench, sitting like a little nodding dog next to Fabio Capello, it absolutely killed me. Then you've got the likes of Dick Bate and Brian Eastick holding such lofty England youth coaching positions at the FA. These people never played the game, they didn't experience it – so how can they coach it? The Jose Mourinhos of this world never played at any level either but I could be a 'Special One' too if I had all the millions at his disposal. I'd like to see him get Colchester promoted, with £640 in the bank for players.

Off the pitch, experience of life is equally important in football management, especially when it comes to winning the trust of your players, which can make or break any manager. I can't imagine Sir Alex Ferguson has told too many of his lads to pull their shorts and pants down in his office when a worried squad member has knocked on his door complaining about a suspected dose after playing away, just 24 hours before flying out on holiday with his wife and kids. But I did that sort of thing and offered an accurate diagnosis, before packing them off to a clinic. My biggest regret is not bringing all of that experience together and having a whole season managing a professional club, just sitting on the bench and making decisions. I'd love to have done the job without the added pressure of having to pick myself to play every week, while keeping a lynchmob of clueless directors at arm's length.

I'm happy, though, living with the love of my life in Spain and my three four-legged substitute children. The 'boys' are terrier Stan, German shepherd and doberman cross, Peter Pup, and cocker spaniel, Ollie. They are all a bit like me. Stan growls at the other two and rips into their ears with his sharp gnashers if they take liberties with his food bowl. Peter Pup shags everything that moves – the other dogs, chair legs and even thin air. But my favourite is Ollie. He is so soft and adorable that you can't help but love him. But he has a destructive side, too. A visiting friend of ours left his bedroom door open and found his £180 glasses and trainers destroyed on returning to the house, with Ollie wearing his cutest big eyes in the middle of the carnage, trying to look innocent. Yep, he's exactly like his Dad.

I still pull my boots on every now and then, returning to Colchester and Southend to play in testimonial games. My Double-winning team – the Boys of '92 – had a reunion match and dinner at Colchester's new Weston Homes Community Stadium in May 2012. Ironically, it was the same week they finally started demolishing Layer Road for a new housing project. It might have been a shithole, but it was a shithole with character – not like this new generation of plastic Lego stadiums, which have no soul. When we climbed back into the Football League 20 years before, the atmosphere was so special, especially the racket generated by the noisy buggers in the Barside, which has now been permanently silenced by the bulldozers. There may have been less hair, more wrinkles and larger midriffs on display in my team, but it was great to see all those old faces again, especially Davey and Robbo. During the 20th anniversary dinner at the club that night, I was inducted into Colchester United's Hall of Fame, which was both very humbling and long overdue! The club presented me with a commemorative tie, and a framed picture and certificate – awarded to Roy McDonagh. They spelt my name wrong, but I had to smile. Some things really hadn't changed in 20 years.

Before leaving Portugal, I played football for my property company in the local Vilamoura seven-a-side league. Playing up front at 52, the lad marking me was a wannabe toughie and gave me a couple of warning shots. No big deal. But after 25 minutes, he stepped it up a gear and elbowed me in the face, sending a crown of stars whizzing round my head and threatening to pull the artificial pitch from under my wobbling legs. I grabbed the player by the neck as he jabbered on at me in angry Portuguese, spitting all over my face. But I didn't punch him, kick him or knee him in the goolies. The red mist never appeared and I let him go, proving I must be mellowing with age. When I returned home early, Liz asked how we'd got on. And I replied, 'You'll never guess what.'

'You didn't?' she said.

I just gave her a cheeky grin. Another red card. Some habits really do die hard.